P9-APJ-764

The Revenge of God

THE REVENGE OF GOD

The Resurgence of Islam, Christianity and Judaism in the Modern World

GILLES KEPEL

Translated by Alan Braley

The Pennsylvania State University Press
University Park, Pennsylvania

First published in France as *La Revanche de Dieu* © 1991 Éditions du Seuil

English translation © 1994 Polity Press

First published in 1994 in the United States of America and Canada by The Pennsylvania State University Press, Barbara Building, Suite C, University Park, PA 16802

All rights reserved. Except for the quotation of short passages for the purposes of criticism and review, no part of this publication may be reproduced, stored in a retrieval system, or transmitted, in any form or by any means, electronic, mechanical, photocopying, recording or otherwise, without the prior permission of the publishers.

ISBN 0–271–01313–3 (cloth)
ISBN 0–271–01314–1 (paper)

Library of Congress Cataloging in Publication Data
A CIP catalog record for this book is available from the Library of Congress.

Typeset in 11 on 13 pt Baskerville
by Photo·graphics, Honiton, Devon
Printed in Great Britain

This book is printed on acid-free paper.

It is the policy of The Pennsylvania State University Press to use acid-free paper for the first printing of all clothbound books. Publications on uncoated stock satisfy minimum requirements of American National Standard for Information Sciences – Permanence of Paper for Printed Library Materials, ANSI Z39.48–1984.

FOR CHARLOTTE, MARIE AND NICOLAS

CONTENTS

ACKNOWLEDGEMENTS

The research which led to the writing of this book could not have been undertaken without the support of the Centre d'études et de recherches internationales (Fondation Nationale des Sciences Politiques) in Paris. Besides giving me institutional and financial support, the CERI is also a unique locus of intellectual exchange and emulation; I would specially like to thank my colleagues in the working group on 'Religion and Politics', as well as Alan Dieckhoff, Denis Lacorne and Jacques Rupnik, who have helped me to negotiate areas with which I was not familiar. In the United States I benefited from the help of the Franco-American Committee for Scholarly Exchange, and above all from the kindness of James 'Hillyer' Piscatori. In Jerusalem, Gilles d'Humières and Emmanuel Sivan befriended me generously. Stephanie Durand-Barracand and Virginie Linhart put together the documentation with great efficiency: it was a pleasure to work with them. And Michel d'Hermies was, as usual, the first and the most critical of the readers of my manuscript.

Lastly I would also express my thanks to all those members of the Christian, Islamic and Jewish movements who granted me interviews which were essential to this enquiry. Many of them will disagree with my conclusions and some will certainly challenge my interpretations. Nevertheless I hope my approach has been a fair one and has provided them with material for future discussions.

The publishers gratefully acknowledge the help of Dr Rosemary Morris in preparing this translation for press.

INTRODUCTION
Religions in a Confused World

The 1970s was a decade of cardinal importance for the relationship between religion and politics, which has changed in unexpected ways during the last quarter of the twentieth century. After the end of the Second World War it seemed that the realm of politics had finally broken away from religion, the culmination of a process of which the philosophers of the Enlightenment are generally held to have been the main initiators. The influence of religion became restricted to the private or family sphere, and now seemed to have only an indirect effect on the way society was organized, like a leftover from the past. This general trend, which proceeded alongside a modernity flushed with the triumphs of technology and having progress as its creed, assumed innumerable forms and intensities, varying according to place and culture. Sometimes it was confined to the elite and to its vision of the world, but this dominant world view masked other processes of change that were at work, more complex changes that had not yet achieved prominence on the public scene.

Throughout the 1960s the link between religion and civic order seemed to grow increasingly tenuous, in a way that clerics found worrying. To check what was taken to be disaffection of the flock towards its pastors and the faith, and an irresistible trend towards secularization, some religious institutions then strove to adapt their message to the 'modern' values of society, to look for points of contact and to emphasize them. The most notable of these undertakings was the Vatican II Ecumenical Council and the *aggiornamento* or 'updating' of the Church it caused, however that event may be reinterpreted at the present time. Similar phenomena occurred in the Protestant world and even in Islamic circles, where there was talk of 'modernizing Islam'.

The reversal of the 1970s

Around 1975 this whole process went into reverse. A new religious approach took shape, aimed no longer at adapting to secular values but at recovering a sacred foundation for the organization of society – by changing society if necessary. Expressed in a multitude of ways, this approach advocated moving on from a modernism that had failed, attributing its setbacks and dead ends to separation from God. The theme was no longer *aggiornamento* but a 'second evangelization of Europe': the aim was no longer to modernize Islam but to 'Islamize modernity'.

Since that date this phenomenon has spread all over the world. It is arising in civilizations that differ in both their cultural origins and their level of development. But wherever it appears it sets itself up against a 'crisis' in society, claiming to have identified the underlying causes of that crisis beyond the economic, political or cultural symptoms through which it is manifested.

From Cairo or Algiers to Prague, from the American Evangelicals to the zealots of Gush Emunim, from Islamic militants to Catholic charismatics, from the Lubavitch to Communion and Liberation, this book is an attempt to detect some of the leading traits of a burgeoning movement that appears at first sight to defy analysis. It aims to cover only the three 'Abrahamic' religions – Judaism, Christianity and Islam – though recent developments in Hinduism and Shinto, to take only two more examples, also present similarities to what is happening in the three 'religions of the Book'.

Even with this limitation, the present work may well seem to be too ambitious. But I am not attempting an exhaustive survey: that kind of information can be found in the many monographs describing the various forms of religious renewal in Christianity, Islam and Judaism during the 1970s and 1980s. My purpose is simply to lay down some markers as a guide for thinking round the phenomenon as a whole.

This essay was born of dissatisfaction with the 'monograph' form: I have spent a dozen years in observing present-day Islam in the field, trying to identify the actors and the trends in this striking reaffirmation, and I am convinced that the causes of this phenomenon were not peculiar to the world of Islam, even though it took its particular colouring from that world. When I observed that certain movements within Christianity and Judaism showed striking similarities to Islamic movements already known to me, I thought it would be interesting to make a systematic comparison of the hypotheses I had constructed on this subject with the diverse forms of Christian and Jewish renewal whose manifestations I was beginning to study. They all seemed to fit into the context of a worldwide discrediting of modernism that was the hallmark of the 1970s.

This may appear to be a peculiar point of view: it is usual to begin by studying the Western religions in order to arrive at the concepts to be used in thinking about what happens elsewhere. Seen from Paris or New York, events in the world of Islam are usually equated with 'Islamic *intégrisme*' or 'Muslim fundamentalism', sometimes to the neglect of the fact that '*intégrisme*' and fundamentalism are two categories of thought rooted respectively in Catholicism and Protestantism, and that they may not, even if used as metaphor, be universally applicable. I believe on the contrary that they over-simplify and sidestep the issue, hindering our overall grasp of these phenomena. And our general inability to interpret present-day movements within Islam is largely attributable to our way of peering at them through the outmoded theoretical spectacles which are all we have to hand, and which simply blur our perception even more. It is time to take up the challenge posed by contemporary religious movements to our traditional ways of thinking about them – and that cannot be done unless they are viewed as a whole.

Starting from the world of Islam enables us to look from an unusual angle on phenomena that form part of our cultural environment and that we thought were self-explanatory. A detour via the experience of something culturally far removed from us has the advantage of overturning the mental laziness and illusion of familiarity which previously prevailed, and of replacing them with new meaning.

Beyond the crisis of modernism

Since Karol Wojtyla became Pope, the Catholic Church has changed course. Evangelical movements have had a profound influence in the United States. Outside the ever-increasing circle of the converted, both these movements have often been denigrated as representing the obscurantism of a bygone age.

And yet if we apply the comparative method to these phenomena we soon find that this widespread view is quite inadequate. For one thing, the members and advocates of these present-day religious movements are not drawn mainly from the 'obscurantist' groups of the population such as the illiterate and aged, country people and so forth; they contain a high proportion of people, young or not so young, who have been through a secular education, with a marked bias towards the technical disciplines. Their way of describing society, their diagnosis of its ills and their recommended cure owe much to the habits of thought acquired in schools which are themselves the product *par excellence* of the modernity whose course they now wish to alter. And the way in which they handle the sacred texts in support of their beliefs takes many liberties with the learned tradition of the ulemas, priests or rabbis, which is always on the side of social conservatism.

For these religious movements all oppose or dissent from the dominant attitude of 'official religion' which they readily criticize. At first sight their leaders and members have more the appearance of 'intellectuals of a proletarian cast', as Max Weber calls them. They all share the remarkable characteristic of challenging the way society is organized: either its secular foundation – as in France – or its secular deviations from a foundation which is in part based on religion, as in the United States or the Islamic countries.

But in every case they complain about the fragmentation of society, its 'anomy', the absence of an overarching ideal worthy of their allegiance. They do not fight against a secular ethic, which according to them does not exist, but consider that in the final analysis the modernism produced by reason without God has not succeeded in creating values. The crisis of the 1970s, by weakening the social cohesion fostered by the welfare state, has brought

hidden human miseries to light. To their eyes it reveals the empti-
ness of liberal and Marxist secular utopias, which have led to
selfish consumerism in the West, and, in the socialist countries
and the Third World, to repression, poverty and a dehumanized
society.

But this opposition is not simply the 'sublimated' or 'reclothed'
expression of a social movement. The revolution in Iran, for
example, cannot be dismissed as an incomplete communist revolution, even if the 'disinherited' (*mustad'afun*) and the 'arrogant'
(*mustakbirun*) of the former are not altogether unlike the 'oppressed'
and the 'oppressors' of the latter. The Italian Catholic movement
'Communion and Liberation', which has excellent anti-communist
credentials, has borrowed several methods of protest against 'bourgeois liberalism' from the far left. But it would be wrong to be
deceived by similarities of language: once the language has been
appropriated it is redeployed in a vast conceptual syntax which
leads elsewhere, to the demand for a link with religion as the
foundation of the social system.

Moreover not all of the contemporary movements in religion,
even if they aim at superseding modernity, have as a short-term
aim seizure of power and revolutionary transformation of society.
Some of them are working to form communities of true believers
here and now who will forthwith break with 'worldly' life styles
and live their lives according to the commandments of dogma or
the injunctions of the Holy Spirit. This is true of the charismatic
groups that are flourishing today in both Catholicism and Protestantism, the Lubavitch in the Jewish world, and the Tabligh,
the largest transnational Islamic organization yet seen.

In different ways they withdraw from the world to bear witness,
by example, to the need for a different way of life, a togetherness
based on personal religious experience. Many have adopted the
most sophisticated techniques of modernity and tried to dissociate
them from the secular culture, to show that there is no necessary
connection between the two.

There are some differences among these contemporary religious
movements, but must we therefore conclude that their almost
simultaneous appearance is due to chance, and that the wish
to discuss them as a global phenomenon proceeds from a false

perspective or a fashionable whim? To see the problems more clearly, let us first briefly mention some of the more significant events of this period.

Signposts

1977, 1978, 1979: during each of these three years, a change of direction occurred in Judaism, Christianity and Islam alike.

In May 1977, for the first time in the history of the state of Israel, Labour failed to win enough seats in the election to form a government and Menachem Begin became prime minister. At these elections the Zionist religious movements, which had suffered a long eclipse, made a breakthrough; in particular they stepped up the numbers of Jewish settlements in the occupied territories, in the name of the special covenant between God and the 'Chosen People'.

In the glum atmosphere that followed the reverses sustained by the Jewish state in the war of October 1973, this phenomenon shows that many Jews were questioning the meaning and the practical expression of their Jewish identity. A significant part of the electorate was critically re-examining the dominant Zionist tradition, for the most part secular and socialist, that had been conducting Israel's policy up to that time.

The religious parties embrace many different outlooks, ranging from anti-Zionism to ultra-orthodoxy, but all of them reject a definition of Judaism in terms of simple belonging. Rather, they judge it by the strictest observance, with an emphasis on understanding of the tradition, the expression of faith, the significance of ritual and the alignment of existence in this world with the precepts of dogma. Since then these movements have been constantly increasing in number, size and importance. Strictly speaking they were not born in the 1960s, but their real emergence on to the political scene dates from that period. Among the Jews of the diaspora this same period witnessed an intensification of Jewish communal feeling, not only in the United States but also in strongly assimilating countries such as France, where voices were even raised in condemnation of 'the emancipation of Jews' as initiated by the French Revolution, on the grounds that under the guise of equality it had sought to destroy Jewish identity, whereas within the walls of the ghetto this identity had flourished.

In September 1978 the Polish cardinal Karol Wojtyla was elected Pope. This ended the hesitancies of the post-conciliar period, during which many Catholics had questioned their identity, confused by a modernization of ritual and doctrine which they could not always understand, while secular society was being attacked from within by the movements of 1968. During the same period the charismatic groups that had come into being in American Catholicism spread to the Old World. Throughout the 1980s they were in the ascendant in both Western and Eastern Europe, forcing the 'Catholic Left', which until then had been apt to think of itself as the 'conscience' of the Church, on to the defensive.

While the truly *intégriste* wing, whose most prominent leader was Mgr Lefebvre, never succeeded in recruiting members outside the most traditionalist extreme-right circles, the charismatics were able to gain many members among the young and the educated in Western countries, and to build up a truly Catholic identity with well-marked boundaries and unashamed proselytism. Viewed at first with some suspicion by the ecclesiastical hierarchy, these groups played a leading part in expounding and illustrating the change of direction imparted to the Church by John Paul II. The political expression of this movement varied from country to country: it was very explicit in Poland and Italy but less so in France. But the proselytizing strength and long-term aims of the various movements are very similar. They proclaim the futility of a society dominated by reason alone, show through communal experience the need to rediscover God and so save mankind, and suggest how society can be rebuilt on a foundation of Christian teaching.

The year 1979 – in Islam the fifteenth century of the Hegira – began with the return of Ayatollah Khomeini to Teheran in February and the proclamation of an Islamic republic, and closed with the November attack on the Great Mosque in Mecca by an armed group opposed to Saudi control of the Holy Places. These two spectacular events opened the eyes of the world to the political potential of Islam, a potential further developed since by some of its adherents. But they were not isolated events: they belong to a

wider sequence which has given Islam a social and political dimension often obscured hitherto by attempts at modernization on the
part of the post-colonial ruling classes.

The 1970s brought Islamic movements to the centre stage, from
Malaysia to Senegal, from the Soviet Islamic Republics to the
European suburbs inhabited by established immigrants. Though
the resurgence of political Islam may have startled many Western
observers accustomed to think of Third-World religions as a pictur-
esque survival, it was only the most visible part of a vast sub-
terranean movement to re-Islamize daily life and customs and
reorganize individual existence according to the injunctions of the
sacred books.

This movement claims to represent a cultural break with the
outlook and motivations of modern secularism, which it blames
for all the ills of Third-World societies, from social inequality to
despotism, and from endemic under-employment to widespread
corruption. Many of its members are highly qualified, especially
in science, and they aim to detach the most advanced technology
– which they intend to master – from the values of secularization
which they reject, in order to promote an ethics which submits
reason to God.

This survey could be extended indefinitely. We may recall that
in 1976 the fervent Baptist Jimmy Carter was elected President
of the United States, and deployed his moral and religious convictions in cleansing the American executive of the sin of Watergate.
In 1980 his rival, Ronald Reagan, was elected largely because he
captured the votes of most of the Evangelical and fundamentalist
electors who followed the advice of politico-religious bodies such
as the Moral Majority. Created in 1979, this movement aimed
at making America – crisis-ridden, weakened by double-figure
inflation and humiliated by the hostage-taking of its embassy staff
in Teheran – into a new Jerusalem.

There too, the religious movements of the 1970s touched all
levels of society; they were not confined to the rural, conservative
southern states, but attracted members both from the black and
Hispanic minorities and from the White Anglo-Saxon Protestants,
and developed a huge preaching and financing network thanks to
their exceptional mastery of television and the most sophisticated
forms of communication. Under Jimmy Carter, and above all

Ronald Reagan, some of them had easy access to the White House and the highest political circles; they used it to promote their vision of a society founded on the observance of 'Christian values' – from school prayers to the prohibition of abortion.

These movements, in all their diversity, began to achieve prominence from the mid-1970s onwards. Most of them had come into being earlier, but none had attracted a large audience until that time. They had not drawn the masses after them, and their ideals or slogans appeared outdated or retrograde at a time of widespread social optimism. In the postwar period, earthly utopias had triumphed: in Europe, which had emerged from the nightmare of war and destruction and had discovered the horror of the extermination of the Jews, all energies were turned to building new societies that would exorcize the morbid phantasms of the past. The building of socialism in the East and the birth of the consumer society in the West left little room for the expression of ideologies seeking to draw upon religion for the guidelines of the social order. The improved standard of living resulting from the considerable advances in technology fostered an uncritical belief in progress, so much so that 'progressiveness' itself became a criterion of value. Nothing seemed unattainable – even the moon, on which American astronauts set foot in the summer of 1969.

This euphoria was not shared by everyone. But in the West criticisms of the social system by the disadvantaged, those left to fend for themselves in the rush for growth, found a sounding board in the slogans of communism, while on the other side of the Iron Curtain dissident thinkers saw the West as the beckoning shangri-la. The polarization of the world by the Cold War only intensified the competing attractions of Moscow and Washington, displaying the two poles as a fundamental dilemma outside which there was no salvation. Believers were called upon to be *committed*, to stand up for the free world or for socialism, and this slowly led to the subordination of faith to the attainment of worldly ideals, of the beyond to the here and now.

The Vatican II Ecumenical Council grew out of this age in which the modern world was viewed with optimism. It tried hard to formulate the Catholic message in the language of secular society, many of whose ideals it espoused, including justice, the right to development and so on, trying to trace their origins in

Christian doctrine. Contemporaries may have noticed mainly how modern the vocabulary was, or may even have thought of this *aggiornamento* as the Church's final surrender; but when, twenty years later, John Paul II set out to reconquer hearts and minds, he started from the Christian roots of the principles enunciated in Vatican II.

In the independent Third-World countries, religion is often held to be a bar to 'progress' – meaning the mobilization of a nation behind its new rulers. Nevertheless, during the struggle against the colonial powers religious affiliation was used as a weapon, even by progressives, when it helped to unite the 'natives' against the 'colonists' and foster a (sometimes inchoate) national identity. But once the new government was firmly in control the clergy were sent back to their books, and the politico-religious movements that had accompanied the new nation on its road to victory were persecuted or destroyed.

Nasser's Egypt, the beacon of Arab progressivism, provides a notable illustration of this process. Nasser, whose seizure of power in 1952 was applauded by the Muslim Brothers from whom he had acquired the rudiments of his world vision, worked implacably to destroy that powerful politico-religious association which was the last obstacle to his autocratic government. And in 1964 the government carried out a radical reform of the Islamic university of Al Azhar, to turn its clerical graduates into transmission belts for Nasser's ideology: their task was to proclaim its virtues as good Islamic orthodoxy. The aim was not to drive religion from the political scene, but to forbid any expression of religion not controlled by the government and to make it into a tool for legitimizing the social order.

During the 1960s this sort of tame religious discourse was a mere auxiliary to the slogans then in vogue – progressivism, anti-imperialism, socialism, positive neutralism, etc. It was aimed largely at sections of the population who did not understand the categories of modern rhetoric, and was somewhat despised by the intelligentsia which supported and expounded the ruling ideology. This situation lasted until the traumatic military defeat by Israel in June 1967 which, in a flash of revelation, threw all the independent Arab societies into turmoil and, by subverting the rules of the ideological game, opened the way for Islamic dissent.

When we look at the religious movements then flourishing in every quarter of the globe, we are led to speculate on the wholesale changes which have affected contemporary societies in the last quarter of the twentieth century, changes whose effects are widely discussed, but whose causes are not always perceived. But if we are going to look at these movements, however strange, aberrant or fanatical some of them may seem to us, we have to take seriously both what they are saying and the alternative societies they are trying to build in response to the confusion they feel in a world from which their landmarks have disappeared.

Our working hypothesis will be that what these movements say and do is meaningful, and does not spring from a dethronement of reason or from manipulation by hidden forces; rather it is the undeniable evidence of a deep malaise in society that can no longer be interpreted in terms of our traditional categories of thought. Taking them seriously does not, however, make us into either their advocates or their fellow-travellers, any more than a person whose eyes had been opened to the condition of the proletariat by reading communist literature had to become a member of the Party.

The contemporary world has left the industrial era behind and entered a new era in which both social relationships and international affairs are being transformed in a way we cannot easily categorize; perhaps the emergence of these religious movements may help us to do so. They are true children of our time: unwanted children, perhaps, bastards of computerization and unemployment or of the population explosion and increasing literacy, and their cries and complaints in these closing years of the century spur us on to seek out their parentage and to retrace their unacknowledged genealogy.

Like the workers' movement of yesteryear, today's religious movements have a singular capacity to reveal the ills of society, for which they have their own diagnosis. This diagnosis itself yields a clue, which must be investigated. Not to do so would be to join the false prophets who descend into the triviality of saying that the twenty-first century (or the third millennium) will either be religious or will not – and that is far from being our present intention.

To interpret what these movements are saying, we have to hear it in the context of their social praxis in a process of mutual illumination. It is not without significance that, in some societies, the most important religious movements develop a strategy of breaking with the established order via a revolutionary seizure of power, whereas in others the pietist form takes over and transforms the system without violence, either by sapping it from within or by exerting pressure on the decision-making bodies.

We shall review four of these contexts, observing in each how the religious movements within them are behaving: Mediterranean Islam, Catholicism in Europe, North American Protestantism, and Judaism both in Israel and among the Jews of the diaspora.

1

The Sword and the Koran

In the Muslim countries of the Mediterranean basin and its
environs, re-Islamization movements took over from groups
inspired by Marxism in challenging the foundation values of the
social order. This was during the 1970s, when violent conflicts
broke out between the two movements for control of potential
sources of revolt. This meant, above all, the universities and the
outer suburbs of large cities, amid the sprawl of shanty towns and
makeshift dwellings. By the early 1980s the Marxists had been
beaten everywhere on the ground, and sporadic Islamist agitation
continued throughout the decade, peaking with the assault on the
Great Mosque at Mecca in 1979, the assassination of Sadat in
1981, and Afghan resistance to the Soviet invasion.

And yet only in Iran did the insurgents succeed in achieving
the aim of all the most radical activist groups, namely to seize
power. The violence of the 1980s, crystallized by the Iran–Iraq
war and the civil war in the Lebanon, or exacerbated by terrorism,
proved unable to undermine the social order or to have the effect
on international relations that the Islamic militants hoped for.
However, there was a 'creeping' re-Islamization 'from below',
affecting customs and life styles, criss-crossing the social fabric of
the countries of the Muslim world. In Algeria (for example) this
process eventually created an immense network of local opposition
which, when the time was ripe, precipitated the downfall of a
dictatorship that had lasted for a quarter of a century.

From Marxist challenge to Islamic 'break'

If we wish to trace the fortunes of the re-Islamization movements to the closing years of the twentieth century, we must first go back to the 1960s and the euphoria of newly independent nations.

Colonial domination had given place nearly everywhere to independent states. From Turkey, whence the foreign armies had been expelled by Ataturk half a century earlier, to Algeria which the French left at the beginning of the decade, native elites took over power and were in unfettered control of relations between the state and society. At first the heady atmosphere of independence spared the rulers from any criticism, by masking or lessening social conflicts. Bearers of modernity and change, the groups in power had a strong legitimacy, due to the part they had played in the victorious struggle against the colonial power, and the new regimes built their symbolism around the important dates and stirring deeds of the wars of liberation and of the events that foreshadowed them.

The first serious difficulties emerged along with the frustrations of managing poverty-stricken economies during the population explosion of the 1960s. In an endeavour to copy the Soviet model, embryonic heavy industries were established from the banks of the Nile to the Sahara, but they soon proved incapable of competing on the world market and turned into financial black holes. Their other – ideological – purpose, namely to create a working class in societies where no such class existed, so as to bring reality into line with Marxist theories, was hardly more successful.

In Muslim countries claiming to operate under market rules, these rules were constantly abrogated by the persistence of feudal mechanisms and the development of large-scale corruption. Very little was done to provide employment or housing for the hordes of younger people who were deserting the countryside for the shanty towns. This Third-World social problem, which, in the widespread poverty it revealed, had something in common with the formation of the proletariat in nineteenth-century Europe, exacerbated the conflicts between the ruling elites and the common people, and began to undermine the political consensus that had prevailed in the early days of independence.

The first to try to make capital from the discontent surfacing in Muslim countries around the Mediterranean were groups inspired by Marxism – even though in the late 1960s there were in those countries virtually no organized Marxist communist parties powerful and independent of the ruling group and capable of leading a revolutionary movement.[1] In self-styled 'socialist' countries with Soviet connections, such as Syria, Egypt, Iraq and Algeria, there were communists in the ruling coalitions, but they were imprisoned, tortured, killed, or forced into exile when their criticisms overstepped the bounds judged acceptable by Nasser, the leaders of the Ba'ath party[2] or those of the National Liberation Front in Algeria. In the conservative or 'bourgeois' states which had no communists in their administration, communist parties and organizations of various persuasions come into being either underground, as in Iran or Turkey, or legally, as in the Lebanon. The various communist groups lacked the resources to overthrow the ruling regimes, either because they had few militant members or because of the severity of the countermeasures taken against them, but their world view somehow fostered aspirations of many of those who would have liked to make far-reaching changes in the social order. No other subversive ideology was so well articulated, containing both a radical critique of the existing order and a blueprint for a better society.

In 'socialist' countries, Marxists in opposition attributed all the ills of society to a betrayal of true socialist ideals by the ruling military oligarchies, whom they accused of having formed exploitative and cynical 'state bourgeoisies'. This was the case with Nasser's Egypt, which Anwar Abdel Malek termed a 'military society' and Mahmoud Hussein called the scene of a 'class

---

1 On the growth of communist movements in the Muslim world, see Maxime Rodinson's book *Marxisme et monde musulman* (Paris: Seuil, 1972), esp. p. 297ff. Also Hanna Batatu, *The Old Social Classes and the Revolutionary Movement of Iraq* (Princeton, NJ: Princeton University Press, 1978). More accessible, the biography of Henri Curiel by Gilles Perrault, *Un homme à part* (Barrault, 1984), evokes the atmosphere that prevailed when communism first appeared in Egypt.
2 The Ba'ath party, which is striving for Arab 'resurrection' from a somewhat secularist angle, is officially in power in Syria and in Iraq. In actual fact its ideological role is very restricted, and follows the *Realpolitik* of presidents Assad and Saddam Hussein in power in Damascus and Baghdad. On this party, see in particular Itamar Rabinovitch, *Syria under the Ba'ath* (Israel Universities Press, 1972) and Nikolaos Van Dam, *The Struggle for Power in Syria* (London: Croom Helm, 1979).

struggle'.[3] These two authors represent an outlook widely shared by the revolutionary intelligentsia and by students in the Muslim world at that time.

In the conservative states, too, the universities were dominated ideologically by student unions, legal or illegal, in which Marxist militants played a leading part. In Morocco, Tunisia, Turkey and Lebanon, there was a burgeoning of leftist groups at the end of the 1960s whose critique of society and vision of the future drew substantially on Marxist-Leninist literature adapted to local conditions.

In Algeria – recently decolonized, and retaining close cultural links with France – the early 1970s saw the emergence of a mass student leftist movement which, led by the communist-oriented PAGS (Socialist Avant-Garde Party) threw its weight behind agrarian reform. This 'avant-garde', inspired as much by the events of May 1968 in France as by Havana or Beijing, believed that reformist agitation would precipitate a revolution in the countryside and speed Colonel Houari Boumedienne's military-'progressive' regime along the path to socialism. These young Algerians thought and wrote in French, the language of the Marxist texts which had inspired them. Most of them had little knowledge of written Arabic. Disturbed by these excesses, the government countered them by bringing back Arabic-speaking students from the Middle East, where they had made contact with the Muslim Brothers.[4] This policy, which was followed by a systematic Arabization of Algeria, helped to weaken the Marxist pressure groups and give the whip-hand to the Islamic movements.

In the Middle East, the years in between the Arab–Israeli wars of 1967 and 1973 were when the Marxist opposition believed that its hour had come. The collapse of the armies of both progressive and conservative Arab states in June 1967 provoked a major crisis of legitimacy for the rulers in power, already weakened by their

---

3   Anwar Abdel Malek, *Egypt Military Society* (New York, 1968); Mahmoud Hussein, *Class Conflict in Egypt, 1945–70* (New York, 1973). Mahmoud Hussein was converted to democracy and to 'the emergence of the individual in the third world' in *Versant sud de la liberté* (Paris: La Découverte, 1989).
4   See Ahmed Rouadja, *Les Frères et la mosquée: enquête sur le mouvement islamiste en Algérie* (Paris: Karthala, 1990), p. 111ff. On Arabization, Gilbert Grandguillaume, *Arabisation et politique linguistique au Maghreb* (Paris: Maisonneuve & Larose, 1983).

general inability to deal with social questions. While Nasser's charisma was withering with the defeat of the Egyptian army at the hands of the Jewish state, a new supreme cause fired the Muslim world – Palestine, which became the symbol of resistance to Israel and Western imperialism. No longer did the rulers in power set the tone: instead, it was a fighting organization, reminiscent of the liberation movements of a decade earlier, which enabled youths who had not known those stirring times to experience them afresh.

The Marxists lost no time in becoming the mouthpiece and the intransigent advocates of the Palestinian resistance and accusing Arab governments of 'betrayal'. This widened their appeal considerably, especially among students. More than ever, it looked as if revolution was in prospect in the Middle East; yet, when the big revolution came in the 1970s, it was not under the banner of Marx or Lenin. It was the birth of the Islamic Republic of Iran – which nobody had foreseen. History played a trick on Western foreign offices by substituting one revolution for another: where they had expected to see a leftist in his keffieh, there was a turbaned mullah brandishing his Kalashnikov. But, beyond the clash of symbols and their obvious contrasts, the way that the triumphant Islamic movements swept the Marxists off the field raises fundamental questions with repercussions beyond the Muslim world.

The aspiration for a better world changed register and passed from the secular domain to the religious. Sudden and unexpected though this religious upsurge may have appeared on the surface, it was in fact the culmination of a hidden process which I shall attempt to trace back to its source.

At that time it was thought – mistakenly – that secularization was a straightforward, unstoppable process, in the Muslim world as elsewhere. Islam was regarded as an outmoded belief held only by rural dotards and backward reactionaries. While this impression may have had some basis in reality, it owed much to the fact that certain secularized intellectuals had a virtual monopoly of opinion-forming, and projected on to society as a whole the changes that had taken place in themselves. Largely for this reason, the opinions of those who continued to insist that the social order must have a religious foundation went unperceived. Far from having suddenly disappeared, they had only lost a battle and had retired to ponder the reasons for their defeat.

In fact, most of the nationalist movements had had a religious component, which had been instrumental in tipping the whole country over into anti-colonial rebellion, and was prominent in the multifarious combats which preceded real independence. The Association of Algerian Ulemas, behind its chief theoretician Abdelhamid Ben Badis,[5] did a great deal to infuse an Islamic tone into the pronouncements of the National Liberation Front. This was all the easier because religious affiliation also served as a criterion of radical differentiation between Algerian Muslims and both the French colonists, many of whom were third-generation Algerians, and the Jews, who had been 'Algerians' from time immemorial.

Of all the movements campaigning for an Islamic state after independence, the best known was born in Egypt. Since their foundation in 1928, the Muslim Brothers[6] had formed a network of sympathizers numbering over a million before Nasser and his comrades, the Free Officers, seized power in 1952. They were among the most fervent supporters of the new regime, and were well acquainted with some of its top leaders, to whom they had taught the rudiments of their political culture. Nasser himself, and above all his successor Sadat, who came from modest, non-Westernized backgrounds, had been steeped in a world view which drew on the Koran when expressing its desire for social change.

But by the end of 1954, Nasser felt secure enough to turn on his erstwhile allies – now his only remaining political opponents – and liquidate them. He did so with unexampled brutality, even compared with the excesses of the colonial armies of occupation. Until the mid-1960s nothing more was heard of the Muslim Brothers; those of its leaders who had not been hanged or imprisoned had taken refuge in the oil sheikdoms of the Arabian Peninsula.

Not until 1965 did the *raïs*, beset by many difficulties, recall

5   Cf. Ali Merad, *Le Réformisme musulman en Algérie* (Paris and The Hague: Mouton, 1963).
6   See Richard P. Mitchell, *The Society of the Muslim Brothers* (Oxford: Oxford University Press, 1969) and Olivier Carré and Gérard Michaud, *Les Frères musulmans (1928–1982)* (Paris: Gallimard/Julliard, 1983).

the Brothers to public notice by denouncing a plot they were supposed to have hatched against him – a pretext for a new campaign of repression which culminated in the execution of the main theoretician of the movement, Sayyid Qutb, the author of a radical Islamic criticism of Nasser's regime, which he had written in a concentration camp. So the Islamic politico-religious movement was still alive, sufficiently so to be targeted for persecution in 1965, but it had not succeeded in regaining an audience comparable with that of the 1940s. This was due not only to the totalitarian nature of the regime but also to the difficulty of getting across, in the 'progressivist' climate of the 1960s, a message whose vision of an ideal society was based rigidly on uncompromising adherence to the holy scriptures. Marxism and its local derivatives had already cornered the market in utopias.

Sayyid Qutb's message, promulgated in the early 1960s, did not find a significantly large readership or mould the thinking of generations of militants until a dozen or so years later, when the radical pessimism of its diagnosis of post-independence Egyptian society matched with the disarray of the 1970s – in Egypt as in the rest of the Muslim world. By then Nasser's Egypt had become in retrospect the prime example of despotism and muddle, the prize cockshy – Nasser's Egypt, once the leading light of pan-Arabism to every 'progressive' eye.

Islam versus jahiliyya

This message, which has earned its author an immense reputation among contemporary Muslims, is to be found mainly in two books written during the closing years of Qutb's life: *In the Shadow of the Koran*, a voluminous commentary on the sacred books of Islam, and *Signposts*, a manifesto that was dubbed 'the "What is to be done?" of the Islamic movement'.[7] Qutb's originality lies in the fact that, from the outset, he radically dissociated Islam from all other human societies of his time, not excluding self-styled 'Islamic' societies. He held that there was no longer any Islamic society,

---

7   See Olivier Carré, *Mystique et politique: lecture révolutionnaire du Coran par Sayyid Qutb, frère musulman radical* (Paris: Presses de la FNSP/Cerf, 1984); Gilles Kepel, *The Prophet and Pharaoh: Muslim Extremism in Egypt* (Berkeley: University of California Press, 1985).

and therefore no point in seeking Islam in a world that had cast it out. There was nothing in the world but *jahiliyya*: this word, which to Muslims means the period of 'ignorance' and 'barbarism' before the Prophet Mohammed preached in Arabia, was applied by Qutb to the twentieth-century societies which seemed to him so contrary to the essence of Islam.

The true Muslim should break with the *jahiliyya* and then struggle to destroy it and build the Islamic state on its ruins. He must follow the example of the Prophet Mohammed and his companions, who in the year 622 AD (year 1 of the Hegira) left Mecca, where the *jahiliyya* prevailed, for Medina, whence they returned as conquerors eight years later, overthrowing the idols and proclaiming Islam.

Qutb's wish to break with the world was very singular. It was contrary to the position adopted by most Muslims – even most of the Muslim Brothers – during the 1960s. They held that there could be no breaking with a society which was, however imperfectly, Islamic, and that believers should preach *within* it for the true establishment of Islam. Qutb, on the other hand, thought that Nasser's 'barbarism' had reached a point of no return, beyond all possible compromise. The symbolic import of this concept of *jahiliyya*, which took Islam back to its origins and bypassed fifteen centuries of Muslim history, was cataclysmic: in the eyes of Qutb and his disciples, *jahiliyya* was idolatry. Men were not worshipping the One God, Allah, but a man like themselves, who had usurped the divine sovereignty which guarantees justice on this earth – the despot, the 'Pharaoh'. He governed as he alone thought fit and ignored the commands of the revealed Book; he was the incarnation of injustice, whereas the true Muslim prince enthrones justice upon this earth because he applies nothing but the Law of God, the *shar'ia*. This ideal could not be realized unless a chosen few of the faithful undertook the reconquest of society after having broken with it.

Qutb was put to death before he had had time to explain exactly what he understood by a 'break': did it involve physical withdrawal from the world and re-creating in the desert an 'anti-society' that would take the *jahiliyya* by storm, or did it mean simply distancing oneself intellectually from it and preserving a cloistered Islamic virtue? His successors in the 1960s battled furiously among themselves on this issue, but it is this idea of a break, in its many interpretations, that is at the root of contemporary movements of re-Islamization. It considers any surrounding society to be a *jahiliyya*, a very model of godlessness, injustice and despotism.

Qutb was executed in 1966 and he never saw his ideas bear fruit. At that time Nasser possessed not only a formidable apparatus of repression, but also a charisma and prestige that remained considerable until Israel's victory over the Arabs in June 1967 destroyed his legitimacy.

The symbolic meaning of that event in the Muslim world was far-reaching. It opened the door to radical challenges to the post-independence regimes, whose military defeat was immediately construed as a sign of overall failure. People began to transfer their allegiance from their own heads of state to the Palestinian resistance – in other words, to militant revolutionary organizations.

A fault line – initially secular in origin – then opened up across the various societies concerned, demolishing the political consensus which had experienced no such shock since independence. For in addition to armed insurrection against Israel which up to that time had yielded little in the way of results, the Palestinian resistance embodied the revolutionary alternative by fighting against the Arab states on whose territories it was living. The effects of this were visible in Jordan, where the confrontation with King Hussein in September 1970 imperilled the king and ended in a bloodbath, the 'Black September' of the PLO.[8] In Lebanon, Palestinian support for the 'Islamo-progressive' movement enabled it to defy the authority of the state and to foment the antagonisms which, in 1975, led to civil war. In Egypt, the Palestinian example galvanized the student and workers' movements who challenged Sadat's power and induced him to take the offensive against Israel;[9] most of the countries in the region were affected in one way or another by the dispute.

---

8 See Olivier Carré, *Septembre noir: refus arabe de la résistance palestinienne* (Brussels: Complexe, 1980).
9 Ahmed Abdallah, *The Student Movement and National Politics in Egypt* (London: Al Saqi Books, 1985).

The Islamization of dissent

Until war broke out between Israel and the Arabs in October 1973, pro-Marxist groups were the chief spokesmen along this sociopolitical fault line. That line did not yet cross the 'Islamic break' of which Sayyid Qutb was the theorist. Only after the war did movements inspired by Qutb's blueprint for the reaffirmation of Islamic identity begin to edge the Marxist left off the field of revolt.

The aftermath of war in 1973 was quite different from what it had been in 1967. Israel had won the actual war, repelling the Arab offensives and penetrating deeply into enemy territory; but she had suffered a first political defeat with the ending of the myth of her invincibility. Furthermore, the Arab oil-producing countries had found oil embargo to be an excellent way of putting pressure on Israel's Western allies, and so on Israel herself.

The war indirectly influenced the development of religious movements through the 1970s, in Islam and elsewhere. By upsetting the balance of the international economy it provoked spirals of inflation and unemployment that destablized sociopolitical systems, particularly in the West, and led to an atomization of society, undermining social cohesion and the welfare state. This was a golden opportunity for religious movements of all kinds, all over the world, to proclaim the values of self-determination.[10] Moreover, the oil states of the Arabian Peninsula, especially Saudi Arabia, used their new and fabulous riches to buy themselves a leading role in world affairs. And one of the priority aims of Saudi Arabia was to propagate Islam – in its Saudi version – throughout the world.

This 'petro-Islam' was the real victor in the war of 1973, but it was scarcely equipped to challenge the social order, even in the name of the Koran. Its spokesmen were generally to be found in the ranks of the 'conservatives'. Nevertheless, while slow to take the measure of the Islamic movements inspired by Sayyid Qutb, it funded them and promoted their spread.

This paradoxical situation, which ended with the passing of the

10   Gilles Kepel, *Les Banlieues de l'Islam* (Paris: Seuil, 1987) relates this development to the spread of Islam in France.

revolutionary torch from the Marxists to the Islamists, must be grasped if we are to understand the re-Islamization movements between the mid-1970s and the early 1990s. After a 'revolutionary' decade, culminating in the 'Islamic' hostage-taking and terrorism between 1985 and 1988, a fresh historical sequence gradually appears in which re-Islamization comes mainly 'from below', from the network of mosques and pietist associations whose tendrils were spreading through civil society.

The decade of Revolutionary Islam

From the mid-1970s to the mid-1980s the re-Islamization movements mostly agreed that seizure of power was a valid objective. This revolutionary interpretation of Sayyid Qutb's programme could take many different forms, ranging from violent action to tactical participation in the seesaw of politics, but all were expressions of ٺ strategy of 're-Islamization from above'. At first it really looked as if the dream might come true: to Muslims, the successes of Saudi Arabia and her allies in the oil war had a symbolic significance, and were generally seen as a sign from God heralding the coming triumph of Islam over the whole world.

At that point the attitude of Muslims themselves to Islam underwent a transformation. Ten years earlier Saudi Arabia had been regarded as a backward region, dependent on the West, and Nasserist rhetoric was the embodiment of resistance to imperialism.[11] After the Arab defeat of 1967 this rhetoric became muted; after the oil victory of 1973 it finally fell into disuse, whereas Islam, championed by the Saudis, was a synonym for victorious confrontation with Israel, America and their allies.

The signs change, but oil was simply the midwife of this reborn Islam, the nerve of the *jihad* that the Islamist groups were to unleash against the *jahiliyya*. The cheques may have been issued in Riyadh, but until the middle of the 1980s those who cashed them had their eyes fixed on Teheran.

---

11   See Malcolm Kerr, *The Arab Cold War: Gamal'Abd al-Nasir and his Rivals, 1958–1970* (Oxford: Oxford University Press, 1971).

From the shanty towns to the university

The startling leap in the price of crude turned the producer countries into an air-conditioned earthly paradise – and into the bankers of re-Islamization – but its effects did not stop there. In the long term it also loosened social bonds in the societies that belonged more or less to the 'petrodollar zone'. The inflows of currency sharpened the contrasts between the countryside and the towns in which the wealth that flowed from royalties was concentrated, and monetary inflation took hold. The flight from the countryside reached an unprecedented scale, and the big cities of the Middle East were flooded with 'decountrified countrymen'[12] who made their abode in outlying shanty towns and other shaky tenements thrown up with scant regard for the building regulations. Government departments were unable to stem this human tide, whose hand-to-mouth existence was organized through unofficial support networks of their own race or province, above all of their religion. Mosques, large and small, were built in these new suburbs long before town halls or police stations; they were surrounded by charitable and educational associations which took over the responsibility for communal life from a state whose infrastructures were collapsing under the weight of population growth and urban immigration. From South Teheran to the *gecekondu*[13] of Istanbul, from the City of the Dead in Cairo to the shanty towns around Algiers, Islamic welfare networks were coming to play an essential part in assimilating those elements of the population who aspired to taste the fruits of modernity and prosperity, but could not get at them.[14]

There was another sector equally affected by the disruption that plagued the Mediterranean basin during the 1970s – the universities. In their eagerness to promote a policy of mass edu-

---

12 This expression was used by Farhad Khosrokhavar in 'Hassan K., a decountrified countryman, speaks about the revolution in Iran', *Peuples méditerranéens*, 11 (1980), pp. 3-30.
13 Literally: 'built during the night'. The word is used for the practice of erecting buildings without a permit between sunset and sunrise, so that the police cannot oppose it. This is common practice throughout the Muslim world.
14 See CERMOC (Centre d'études et de recherches sur le Moyen-Orient contemporain), *Mouvements communautaires et espaces urbains au Maghreb* (Beirut, 1985); Ahmed Rouadjia, op. cit.; Gilles Kepel, *The Prophet and Pharaoh*, op. cit.

cation which they thought essential to economic takeoff, governments in the region had opened higher education to the ever-growing hordes of young people, many of whom had left the countryside for the precarious life of the sprawling suburbs. In most of those countries the educational structures were unable to cope: a badly paid and understaffed teaching body (for teachers went abroad in search of better salaries) was faced with crowded lecture halls. In such circumstances underpaid teachers organized expensive private 'revision' lessons during which the examination subjects were dealt with, or sold photocopies of their lectures, and so on.

The universities were symptomatic of the foundering of the welfare utopias run by the independent states. As a free service they could not meet the huge demand on a basis of equality, and only corruption could restore the balance by offering a better education to those who could afford to pay.

It was at this point that the Islamist movements made their most significant social breakthrough, by organizing free revision classes and extra tuition and by selling copies of lecture notes at low prices. They shielded women students from often distasteful contact with the men by special pick-up coaches or by insisting that the sexes occupy separate benches in the lecture rooms. Thus they provided a whole range of 'services' to students. They began by remedying the most obvious deficiencies, and gradually instilled an attitude of 'Islamic break' with the surrounding world. They were favourably regarded both by the oil sheikhs, who (up to the Iranian revolution) were ready to pour money over anything that claimed to be Islamic, and by the governments concerned.

In both Egypt and the Mahgreb, governments treated the Islamist groups favourably in order to 'break the leftists'[15] who were keeping up an agitation on the campuses reminiscent of that in the European universities. By the mid-1970s they had completed the task just about everywhere, and pictures of Lenin finally vanished behind the slogan *Allah Akbar*, 'god is great'.

The Islamist militants in the universities cleverly linked charity and social concern with their political and religious aims: for

15 For the Mahgreb, see particularly Ahmed Rouadjia, op. cit., and François Burgat, *L'Islamisme au Mahgreb: la voix du sud* (Paris: Karthala, 1988).

example, they offered impecunious women students a complete set of clothing for a ridiculously low price. It was, of course, 'Islamic dress' – veil, long dress, gloves and so forth. When, in the mid-1970s, they were allowed to stand in university elections, they filled most if not all the positions for student representatives. They trounced both the official candidates and the Marxists in opposition – though they generally resorted to intimidation when ordinary electoral propaganda proved unavailing. Like the extreme leftist militants who trawled the 'mass organizations' for recruits to the proletarian revolution, the Islamists found among the 'disinherited' whom they helped the warriors of revolution in the name of God.

The first significant clashes between Islamist groups and government occurred in Egypt, where a plot was unearthed as early as 1974. But it was in 1977 that Sadat's government made a spectacular swoop on a sect that had carried Sayyid Qutb's idea of an 'Islamic break' to its furthest extremes. Led by a young agronomist who had been imprisoned under Nasser, its disciples practised the separation between the 'true believers' and impious society (*jahiliyya*) by living in closed communities in caves in Middle Egypt and, above all, in the shanty towns round Cairo.

Leaving their families, their studies and even their spouses (since ties contracted under the *jahiliyya* were not binding), the disciples led an 'Islamic' existence, regulating their daily life on the pattern of the Prophet as interpreted by their leader, Shukri Mustapha. Refusing civil-service jobs so as not to serve the godless state, they earned their living as itinerant traders or lived on remittances sent by those whom Shukri had sent to work in the oil states of the Arabian Peninsula. The social organization of this sect reflected not only Qutb's ideology, but also the typical survival strategies of poor people in the overpopulated Islamic countries of today.

Emigration to the Gulf or to Europe is still the most popular way of earning a living in a saturated employment market. Shukri put a different gloss on this necessity by Islamizing it. The Arab word for emigration, *hijra*, also means the 'hegira', the flight of the Prophet to Medina. For Shukri and his disciples, the communities living in the suburbs or the caves were Medina all over again. Their wish was to begin the fight against the *jahiliyya* as soon as they were strong enough, and to march on Cairo, there to restore

Islam as they interpreted it, just like the Prophet returning in triumph to Mecca.

But things did not turn out quite as they wished. In 1977 the Egyptian government arrested some of the disciples. Shukri retorted by taking hostage a religious dignitary, whom he subsequently had murdered. Thereupon the sect was broken up and its main leaders executed. This was the first setback suffered by the Islamist strategy for seizing power. But Shukri and his followers were extremely poor analysts of the political situation, and by applying Qutb's teachings to the letter they made themselves very easy targets for repression.

It was in 1979 that all the hopes of the movements for re-Islamization 'from above' began to be realized – but not in the Sunni Arab world, and not by Qutb's followers. It was in Shi'ite Iran that the Islamic revolution came to power, in February, when Ayatollah Khomeini returned to Teheran. But Khomeini's victory was due to a twofold chain of causation which had no equivalent in the Sunni world, where, in consequence, it could not be repeated.

The special features of the revolution in Iran

To begin with, there were some unique and paradoxical features about the economic and political situation in Iran under the Shah. The fabulous riches flowing from oil had enabled this very populous country to afford well-endowed infrastructures of all kinds. Unlike their counterparts in Egypt and Syria, the universities in Iran were not staging posts on the way to unemployment. The teaching staff, who were properly paid, did not all yearn to emigrate in order to improve their standard of living, and they turned out well-qualified graduates. Students who showed promise were sent to the United States for their postgraduate education, with study grants from Iran. The managers and technocrats of the Islamic republic were recruited mainly from these graduates of American universities, once they had let their beards grow.

However, there were structural obstacles that prevented these well-educated elites from making full use of their qualifications and fulfilling their aspirations. The heavy hand of dictatorship, accompanied by savage repression, stifled all freedom of expression, and the fact that the oil revenues, and all that they made possible, were monopolized by unscrupulous operators at the imperial court engendered considerable frustration among these young graduates relegated to the sidelines. Also, the oil wealth had attracted masses of peasants from the country to the suburbs, where they packed into shanty towns, much as in the Sunni Arab world. These were the 'disinherited' who were mobilized by the Islamic revolution.

There was also another feature peculiar to the situation in Iran, connected with the relations between the religious clerics and the government, which were different from those in the Sunni world. In Shi'ite Islam there is a kind of hierarchized clergy, led by certain doctors of the Law, who are adept at interpreting the sacred texts as they see fit. These clergy enjoyed a considerable degree of independence from the government. They had managed to hold on to their vast wealth, especially in land, despite the Shah's attempts to wrest it from them during the 'White Revolution'. As for ideology, Shi'ites hold that no ruler will have legitimacy until the advent of the hidden Imam, the Mahdi, who will conquer the world, 'filling it with justice and truth as it is now filled with lies and injustice'. It is to the Mahdi, whose coming the doctors of the Law await, that Shi'ites owe obedience, though they may, for reasons of convenience, give temporary outward allegiance to the ruling power, an allegiance which can be ended at any moment by the clergy.

This fundamental illegitimacy of the ruler provided a valuable doctrinal basis on which Khomeini could call for the overthrow of the Shah's regime. What triggered the revolution in Iran was the alliance formed between those among the clergy who followed Khomeini and the Islamist student elites, products of the efficient educational system in Iran but frustrated in their attempts to rise in the social scale. This revolutionary alliance was able to assume the leadership of the movement; the 'disinherited' from the crowded suburbs, galvanized into action by pro-revolutionary mullahs, supplied its foot-soldiers.[16]

16   On the Iranian revolution, see in particular Yann Richard, 'Clercs et intellectuels dans la République islamique d'Iran', in *Intellectuels et militants* . . ., ed. Y. Richard and G. Kepel, op. cit.; B. Hourcade and Y. Richard, 'Téhéran au-dessous du volcan', *Autrement* (Paris), 27 (November 1987); Shaul Bakhash, *The Reign of the Ayatollahs* (2nd edn, New York: Basic Books, 1986); Shahpur Haghighat, *1979, Iran: la révolution islamique* (Brussels:

Although the Iranians were certain that their revolution would spread throughout the Muslim world, they were not widely emulated except by members of another Shi'ite population, in Southern Lebanon, where the pro-Khomeini militants of Hizbollah were enrolled by volunteers from Teheran.

The failure of the Sunni Islamist revolutionaries

In the Sunni world, movements trying to bring about Islamization from above emerged defeated from all their violent confrontations with the state. In November 1979, the dawn of the fifteenth century of the Hegira, an Islamist group stormed the Great Mosque at Mecca, the holiest city of Islam. The aim of this spectacular attack was to protest against the corrupt rulers in Riyadh, who, they said, worshipped no god but the rial (the currency of Saudi Arabia) and were lukewarm in the defence of Islam. After a murderous struggle the attackers, who had taken refuge inside the mosque, were captured and subsequently executed.

In October 1981 Anwar Sadat was assassinated at Cairo by militants of the Islamist group Al-Jihad ('the holy war') while at Assyut, at the other end of Egypt, their accomplices seized official buildings, killing many policemen.

The theorist behind Al-Jihad was an electrical engineer named Faraj, who, unlike the agronomist Shukri Mustapha, thought there was no hope of building a counter-society, a new Medina, on the fringes of Cairo the megalopolis. Faraj thought such a society would be an easy target for persecution by the godless state. Once the despot had been killed, however, there would be a mass uprising of the Muslim people of Egypt, and the soldiers themselves would turn their arms against the *jahiliyya*. He was sure that Egyptian soldiers, like the Shah's army in Teheran, would refuse to fire on the crowd. But Sadat's killers were immediately apprehended, sentenced and executed, as were the ringleaders of the Assyut rising. The Islamist revolutionaries had not succeeded in linking up with the mass of the 'disinherited', although the

Complexe, 1985).

suburbs of Cairo contained all the ingredients for a social explosion as dramatic as that in the suburbs of Teheran.

Events took the same course in the other Sunni countries in which Islamist revolutionary movements had surfaced. In February 1982 local members of the Muslim Brotherhood instigated a revolt in the Syrian town of Hama, but it was recaptured by government troops after the air force had bombed the districts in which the uprising was concentrated.[17] Even in Afghanistan, the Muslims who rose against the Soviet invasion, in the hope of overthrowing a communist regime imposed from abroad, failed to take over power, though they controlled the countryside until 1992.[18] And the sporadic plots and revolts that occurred thereafter in the other Muslim countries of the Mediterranean Basin never led to a seizure of power, as happened in Iran.

These repeated defeats of Islamist revolutionary movements are due primarily to the present structure of religious life in Sunni Islam. Unlike their Shi'ite counterparts, the Sunni doctors of the Law, the ulemas, have not preserved any real independence from established governments in post-independence states. Traditionally, they occupied a 'bipolar' position:[19] on the one hand they lectured the Prince and exhorted him in the name of God to treat the *umma* (the Muslim community which it was his task to govern) more justly, especially its poorest members; on the other, they enjoined civil obedience on the *umma*. They had a potent weapon at their disposal, the *takfir* (more or less equivalent to excommunication) that they could pronounce against the Prince if, by his conduct or way of governing, he endangered the existence of Islam. They had the task of assessing such danger, which might take different forms, one of which was intolerable oppression. To pronounce his banishment from the *umma* would have been to unleash, against him and his soldiery, a *jihad* in which all believers were urged to take part.

The great ulemas of medieval Islam whose names have come

---

17   Cf. Michel Seurat, *L'Etat de barbarie* (Paris: Seuil, 1989).
18   Olivier Roy, *Islam and Resistance in Afghanistan* (Cambridge: Cambridge University Press, 1987).
19   This is the term used by Pierre Bourdieu, 'Genèse et structure du champ religieux', *Revue française de sociologie* (December 1971); cf. Gilles Kepel, 'L'Intelligentsia, les oulemas et les islamistes en Egypte', *Revue française de science politique*, 35 (June 1985).

down to us, such as Ibn Taimiya[20] (1263–1328), one of the key figures in the Sunni faith within Islam, were renowned for their refusal to truckle to the rulers of their day. Very early on in Sunni Islam the problem of the legitimacy of the Prince arose, since most of the rulers were not chosen on the basis of their personal qualities, like the Prophet, but had taken power after a coup or succeeded to the throne on a dynastic principle unsupported by the sacred Texts. This being so, the ulemas had thought it prudent to enquire not into the source of their power but the way in which it was exercised. If the Prince was a defender of Islam there was no sense in proclaiming a *jihad* against him, for this would have carried the risk of plunging the community of believers into rebellion and virtually inviting the enemy, Christian or other, over the frontier.

After independence the ulemas of the Sunni world found themselves in a position of extreme weakness *vis-à-vis* the new governments. For these governments had generally taken care to dispossess them of the assets under their control (*waqf, habous*)[21] which were nationalized or redistributed. In some countries, such as Nasser's Egypt, the state monitored institutions for religious studies very closely: the Al Azhar university was 'reformed' from 1964 onwards to make it nothing more than a propaganda instrument for Nasser. The overall effect was to prevent the ulemas as a body from structuring themselves, as the Shi'ite clergy had done, into an independent force which might some day pass into resolute opposition to the regime, taking the 'disinherited' along with it. The Sunni ulemas formed a very heterogeneous body, racked with internal antagonisms, and their most prominent members, like the 'muftis of the Republic' or the sheikh of Al Azhar, had very little power to withstand the wishes of the government.

Few of the militant Islamists in the Sunni world had come up through the ranks of the ulemas. On the contrary, the typical

20 On Ibn Taimiya, see Henri Laoust, *Essai sur les doctrines politiques et sociales d'Ibn Taimiya* (Cairo: IFAO, 1939); on his present-day influence, see Gilles Kepel, 'L'Egypte d'aujourd'hui: mouvement islamiste et tradition savante', *Annales ESC*, 4 (1984); Emmanuel Sivan, 'Ibn Taimiya, father of the Islamic revolution', *Encounter* (May 1983).
21 Words designating endowments dedicated 'to God' by believers, the revenue from which was used to support charitable or pious institutions (koranic schools, mosques, etc.). Administered by the ulemas, they provided them with an income and financial independence of government.

militant is a student in a modern, secular faculty, biased towards the applied sciences. They are typically agronomists, electricians, doctors or engineers who are near completing their studies, and have found their own way into the sacred Texts, which they read and interpret without reference to the learned commentaries of the ulemas and their social inhibitions. Scions of the first generation to be literate in Arabic, they look in the Koran for the quotations which seem best to express their revolt against the established order and call the *umma* to wage a *jihad* against the ungodly Prince.

The group manifesto of Sadat's assassins expresses this attitude in its most extreme and coherent form. Its title is 'the hidden imperative', meaning that the imperative of waging a *jihad* against the non-Islamic government has been hidden by ulemas who are nothing more than its cloistered lackeys. It was therefore the task of Islamist militants to act in place of the ulemas by starting a holy – civil – war against the government.

Whereas in Iran the young Islamist intellectuals made an alliance with the Shi'ite clergy, in Sunni countries the violent opposition between Islamist militants and ulemas contributed largely to the failure of attempts at revolution 'from above'. For unlike the Iranian mullahs, the ulemas did not broadcast appeals for revolution to the 'disinherited' during their Friday sermons in the immense network of mosques. There was only sporadic agitation in the universities and suburbs, and this was always suppressed; it never led to a seizure of power.

These setbacks to the Islamist movements around the Mediterranean Basin meant that Iran, embroiled in a costly war with Iraq, was the only successful example of 're-Islamization from above'. But in the mid-1980s this process got out of hand and ended in international terrorism, spearheaded by the Shi'ite Hizbollah in the Lebanon and backed mainly by the Iranian government. The rulers in Teheran saw the taking of Western hostages and terrorist attacks in Europe as the most logical way of putting pressure on Iraq's allies and military suppliers; it was the continuation of diplomacy – later of war – by other means. Nevertheless, despite some shrewd blows at European security, Teheran lost the battle of terrorism just as it decided not to continue with hostilities against Iraq. The *jihad*, which was supposed to spur the 'oppressed Muslims' of the world into attacks on infidel nations, and which had filled the television news for several years, was espoused only by gangs in Beirut specializing in racket ransom – Islamic style.

Re-Islamization 'from below' and its ambiguities

The Salman Rushdie affair was Khomeini's last attempt to relaunch the international *jihad* before his death in June 1989. In calling for the murder of this British writer of Muslim origin, whom he accused of apostasy for having shown disrespect to the Prophet in his novel *The Satanic Verses*,[22] the imam was hoping to restore Iran, weakened by her inconclusive war against Iraq, to a leading role in the Islamic world. He put political pressure on European countries with Muslim populations by trying to incite them to violence. At the same time he helped to destabilize the countries of the Indian sub-continent, where Rushdie had been born, causing riots that resulted in many deaths.

But the Rushdie affair in fact went beyond the logic of 're-Islamization from above' which characterized the decade of Islamic revolution from the mid-1970s to the mid-1980s. All Teheran had done was to pick up and amplify a movement that had originated outside its traditional control and sphere of influence, among the Indian and Pakistani immigrants in the suburbs of Thatcherite Britain, who were organized along communal and pietist lines.

To understand the switch from 'above' to 'below' that charac-terized re-Islamization movements in the late 1980s, it is necessary to revert to the meaning of the Islamic 'break' (*'uzla* or *mufasala* in Arabic). For most of Sayyid Qutb's followers, this break meant a struggle against the *jahiliyya* incarnate in the 'infidel' despot, followed by a seizure of power and the inauguration of an Islamic state subject to the *shar'ia*. The suggested means of doing this varied enormously, from the alternative society of Shukri Musta-pha's group in Egypt to terrorism, with the formation of Islamist political parties as an intermediate solution.

---

22 Salman Rushdie, *The Satanic Verses* (London: Viking, 1988).

Living with the Islamic 'break'

But there is also a different interpretation that focuses on *ways* of breaking with one's society. These ways are very precisely codified; they govern the process of 'withdrawal' by the faithful from their 'godless' environment down to the smallest detail. They relate to everyday life, to ways of eating, dressing, praying, relations with the opposite sex and children, education, and so on. Their ultimate aim is to re-Islamize society as a whole, but in the meantime they allow networks of communities to be formed which already live according to the *shar'ia* in its strictest interpretation. This honeycombing of small areas of society through space and time is what is meant by 're-Islamization from below'.

This approach owes its origin to a pietistic association that was founded in India in 1927, the Jama'at al Tabligh ('Society for the Propagation of Islam').[23] Its founder, Muhammad Ilyas, was disturbed at seeing Muslims, who formed a minority on the subcontinent, 'contaminated' by the Hindu society around them. Unless something drastic happened they would soon become indistinguishable, and Islam would disappear in an unacceptable syncretism. In order to combat this process of assimilation, the Tabligh redefined the Islamic 'break', the radical differentiation between 'Muslims' and 'the strayed' (*khasirun*), as a literal imitation of the conduct and attitudes of the Prophet. Pious Muslims believe that the Prophet Mohammed is the supreme incarnation of the virtues of Islam, and that everyone must try to be as like him as possible. His followers can imitate him in spirit, and find in his political tactics the inspiration for contemporary conflicts, as did the revolutionary Islamist militants who took the flight to Medina and the subsequent victorious march on Mecca as the model for their own political action. They can also copy Mohammed in the smallest of his actions, consecrated by his status as God's Messenger.

This latter way was the one chosen by the Tabligh. Its disciples followed the precepts of a pietist manual entitled *Ryadh al Salihin*

23   On the Tabligh, cf. Gilles Kepel, *Les Banlieues...*, op.cit., and the bibliography to chapter 4. Also Felice Dassetto, *Le Tabligh en Belgique: diffuser l'islam sur les traces du Prophète* (Louvain: Sybidi papers, 1988).

('The garden of pious believers'), consisting of a compilation of verses or sentences from the sacred writings of Islam regarding the Prophet, divided according to subject. Thus, readers wanting to know how to dress find in the 'chapter on dress' that the Prophet preferred to dress in white, that he wore a turban of such and such a size, and so on. A member of the Tabligh reorganizes the whole of his life by the most scrupulous mimicry of this, the only legitimate model. Conversely, everything in the legal organization of society that differs from this archetype has to be rejected as sin and corruption.

In the India of the late 1920s the danger of adulterating Islam, of 'straying', was identified with the Hindu masses. In fifty years the Tabligh spread across the world, until in the 1980s it had become the largest Islamic transnational organization. It continually redefined 'straying' as any aspect of modern life that was not exclusively inspired by reference to the Prophet. Candidates for 'straying' have included various nationalist and socialist movements that have taken root in Islamic countries. When from the 1970s onwards groups of Muslim immigrants settled in Europe, they found themselves isolated, paradoxically rediscovering the situation that had originally faced the Tabligh in India. This gave a considerable boost to the Tabligh, which has exercised a decisive influence on the organization of Islam north of the Mediterranean.

Over and above the doctrinal dimension, the Tabligh and similar movements answer to a social need. By its influence over the groups of 'true believers' who were breaking with the 'godless' societies they lived in, it offered a refuge to individuals who felt wholly at sea in an atmosphere of rapid modernization, flight from the countryside and the breakdown of the old, close-knit rural society. Re-Islamization 'from below' is first and foremost a way of rebuilding an identity in a world that has lost its meaning and become amorphous and alienating. Until the mid-1980s the disciples came mainly from the less educated strata of society, rather than those of the Islamist student militants – unemployed labourers or young people with no prospects, fathers upset by children over whom they had lost their traditional authority, often turning, in their distress, to drink, drugs or crime, until brought back to the path of true religion by the itinerant preachers of these movements.

Unlike the revolutionary Islamist militants, they usually received tolerant treatment from governments, who looked upon them as conservative elements likely to make for social peace in the short term. They provided services, did works of charity, looked after children in koranic schools, and gathered the unemployed together in the mosques, where they were taught to pray and reorganize their lives into a literal imitation of the Prophet: thus it seemed they were preserving them from delinquency and other anti-social behaviour, as well as from revolutionary Islamist militancy. The very states of the Muslim world which had promoted the rise of Islam during the first half of the 1970s so as to eliminate left-wingers from the universities were endeavouring, ten years later, to help the pietist associations in order to counter the influence of the Islamists. Governments in Western Europe, alarmed by pro-Iranian activism among immigrant populations, did the same. More generally, these pietist communities seemed to offer social peace at low cost, sparing governments the highly priced investments needed to end poverty and marginalization. Allowing a mosque to be created in a garage or in the basement of a tower block was much cheaper than financing vocational training courses.

By the end of the 1980s the movements of re-Islamization 'from below' were at the head of powerful networks, which sometimes controlled whole districts and had become the indispensable intermediaries between the public authorities and marginalized social groups. At that point a change occurred in relations with the government: these movements began to take part in political life, a field into which they had seldom ventured before. This happened not only in Muslim countries, but also in Western Europe. It goes a long way to explain the Rushdie affair in Britain, the 'Islamic veil' controversy in France[24] and also the Palestinian Intifada and the emergence of the Islamic Salvation Front in Algeria.

24   On this affair, see below pp. 39–40.

Islamic communities in Europe and the triumph of the Tabligh

The Rushdie affair began in Mrs Thatcher's Britain, a country whose Muslim population, most of whom came from the Indian sub-continent, lived in communities where the religious aspect was much more prominent than it was among their co-religionists in France or Germany. The European headquarters of the Tabligh is in Dewsbury, near Bradford, the declining industrial town in which the imams publicly burnt copies of *The Satanic Verses*. The working-class suburbs and inner cities in which the immigrants live are covered by a huge web of Islamic associations of various shades of feeling and opinion.

This formation of immigrant communities was encouraged by the British authorities, whereas other countries (France, for example) promote individual integration. These differing attitudes towards foreign immigrants have a basis in history: they merely prolong the attitude taken by the respective states towards the peoples living on their territory. France, first under the absolute monarchy and then influenced by the Jacobinism of the Republic 'one and indivisible', took care to level out regional peculiarities, whether linguistic or religious. As regards the latter, an original system of secularism, most completely expressed in the law on the separation of Church and state, tends to limit the expression of confessional allegiance to the private sphere. The very name of the United Kingdom, on the other hand, indicates that it is a federation of nations – chiefly English, Welsh, Scottish and Northern Irish – which have each retained a political identity. Similarly, religion is not a purely private matter: the sovereign is head of the Anglican Church, and Anglican priests can celebrate marriages which are recognized in law, without the need for a civil ceremony (which is required for adherents of other confessions). There is no exact equivalent in English of the French word *laïcité*.[25]

In Britain this tradition was reinforced by the economic liberalism of Mrs Thatcher, anxious to limit state welfare expenditure

---

25 Secularism, undenominationalism – Translator.

which had been considerably increased during the years of Labour government. Cuts in the welfare budgets affected the poorer sections of the population, including immigrants and (of most interest to us) Muslims. This led to a very strained situation, most strikingly exemplified in the Brixton race riots.

Two factors combined in Britain to create a particularly fertile ground for re-Islamization 'from below'. Firstly, immigrant communities had a recognized existence. Secondly, the reduction of state welfare provision encouraged Muslims to turn to self-help networks run by the mosques. The break with the surrounding British *jahiliyya* found a territorial basis in districts that were developing into a sort of ghetto, organized around the mosques and controlled by the imams. These latter were particularly keen to avoid any 'contamination of healthy Muslim youth by the corrupt morals of a depraved West' while simultaneously trying to contain the social ills engendered by unemployment, such as crime and drug addiction.

In the June 1987 elections the re-Islamization networks tried to make political capital out of their investments in communal social control. In a leaflet entitled 'The Muslim Vote' they urged their co-religionists to vote[26] only for candidates who undertook to support a 'charter of Muslim demands' whereby 'the elementary rights of some two million Muslims living in the United Kingdom should be recognized and implemented by the next government'. This charter contained a number of different proposals aimed at strengthening communal segregation and increasing the effective control of Muslims by re-Islamization movements. One of the demands was that books presenting an 'unauthentic' image of Islam should be banned.

When the Rushdie affair exploded, at the end of 1988, the ground had already been largely prepared. The Bradford imams who started the book-burnings were intellectually close to a Pakistani Islamist group, the Jama'at-i-islami, founded by a theoretician close to Qutb, A. A. Mawdudi (who died in 1979). They took the view that Rushdie, who was accused of having shown disrespect to the Prophet, was a flagrant example of disobedience by a person

---

26   Commonwealth citizens resident in the United Kingdom were automatically entitled to vote, until this legislation was modified to make it more restrictive.

of Muslim origin towards the communal prohibitions decreed by these same imams. It was the worst kind of temptation for young Indians and Pakistanis living in the United Kingdom, who, if they followed Rushdie's example, might become Westernised, and escape by way of 'blasphemy' and 'apostasy' from the social control of the 're-Islamization from below' networks. As long as the matter was confined to Britain, it constituted a test of the imams' ability to obtain political concessions from the state: in return for stopping the agitation in the ghettos, they wanted the book banned. They had set themselves a precise aim: to establish themselves more firmly as intermediaries who could demand, as the price of social peace, concessions that would strengthen their communal position.

When Khomeini took over and ordered Rushdie's execution, he placed the affair once more within the framework of the revolutionary Islamism of the preceding decade. He was acting in furtherance of Iranian policies, at a time when Teheran was attempting to regain the ideological leadership of the Muslim world and to overcome the setback in the war against Iraq. But in doing so he raised the stakes above any possibility of negotiation with Britain, which could not tolerate a death threat to a British subject. Khomeini's startling intervention was, in effect, paradoxical: it applied an outdated historical logic to a phenomenon that is better seen as heralding a fresh phase of re-Islamization, Islamization 'from below' rather than 'from above'.

The affair of 'the Islamic veil', which erupted in France in the autumn of 1989, immediately following the Rushdie affair, exemplified the same process. It showed how far the networks of re-Islamization 'from below' had spread in France, to the point where some of its supporters wanted to stage a trial of strength by confronting the French state on the sensitive ground of *laïcité* (see footnote 25, page 37). They wanted 'positive discrimination' in favour of Muslim girls in French state schools, allowing them to wear the veil and to be excused physical training and music, thus implementing in daily life the break with the surrounding French *jahiliyya*.

At the outset, the situation in the United Kingdom was quite unlike that in France. The row in Britain was triggered by a person of Muslim origin transgressing a communal prohibition, whereas in France there was an attempt to introduce communalism into the religiously neutral sphere of school. Although the Tabligh had strongly influenced one of the Muslim groups involved, the offensive was taken by Islamist groups composed of students from the Maghreb. Their involvement in the veil dispute evidenced a change of tactics that showed they had adopted the policy of 're-Islamization from below'.

At the very beginning of the 1980s the 're-Islamization from above' movements in France had been drawn into activism on behalf of Iran, and though this activism escalated into violence it gained no foothold whatsoever outside restricted student circles; the police had found little difficulty in breaking up their cells. The Islamist associations that then took up the running consisted of Mahgrebi followers of Sayyid Qutb who, aware of their weakness, concentrated on winning sympathizers and never sought a showdown with the French authorities. Indeed, their imams even exhorted believers not to go on strike in the factories where they were working, so as not to invite repression, perhaps followed by expulsion, which would have decreased the numbers of the combatants.

When the veil affair blew up, these same militants abandoned their low profile and went into negotiations with the principal of the school in question, gaining the sympathy of some Catholics who regarded them as allies in their fight for a 'new *laïcité*' in which religion would once more feature in public life. They issued a press release attacking the French prime minister – something they would not have dared to do a few years earlier. Although the Muslim schoolgirls at Creil were made to give up the veil in order to pursue their studies, the affair showed the great potential of re-Islamization 'from below' in France.

By making themselves the spokesmen of 'Islam' and by negotiating a 'positive discrimination' which would allow practising Muslims to withdraw, in certain domains, from the laws of the Republic and obey the *shar'ia*, militant Islamists succeeded, for the first time, in bringing a demand relating to everyday life into the political sphere. Contrary to the traditional revolutionary strategy which favoured total confrontation with the state, they had learned to negotiate partial demands and had found powerful allies in the hierarchy of the Catholic Church and among the leading rabbis. For, as we shall see below, these latter were no less determined to seek a renewal of the Christian and Jewish faiths in the teeth of *laïcité*.

The Intifada and re-Islamization

The phenomenon of re-Islamization 'from below' also spread in the Muslim world proper during the second half of the 1980s. In Palestine, the Intifada was in part such a movement, while in Algeria the successes of the Islamic Salvation Front (FIS) were based on Islamic infiltration into everyday social life, which was later to spill over into politics. The context and scope of these two phenomena are different in kind from the Rushdie or 'Islamic veil' affairs, but they all form part of the same historical sequence.

In 1990 the Palestinian uprising was in its third year. Unlike the earlier short-lived rebellions against Israeli occupation, this was a groundswell movement, not limited to the universities or to select groups but touching society as a whole. Until the Intifada was unleashed, the PLO leaders in exile had the greatest claim to leadership of the Palestinian population 'within'. Although some of the leaders of Fath, including Yasser Arafat himself, had in their younger days been Muslim Brothers, until the mid-1980s the Palestinian cause was the last living expression of Arab nationalism in which the vocabulary of 'Islamic mobilization' played only a minor part.

In addition to the significant number of Christians in the PLO leadership, and in particular at the head of the PFLP and the DFLP,[27] the Resistance still had the advantage of embodying an ideal of *national* liberation – unlike the Arab heads of state in the Middle East, who had irretrievably lost face after the military defeat of 1967. The leaders of these movements were not exposed to radical challenges during the decade of revolutionary Islam, even though 're-Islamized' people felt a certain loss of confidence in the Palestinian resistance as being too 'secularized'; for them the Afghan *jihad* against Soviet atheism became the supreme cause.

Some militant Islamic groups came into being in Palestinian universities – when they were not closed by order of the Israeli

---

27 Popular Front for the Liberation of Palestine and Democratic Front for the Liberation of Palestine, Marxist-oriented, led by George Habash and Nayef Hawatmeh respectively.

military authorities – and they even achieved some successes in student elections, but they were never really able to challenge the authority of the PLO. Moreover any criticism, even if couched in koranic language, played into the hands of the Israelis, who treated the Islamists with a degree of restraint which made the broad mass of Palestinians somewhat suspicious of them.

Once the Intifada had begun, a plethora of people's committees controlled the day-to-day uprisings, thereby infiltrating the whole anti-Israeli movement. Strikes and boycotts of Israeli products and services of every kind from food to administration, including traffic laws and public order, called for a new kind of social cohesion founded on mutual assistance and charitable networks. The mosques played a large part in this process. Young Islamist militants also took part in the uprising from the beginning, identified by various initials – including *Hamas*, an acronym for Islamic Resistance Movement, and meaning 'enthusiasm'.

They belonged to the 'third generation' of the resistance. Their illustrious elders, now in their sixties, had looked to Jordan; the forty-year-old intellectuals in between represented the PLO. Unlike the latter, the youngsters were not members of the moneyed or learned elites native to Jerusalem; they came from the refugee camps, from the Gaza Strip and the rural parts of the West Bank, poverty-stricken areas not known as breeding grounds for activists. Furthermore, the forces grouped in the unified national command (UNC) looked to the PLO and not exclusively to Islam. But the fact that after three years the uprising had run out of steam, and had made no concrete gains, was bound to weaken the position of the UNC in the long run and to strengthen re-Islamization movements which, at the base and in urban areas, controlled the social environment and the self-help networks that had grown up around the mosques.[28]

28 On the Intifada, see the works of Jean-François Legrain, especially: 'Les Islamistes palestiniens à l'épreuve du soulèvement', *Maghreb-Machrek*, 121 (July 1988); 'Mobilisation islamiste et soulèvement palestinien', in *Intellectuels et militants*, ed. G. Kepel and Y. Richard, op. cit.; 'Le Leadership palestinien de l'intérieur' (Husayni document, summer 1988), in *L'Etude du monde arabe contemporain: approches globales et approches spécifiques* (Cairo: CEDEJ, 1990); (with P. Chenard) *Les voix du soulèvement palestinien: critical edition and French translation of the communiques of the National Unified Command and of the Islamic Resistance Movement* (Cairo: CEDEJ, 1990).

*The Islamic Salvation Front: from the local mosque to the
fringes of power*

In Algeria the strategy of re-Islamization 'from below', by the
infiltration of society, was remarkably successful; it achieved its
political breakthrough in the municipal elections of June 1990
with the victory of the Islamic Salvation Front (FIS) and later in
the national elections of 1992. This was the first time a re-
Islamization movement had gained a majority in a Muslim country
where free elections were held. To understand why, we must go
back to the beginnings of the movement in Algeria, about which
very little was known until a university professor in Constantine,
Ahmed Rouadjia, researched it.[29]

At the beginning of the 1970s the Boumedienne government,
which had encouraged French-speaking pro-Marxist students to
propagate the ideology of agrarian reform, became worried by
their activism and as a counterweight introduced some Arabic-
speaking students who had been educated in the Middle East and
were influenced by the Muslim Brothers. This policy of the Algerian government is comparable with the policies followed in the
other Arab capitals at the same period. Right through the 'decade
of revolutionary Islam', Islamists and left-wingers fought it out in
the Algerian universities – with victory going, there as elsewhere,
to the Islamists.

Nevertheless, in a country so tightly controlled by the National
Liberation Front, it was only with great difficulty that the movements of re-Islamization 'from above' succeeded in countering
repression. The armed Algerian Islamic movement, founded in
1982 and better known as 'Bouyali's band' (from its founder's
name) went in for raids and various acts of violence, keeping
underground until its leader was gunned down by the police in
1987. But it appears to have been the only one of its kind, contrary
to the situation in Egypt, for example, where scattered groups of
revolutionary Islamists had begun to form by the mid-1970s.

From then onwards, Islamic networks in the universities and
later in the suburbs began to form around a movement for building

---

29 Ahmed Rouadjia, *Les Frères et la mosquée*, op. cit., from which most of the information
used here has been obtained.

'wild' mosques which soon became very widespread. Unlike the places of worship established by the state, these mosques were built by district committees in the municipal housing estates and shanty towns which were spreading around cities in Algeria as the population grew. Erected on any available piece of land – parks, land acquired for roadbuilding, etc. – and made from anything to hand (chiefly corrugated iron), these mosques were converted into permanent buildings as soon as the opposition of the local authority had somewhat abated. They were very important to a country whose social infrastructures were chronically inadequate, but whose government agents were everywhere, exercising an intolerably tight ideological control. They did something to meet social needs, dispensed charity – and also organized 'grassroots' opposition to the party apparatus. This latter dimension was particularly important in Algeria, which was subject to a totalitarian regime until the riots of autumn 1988, unlike countries such as Morocco, Tunisia or Egypt, where government authoritarianism was tempered by some freedom of expression and of publication.

In a situation of this kind, the local mosques were among the very few places offering escape from the omnipresent censorship and repression. In that world the break with the surrounding *jahiliyya* took the usual forms – 'Islamic' socialization, observance of 'good behaviour', charitable activities and so on – but it developed into rigid forms of communal control; for example, it put an end to the sale of alcohol in 're-Islamized' districts.

Furthermore, re-Islamization 'from below' always went hand in hand with opposition to the use of French. This bitter struggle waged by the Algerian re-Islamization movements against a language has no parallel anywhere else. Behind the stated preference for the 'language of the Koran' and the animosity towards the 'colonizer's language' (Islamist Algerians prefer English, a 'truly modern language') there looms a conflict whose social dimensions are poorly concealed by the ideological justification.

The policy of teaching exclusively through Arabic, which has been in full swing since the mid-1970s, has accentuated the disproportion between a high demand on the labour market for skills dependent upon a knowledge of French and a huge supply of people qualified only in Arabic, whose future prospects are dim. For them, the fight against French is a problem of openings and jobs at least as much as a theological question. But by making this theme one of their favourite propaganda slogans, the re-Islamization movements have demonstrated their skill at expressing a social problem in religious terms.

In their holy war against French, the militants of re-Islamization in Algeria have found allies in some government circles. Even within the National Liberation Front, conflicts between those who demanded a total monopoly for the 'national language' (literary Arabic) and those who also spoke French or Berber very soon sent the former into the arms of the 'bearded ones', the *barbus*. In these circles, dubbed the 'Barbefelen' (bearded FLN) by Algerian humorists, were to be found most of the ulemas, who were few in number and not strongly organized. Contrary to the situation in Egypt, there was no violent antagonism between them and the Islamist movement. In order to make up for the shortage of Algerian doctors of the Law, the government 'imported' from Egypt an imam imbued with the ideology of the Muslim Brothers, Muhammad Al Ghazali. He was put in charge of the Great Mosque at Constantine, and was one of the most important links between the ulemas and the militants of re-Islamization.

When the riots of November 1988 broke out, those militants simply joined in an event which they had not instigated. But the opening of the political system enabled the Islamic Salvation Front, the FIS, to be set up. Viewed sympathetically by the 'Arabo-Islamic' tendency within the NLF, which afforded it access to government circles, it very quickly showed itself capable of federating the numerous forces that had sprung up at local level from the 're-Islamization from below' networks. And its road to power was greatly smoothed by the fact that the June 1990 elections were municipal, not national: this enabled the Front to tighten its local hold still further.

Since the mid-1970s, when re-Islamization movements appeared on the political scene in the Muslim world, they have passed through two major historical phases. After a decade in which it seemed that power was within their grasp and when the Iranian revolution appeared to set the pattern, a new phase began at the end of the 1980s, with the stress on re-Islamizing individuals rather than states. Both these procedures had the same aim,

namely to re-Islamize society in Muslim countries and to
propagate Islam everywhere until humanity was converted into
'ummanity'. But the ways in which Islamists, on the one hand,
and pietists, on the other, propose to break with the 'godless'
environment operate at different levels.

Because the former stress the political dimension, they have
encountered repression from existing states, and nowhere except
in Iran have they succeeded in conquering civil society. The latter
group, by focusing their efforts on everyday life, have succeeded
better in eluding the vigilance of the *jahiliyya* states because their
activities promote social stability. For they built up structures in
the community that protected individuals from the buffetings of
modern life, which are often devastating for the 'disinherited'. And
yet, despite their inclination to shun politics, movements of re-
Islamization 'from below' have sometimes come to occupy a dominant position in civil society. This is the case in Algeria in particular, where a totalitarian state has imploded after some three decades of dictatorship. In that country movements of re-Islamization
invaded the political sphere from below and were gradually trans-
muted until they reached the fringes of power, without need for
a revolution.

At the end of 1990 this new phase was only just beginning.
But whatever may happen in the future, it would be a mistake to
think that re-Islamization 'from below' is less radical, in its rejection of the secular and democratic organization of society, than
the Hizbollah and other soldiers of the *jihad* who made the running
in 1985. As Ali Belhaj, star preacher of the FIS, is always
reminding us, democracy is only a kind of *jahiliyya* which robs
God of His power and bestows it on His creatures. And the imams
of the Tabligh have the very same motive for shielding 'healthy
Muslim youth' from the temptations of the ungodly West by
developing the Muslim community.

But, as we shall now see, from the mid-1960s onwards other
religious cultures have also been making a break with secularism.
In the Christian and Jewish worlds, strategies 'from above' and
'from below' have also been deployed, with results that can be
compared with the Muslim phenomena so far discussed.

2

Mission Field Europe

In Catholic Europe, the last quarter of the twentieth century opened on a paradox: never before, it seemed, had society been so massively secularized and de-Christianized, and yet re-Christianization movements were springing up everywhere. Some charismatic communities encouraged university graduates to discover the inspiration of the Holy Spirit; others performed scores of miraculous cures. Elsewhere, organizations such as 'Communion and Liberation', aiming to re-create a Christian society after the 'failure of secularism', mobilized hundreds of thousands of young Italians, while in Eastern Europe, after the collapse of the Soviet Union, social movements and parties were taking shape which, after forty years of state atheism, based their political identity on a reaffirmation of their Catholicism.

Whereas the Vatican II Council (1962–5) appeared to limit the Church's aim to proclaiming the presence of God in a world grown blind, the pontificate of John Paul II, which began in 1978, has been marked by a reaffirmation of Catholic values and identity. These are now based upon an a priori break with the principles of secular society, and are intended to restore to the 'post-modern' world a meaning, an ethic and an order which, it is claimed, have vanished in the collapse of all its certainties.

In the West, the oil crisis that began in October 1973 enforced economic restructuring which called in question many group loyalties taken for granted in the industrial era, such as trade unionism, while pressing anxieties were developing as to the near future of the planet, under threat from pollution and the arms race. At the same time the electronic revolution, bringing a mass of images and information into every home, was transforming ethical standards as never before. Methods of learning, the transmission of values, the integrity of the family unit and its relationship to the public domain were abruptly transformed in a way which many individuals felt powerless to control.

In Eastern Europe the disintegration of communism, which reached the point of no return when the Berlin wall was breached in 1989 and subsequently demolished, freed the minds of millions from strict Marxist control. In Poland the affirmation of their Catholicism by the leaders of Solidarnosc, symbol of the only durable resistance by any civil society to Soviet influence, and the subsequent appointment of a Catholic prime minister in 1989, appeared to show that the collapse of communism would inevitably be followed by a return of religion to the political scene. Poland even seemed to be providing a model or source of inspiration for the 'second evangelization of Europe' – one of the main objectives of John Paul II's pontificate.[1]

Some churchmen saw in these events the end of the modern era, which had begun with the Enlightenment in the eighteenth century when reason, self-confident and emancipated, had been rather too quick to reject religion. Some of the pronouncements at Vatican II, reflecting the social optimism of the 1960s, had attempted to reimpose a Christian logic on the 'progressive values' of secular ideology. The new Christianity of the last quarter-century is different: it has offered a Catholic ethic to a 'world adrift', the only ethic which has any sort of a future. 'We are at the beginning of the Christian era', wrote Cardinal Lustiger. 'In our time the West (and probably the whole world) has become such an enigma to itself, is faced by such fearfully unprecedented problems and such terrifying ordeals, that it must at long last consider the possibility that only the coming of Christ will give it the arguments and the strength to assume its destiny. . .'[2]

In analysing the re-Christianization of the past fifteen years we must first review its intellectual and social genesis. We shall then see how extensively Vatican II has been re-read to counter the

1   See Patrick Michel, 'Y a-t-il un modèle ecclésial polonais?', in *Le Retour des certitudes: événements et orthodoxie depuis Vatican II*, ed. Paul Ladrière and René Éuneau (Paris: Centurion, 1987), pp. 142–57.
2   Cardinal Jean-Marie Lustiger, 'La nouveauté du Christ et la post modernité', *Revue catholique internationale Communio*, XV, 2 (1990), pp. 13–14.

progressivist or crypto-Marxist interpretations of 'left-wing Catholic' groups and of liberation theology. We shall also note how the changes in society since 1970 have been interpreted in the light of Christian eschatology. Then we shall observe how this re-Christianization has been put into practice in the field.

It has taken the form of Catholic movements aiming to put pressure on governments, or to attain power themselves, in order to change society 'from above' in accordance with their own idea of the Church's teachings, and to combat secularism. But it has also prompted an upsurge of charismatic groups whose members endeavour to live an everyday 'Christian' life within a community imbued with the Holy Spirit, withdrawing from the customs and motivations of the society around them.

Unlike re-Islamization, which occurred in countries in which only the top levels of society had been (incompletely) secularized under Western influence, the re-Christianization movements appeared in societies most of which had been living a deeply secularized existence for more than a century. This had been enshrined in institutions and laws, but it had found its ultimate expression in an unprecedented indifference towards religion, especially among the young, and in a considerable decline in the numbers of those offering themselves for the priesthood, especially after the events of 1968. Thus, unlike the Islamic or pietist movements which, when they make use of a koranic vocabulary, are easily understood by a Muslim population still very aware of their religious background, re-Christianization movements have to teach young people the meaning of their Gospel references, since most of them have had no contact with Christianity.

This ignorance of Christianity, so widespread among the European young except in such 'bastions' as Poland or Slovakia, is one of the reasons why religious movements in Catholic Europe have had less overall impact than in the Muslim world. The other reasons, as we shall see, have to do with democracy, almost non-existent in Muslim countries: for in a democracy there is room for a political activity which gives religion little chance of gaining a stranglehold on civil society, even after forty years of communism.

Despite the manifold differences between contemporary Muslim and Catholic societies, it is remarkable that from the mid-1970s onwards parallel phenomena have appeared in both. First a conflict arose between the secular ideas of utopia (accepted by some theologians and believers) and newly affirmed religious doctrines. Such doctrines weighed the social system against a transcendent order and decided that a 'break' with secular values was required, a rejection of the world. Then new movements took shape which aimed at an eventual re-Christianization of society either 'from above' or 'from below', re-enacting 'the birth of Christianity', rather like the dedicated re-Islamizers who draw their inspiration exclusively from the 'generation of the Koran', the generation of the Prophet.

The legacy of Vatican II

The Vatican II Ecumenical Council, held from October 1962 to December 1965, set about an *aggiornamento*, or updating, of the Catholic Church at the behest of Pope John XXIII on whose initiative it was convened. Its internal revision of that ancient and complex institution, which engaged the efforts of bishops the world over, resulted in the promulgation of sixteen conciliar documents. They concerned both the reorganization of the Church itself and the redefinition of its relationships with the outside world. The 'dogmatic constitution on the Church' (*Lumen gentium*),[3] and the 'pastoral constitution on the Church in the contemporary world' (*Gaudium et spes*) well illustrate this dual focus.

Each document was the fruit of patient compromise between the forces present in the council – the two successive popes, John XXIII and Paul VI, the Roman Curia, bishops from the West, the East and the Third World, representatives of assorted theological trends – and each left room for interpretation. This made it easier for the texts to be adopted almost without dissent, except from Mgr Lefebvre and his friends (who formed only a tiny minority of the Fathers in council). But a few years later the legacy of Vatican II was causing fierce arguments between those who

3   By tradition these documents are designated by the first words of their Latin text; thus: '*Lumen gentium cum sit Christus . . .*' (Christ being the light of the nations . . .) or '*Gaudium et spes, luctus et angor hominum huius temporis . . .*' (The joys and hopes, the griefs and torments of the men of our time . . .).

saw it as simply the first step towards opening the Church to the world and those who said 'thus far and no further'.

The historian Emile Poulat sees Vatican II as a continuation of the Church's resistance to modernism – as a stance of 'non-negotiability' enabling the hierarchy to withstand the challenges put to it since the nineteenth century both by modernism and by 'liberal Catholicism' in its various manifestations. The Church, 'sure of its truth and its mission', was concerned to 'adapt its methods and resources to its present tasks in new circumstances. "Updating" was essentially revision in order to pre-empt recasting.'[4]

In its various historical avatars, Catholic intransigence betrays a fear that 'the Church may be drawn into the modern spirit' unless adaptations and changes are carried out 'with constant reference to the official teaching of the Church' – if they borrow 'criteria and standards from this world itself'.[5] In other words, this attitude aims to safeguard the institution, while consenting to give up a minimal number of dogmas or rites so antiquated as to be largely counter-productive – even to driving away the faithful.

On a time-scale of centuries, Vatican II can be interpreted in this way. But on the scale of a human lifetime, the council appears as a product of the balance of forces represented by its various participants. As regards church organization, what was at stake was not primarily the loss of the cassock and the Latin mass. It was much more the role of the hierarchy – and of the Pope as its head – and also the position to be accorded to the laity. How compatible was the collegiality of bishops with the primacy of the Pope? At what point should the writ of Rome yield to the specific circumstances and needs of local churches? And within the local churches, what weight was to be given to the experience and demands of the laity, at a time when vocations to the priesthood were becoming fewer?

In the sphere of church–world relationships, *Gaudium et spes* is an attempt to place the leading ideas of the time, such as development and social justice, once more within a Christian

4   Emile Poulat, *Une église ébranlée* (Paris: Casterman, 1980), p. 266.
5   Danièle Hervieu-Léger (assisted by Françoise Champion), *Vers un nouveau christianisme?* *Introduction à la sociologie du christianisme occidental* (2nd edn, Paris: Cerf, 1987), p. 255.

perspective. With the biggest increase in the Catholic population taking place among the impoverished masses of Latin America, the Church could not be seen simply as the defender of the established order, or it would lose its influence to other forms of religious expression, chiefly sectarian.

In Europe, the 'working class' seemed to have no time for a social Christianity which Marxists denounced as a weapon of the bourgeoisie. And in 1965, when the council ended, it was all the more important to affirm that man, as God's creature, cannot be reduced to a factor of production exploitable at will, since Rome had irrevocably condemned the experiment of the worker-priests in 1954.[6] For as soon as Catholic priests relativized the sacral priesthood by going to work in factories (some even joined the Communist Party), they ceased to exercise their vocation entirely under the Church's authority, allowing it to be 'corrupted' by worldly considerations. Despite the impeccable institutional logic of this condemnation, it did somewhat tarnish the image of the Church.

Liberation theology and socialist messianism

In the years following the Council, Europeans, especially Catholics, were confronted by the 1968 student movement, which questioned established values to an extent that made the bold decisions of Vatican II look extremely timid. In this context, some Catholics committed to social action saw the council as a first step on the road to revolution. Many of them identified with the Latin American priests and laymen who fought for justice alongside the poor of the shanty towns in the name of 'liberation theology'. Gustavo Gutiérrez, one of the leading liberation theologians, complained that '*Gaudium et spes* has avoided making any pronouncement on the relationship between temporal progress and supernatural redemption. It is satisfied with general statements [. . .] and has avoided radical criticism of the unjust system on

6 See François Leprieur, *Quand Rome condamne* (Paris: Plon, 'Terre humaine' series, 1989).

which the life of society is based. In other words, it has glossed over the conflictual aspects of political life.'[7]

Liberation theology was not the only manifestation of the 'progressivist mentality' to shake the Church between the end of the council and the death of Paul VI in 1978. But it represented a fairly coherent intellectual construct and appeared to have won over many of the faithful, so that the hierarchy regarded it as the outstanding embodiment of the 'Marxist danger' of making the Church into a tool, of tainting its message with left-wing sentiment. This is why the burgeoning re-Christianization movements were to define themselves politically and socially by their opposition to that theology.

Gutiérrez believed that: 'It is largely because it has been stimulated by Marxism that theological thinking has been turned back to its origins and made to reflect upon the meaning of the transformation of this world and on the action of man in history. [. . .] Theology so understood has a necessary and permanent part to play in freeing people from every kind of religious alienation, often nourished by the institution of the Church itself, which prevents an authentic approach to the word of the Lord.' And 'only a radical destruction of the present order of things, a profound change in the system of ownership, the accession of the exploited class to power and a revolution in society will put an end to dependence. Only these things will effect a transition to a different society, a socialist society, or at any rate will make such a transition possible.'[8]

Apart from the very dated language of the late 1960s, these declarations have two main emphases: they reject an unjust social order which is intolerable for the poor and lowly, and aspire to a new order, a socialist society that will embody justice. The specifically Christian vocabulary is overlaid by Marxist terminology, and that is the real clue to its interpretation; by contrast, according to Gutiérrez and his friends, 'religious alienation' is the inevitable result of the official Church's determination to box in all interpretation with learned glosses chiefly intended to legitimize

---

7 Gustavo Gutiérrez, quoted by Jan Grootaers, *De Vatican II à Jean-Paul II: le grand tournant de l'Eglise catholique* (Paris: Centurion, 1981), p. 50.
8 Gustavo Gutiérrez, *Theology of Liberation* (New York, 1990).

the established order. Liberation theologians, for their part, go directly to the holy scriptures, in which they find parables to justify their commitment to socialism. Thus, the exodus of the Hebrews from Pharaoh's Egypt symbolizes the necessary emancipation of the oppressed classes and the struggle against the exploitative bourgeoisie and imperialism.

This ideology involves a break with the existing order, but it believes that building socialism is the fulfilment of the Christian mission. The main divide is not between a fundamentally secular society and a Christian society, but between the oppressors and the oppressed, along the lines of a class war that runs through Church and world alike.

Taken to its logical conclusion, this comes down to splitting the Church, denying its autonomy and subordinating the Christian message to a secular messianism: the building of socialism is a substitute for the coming of Christ. Although any such intellectual construct is unacceptable to the Church, Rome has treated liberation theology far more gently than the worker priests of twenty years earlier. Vatican II had done a lot to change attitudes, it is true; and there had been changes in the Roman Curia. The movement was something of a mass phenomenon in Latin America, whose large Catholic population gave the Church worldwide enough weight to challenge the other Christian confessions and, above all, Islam. And after all, the movement did profess allegiance to *a* theology – which seemed a lesser evil than embracing secularism.

The surest way to counter the influence of the movement seemed to be to resume control of the Episcopal Conference in Latin America and to appoint bishops hostile to liberation theology: accordingly one of its main representatives, Leonardo Boff, was summoned before the Congregation for the Doctrine of the Faith and temporarily gagged. But the Vatican was not blind to the potential of this desire to 'break' with an unjust social order – as long as the impulse behind it remained Christian. So although the first of the Congregation's instructions, issued in 1984, was intended to halt a worrying line of development, the second, issued in 1986, though reiterating the warnings on doctrine, expressed approval of pastoral work which gave priority to the poor. The

Pope took the same line in an address to the Brazilian bishops in April of the same year.

The vexations of liberation theology have often been seen as a conflict between the 'conservatives' represented in particular by Cardinal Ratzinger, Prefect of the Congregation, and the 'progressives', but such a view simply transposes the fault lines in society to the Church. We must go on to ask how the reaffirmation of purely Catholic identity and values which is displayed in the re-Christianization movements has been able to take over a 'break' that was formerly based on secular thinking.

Disillusion with secularism and the Catholic 'break'

The re-Christianization that took hold from the mid-1970s onwards started out from a pessimistic judgement on the future of a secularized world. The fear was that scientific and technical progress would escape from man's control and deny his status as a creature of God; that he would be first enslaved and then destroyed. Unlike the 'progressive Catholics' who regarded the classes 'exploited by the bourgeoisie' as the only enslaved creatures of God, the new Christians held that *all* men and women were now endangered, and that no earthly messianism could save them. And compared with the optimistic spirit of Vatican II, they believed much more strongly that conflict with the secular world order was unavoidable. They blamed the supremacy of reason over faith through a period in history that had begun with the Enlightenment and ended around 1975. This Catholic critique of reason utilizes certain trends in the human sciences and in secular philosophy, including psychoanalysis, structuralism and the thoughts of Heidegger. But these play only a very minor role; the object is no longer to fertilize theological reflection by the human sciences à la Gutiérrez, but to point out that they support the challenge to the supremacy of reason which theology poses and, they say, always has posed. Theology then becomes part of a general disenchantment with modernity, a 'disillusionment with secularism'. This theological diagnosis of our contemporary malaise is expressed in formulae – in a whole rhetoric – which is consonant with some of the questionings and anxieties that are surfacing in European societies.

Cardinal Lustiger and Cardinal Ratzinger embody, each in his own way, this consonance of the Church's discourse with post-modernism. The story of Cardinal Lustiger's life could be a perfect example of the relevance of the Christian vocation. He was a Polish Jew, converted during the Second World War, a 'son of secularism', educated at the Lycée Montaigne with the children of the intellectual bourgeoisie of Paris, and gained his degree at the Sorbonne, a secular university. Jean-Marie Lustiger comes from a different world from Father Alexander, the country priest who was made famous by *Horsain* ('The Outsider').[9] His auto-biography in dialogue, *Le Choix de Dieu* ('The Choice of God') shows him to be an intellectual who has mastered modern learning, in particular the most sophisticated social sciences, has seen what they can and cannot do, and who finds in the Catholic faith[10] the means of doing what they cannot do.

Now Archbishop of Paris, he says of himself: 'I belong to that generation which has plucked the bitter fruits of Reason's preten-sions to unfettered sovereignty.'[11] The end result of this 'arrogance of reason' which ignores God and will answer to nobody but itself was Nazi and Stalinist totalitarianism. It was born in 'the Age of Enlightenment [which engendered] totalitarianism, meaning the divinization of human reason and its refusal to accept any criti-cism.'[12] Enlightenment thinking becomes the source of all evils, the scapegoat, according to the logic made fashionable by Hannah Arendt, who blames the French Revolution for all the totalitarian sins of the twentieth century while endowing that other child of the Enlightenment, the American Revolution, with all the virtues.[13] Cardinal Lustiger, for his part, condemns them all *en bloc*, even blaming this Source of all Ills for the extermination of European Jewry: 'I believe that Hitler's anti-semitism derives from the anti-

9 Bernard Alexandre, *Horsain: vivre et survivre en pays de Caux* (Paris: Plon, 1988).
10 On the arguments raised in certain Jewish circles against the conversion of Jean-Marie Lustiger and the meaning he has attributed to it, see the pamphlet by Raphael Drai, *Lettre ouverte au Cardinal Lustiger* (Alinéa, 1989).
11 Jean-Marie Lustiger, *Le Choix de Dieu: entretiens avec Jean-Louis Missika et Dominique Wolton* (Fallois, 1987; Le Livre de Poche, 1989), p. 210.
12 Ibid., p. 161.
13 See, inter alia, Hannah Arendt, *On Revolution* (New York: Viking Press, 1963).

semitism of the Enlightenment and not from any Christian anti-semitism.'[14]

Reason, being 'arrogant', makes man the idol of man, with all that that implies of despotism and oppression. But nothing is said here about the class war, the theme of the liberation theologians. Forgetfulness of God is the root of all social evil – a theme that was also common to the theoreticians of re-Islamization and of re-Judaization at that time.

The findings of the human sciences and the life sciences no longer pose a threat to faith (as was alleged when positivism was in vogue). What they do call in question is the autonomy of reason – a reversal of meaning that is also found in contemporary militants of Judaism and Islam. The Cardinal recalled:

> I was born after the nineteenth century, We learned, with Old Father Marx, Freud and Einstein and some others, that all that stuff wouldn't stay the course. We have seen with our eyes and found to our cost why it wouldn't stay the course [...] this chimerical idealization of reason, this 'arrogant' reason that doesn't know its own limitations.[15]

But Freud, Einstein and 'Old Father Marx' have exhausted their historical role once they have seen off the Enlightenment. We should have no use for what they said against religious belief. As regards social organization, whenever politics tries to cut loose from the Christian ethic it inevitably ends in totalitarianism, whose supreme embodiment is communism. Some people thought at the end of the 1960s that that doctrine was about to triumph, but in reality it was obvious to an alert Catholic observer that the revolutionary clamour signified its imminent decline:

> It was the generation of '68 that dared at last to spit in the idol's face. In the Place de la Sorbonne I saw with my own eyes and heard with my ears Cohn-Bendit call Aragon a 'Stalinist scoundrel'. It was wonderful! In this sea of waving red and black flags, amid all that myth of Marxist revolution! Today, I said to myself, the idol was shattered! May 1968, then Solzhenitsyn and Poland. The

14   J.-M. Lustiger, op. cit., p. 101.
15   Ibid., p. 160.

new holy scriptures on which the French intelligentsia had fed since 1917, under the magic spell of a new religion and a new eschatology, were demolished. The world was released from the spell and Stalin was dead.[16]

The way was open for re-Christianization; we were about to see the beginnings of the Christian era.

However, in the secularized societies of Western Europe, the first obstacle on the road to re-Christianization was that religion had been relegated to the private sphere. In France, legal sanction was given to this process in 1905 with the law separating Church and state. It has been less strictly codified in other countries, but the results have been similar. Hence one of the first tasks in re-Christianization was to campaign for the return of religion to the sphere of public law and, for this purpose, to bring about a 'new secularism'.

It is in the works of Cardinal Ratzinger that the need for this struggle has been expounded most forcefully. This German theologian, whom John Paul II appointed Prefect of the Congregation for the Doctrine of the Faith, is responsible for the 'line' of the Catholic Church, and his ideas have made him unpopular with some of the 'progressive' circles who think he is out to bury the hopes that were raised by Vatican II. He vigorously defends the unity of the Church against 'dissensions' and the 'decadence' characterizing the post-conciliar period, in which national churches have achieved a degree of self-government which he thinks prejudicial to the unity of Catholic teaching.[17] He also reaffirms that 'On the basis of [the] theology of martyrdom the primacy represents the guarantee of the opposition of the Church in its Catholic unity to all particular secular power.'[18]

As regards relations with the 'world', the Cardinal sees the Church as the sole recourse against the totalitarianism of states dedicated to enslaving mankind. 'The battle over crosses in the schools which is being fought in Poland today [1984] and which was fought by our parents in Germany in the period of the Third

---

16   Ibid., p. 234.
17   On the 'Ratzinger period' as a 'critique of self-government, illustrated by the controversies about the catechism in France', see Danièle Hervieu-Léger, op. cit., pp. 323–9.
18   Cardinal Joseph Ratzinger, *Church, Ecumenism and Politics* (Slough, 1988), p. 38.

Reich is completely symptomatic. [. . .] The cross in schools is the sign of a last bit of freedom which they do not want the totalitarian state to take.'[19]

But if the Cross is to defend humanity it must not, it cannot, be relegated to the private sphere by a secularism that in the last resort proceeds from the same totalitarian source. 'This retreat into the private sphere, this categorization in the pantheon of all possible value systems contradicts faith's claim to truth which is as such a claim to public validity.'[20] It is moreover something specific to Christianity, which, unlike the other religions of antiquity, refused to sacrifice to the cult of the Roman emperor, the archetype of the non-Christian state: 'however small the number of its adherents may have been at first, Christianity from the start laid a claim to public legal status and placed itself on a legal level comparable with that of the state. For this reason the figure of the martyr is to be found in the innermost structure of Christianity.'[21]

The recovery of this 'public legal status' is one of the fundamental aims of contemporary re-Christianization. Ideally it would be effected 'from above'. The state would moderate its claim to totality and bow to a transcendent principle: 'The state must recognize that a basic framework of values with a Christian foundation is the precondition for its existence [. . .] It must learn that there is a continued existence of truth which is not subject to consensus but which precedes it and makes it possible.'[22]

According to Ratzinger, this claim is not comparable to the desire of re-Islamization movements to build a state governed by the law of God as expressed in the Koran. In the Catholic world, the state is indeed subordinate to the truths of the Gospel, but it still has its own sphere; the Christian social order is dualistic, although the political authority, being secular, is inferior in dignity to the sacred authority. Only if this autonomy is maintained can there be respect for freedom and human rights – a notion which the Church claims to have fathered:

19   Ibid., p. 219.
20   Ibid., p. 218.
21   Ibid., p. 214.
22   Ibid., p. 219.

The modern idea of freedom is thus a legitimate product of the Christian environment; it could not have developed anywhere else. [...] Dualism, which is the precondition for freedom, presupposes for its part the logic of the Christian thing. [. . .] When the Church itself becomes the State, freedom disappears. But also when the Church is done away with as a public and publicly relevant authority, then too freedom is extinguished.[23]

Nowhere in late twentieth-century Europe has the Church become the state, and it seems scarcely likely to do so. The doctrinal symmetry constructed by Ratzinger leads in practice to just one imperative, the struggle to restore the Church as a public corporation – and that is the aim of re-Christianization.

Re-Christianization in Western Europe

Not until 1989 was the Iron Curtain lifted over Europe, a Europe of infinite variety. Amid this variety there were two societies in which re-Christianization movements attempted to wage this struggle 'from above', by putting pressure on the state. One of these was Poland, where the Church played a supremely important political role during the last years of communism; the other was Italy, where the Communion and Liberation movement arose and flourished. Both had their difficulties, which by the end of the decade had turned them towards re-Christianization 'from below', a method already in practice elsewhere. Such methods included both the charismatic movement, whose adherents live in separate communities, and the restoration of Catholic influence over particular institutions such as the school, which is an interface between the family and civil society, between the private and public spheres. But, unlike the re-Islamization movements, which met with no real opposition in Muslim societies, the re-Christianization movements found their impact limited by the democratic culture of European societies, even in Catholic countries emerging from communism. And that has sustained, even among the Catholics of the Old Continent, a current of opinion which holds that contemporary

23   Ibid., p. 162.

re-Christianization, whether proceeding 'from above' or 'from below', is not, in any form, the appropriate Christian response to the challenges of our times.

The experience of Communion and Liberation

Although dating from the 1950s, the re-Christianization movement Communion and Liberation did not really take off until the late 1970s. It was founded by a priest in the Milan diocese, Father Luigi Giussani, who was anxious to reaffirm the foundation values of Catholicism in an Italian society deeply secularized by modernism. For a long time little notice was taken of it in the Church, which was busy preparing for, and then conducting, Vatican II.

Father Giussani and his followers believed that the world acquires its 'religious meaning' only for people who expressly confess their faith in the Revelation event and accept its mystery. That establishes a radical break between Christian society on the one hand and secular society on the other. Those who play down this antagonism, and believe that the world can achieve its Christian future without any need for an affirmation of Catholic identity in society, are in danger of being sucked in and crushed by secular ideology.

Rebuilding a society on Christian foundations means fighting for the visible presence of the Church in a world where man has withdrawn far from God; it means laying the foundations of a common life 'set on a hill', guided by the precepts of the Gospel, a life to which in the end all people will be attracted. It means re-creating a 'communion' which alone can guarantee the full 'liberation' of mankind – the meeting with Christ the Saviour.

This plan echoes the ideas of Cardinal Lustiger and Cardinal Ratzinger; but Communion and Liberation has the special distinction of having put it into practice in present-day Italy. The movement has contrived to express an 'uncompromising' theology in a sociocultural praxis very relevant to the upheavals of the last quarter-century, and in particular to the needs of those whom modernism leaves by the wayside.

The critique of the 'dominant culture'

In a book of interviews, Father Giussani relates two anecdotes to illustrate the cultural context of the 1950s, which induced him to start his movement. As a young seminary teacher, he was once in a train with a group of students who told him how uninterested they were in the Church, how they even despised it.[24] He was so disturbed by this that he left the seminary and decided to devote himself to propagating the Christian message in the world, outside clerical circles. He became chaplain at the Lycée Berchet, the prestigious school for middle-class children in Milan, and before long he noticed a group of young people in animated conversation. Their comradeship and sense of unity made a strong impression on him, and when he enquired who they were he found that they were communists. 'That struck me forcibly. How was it that Christians were not capable of displaying such unity, when Christ said that this would be the first, most obvious sign by which believers in Him would be recognized?'[25]

Taken together, these two 'parables' tell us 'how it began', this movement for Catholic revival, later to be known as Communion and Liberation. An anaemic Christianity which left young people indifferent was contrasted with a communism that had rediscovered the real virtues of cooperation and commitment to an ideal society, virtues that had been neglected by Christian militants.

The group that Father Giussani founded in the 1950s was named Student Youth (*Gioventù studentesca*) and most of its members were recruited among the schoolchildren and students of Milan, the industrialized, secular capital of Northern Italy. Its avowed enemy was the 'secularism' which had adulterated people's sense of Catholic identity and given birth to atheistic Marxism. But Father Giussani's real target was the root of the evil, the culture of the Enlightenment; Marxism, which he termed 'the dominant culture of the intelligentsia [. . .], the scholasticism of the modern

---

24   Luigi Giussani, *Le Mouvement Communion et Liberation: entretiens avec Roberto Ronza* (Paris: Sarment/Fayard, 1988), p. 11. This document is essential for a knowledge of the movement. There is also the study by Salvatore Abruzzese, *Comunione e liberazione: identité catholique et disqualification du monde* (Paris: Cerf, 1989).
25   Luigi Giussani, op. cit., p. 21.

cleric',[26] was only its latest manifestation, doubtless the most hateful but not the least fascinating. Communist activism, communist organization, its strong place in society and its skill in manipulating the Italian political system, were an inspiration to this new and different breed of Christian militant.

As Father Giussani himself tells it, the history of his movement has three stages, as in Hegelian dialectic. First was the stage of 'Student Youth', from 1954 to the late 1960s; then 'the stage of negation', a time of deep crisis and internal dissension subsequent to Vatican II and (in particular) 1968; finally (1970 onwards) came the creation of Communion and Liberation as such, the 'transcendence', the third term in this dialectic of success.

Throughout its four decades of existence, the movement has combined theoretical reflection and social activity in constant interaction. During the stage of Student Youth, the primary aim was to differentiate the group from Catholic Action, the main Catholic presence in society and among the young – Catholic Action being a direct arm of the Church. In Giussani's eyes, that institution had become an empty shell, devoid of creative social thinking and without any exciting initiatives that could compete with the secular 'dominant culture' and the attractions of Marxism. In the diocese of Milan, at that time the largest in the world in terms of registered baptisms, a typical Catholic Action meeting would attract some five to seven people – as Giussani sadly relates. To attract young people to its premises the organization invested mainly in ping-pong tables, and the atmosphere was compounded of churchiness and outdated moralism, keeping the boys and girls strictly apart.[27]

Student Youth, on the other hand, recruited on the basis of a strongly motivated membership which put into daily practice an ideal of living that drew its inspiration solely from the holy scriptures. Its first characteristic was the exhortation to meet together 'with everything that makes up our life, in the presence of Christ: thus, we endeavour to illustrate in our life the doctrine of the mystical body as formulated by Saint Paul.'[28] These groups, whose

26 Ibid., p. 15.
27 Ibid., pp. 18, 20, 26–8.
28 Ibid., p. 33.

members are brought to realize that they belong to the whole community and measure their problems, their hopes and their openness by the yardstick of the shared ideal, are called 'honeycombs'.[29] The intensity of the human interactions that take place there reminds some observers of group therapy (which doesn't bother Father Giussani). These times of community sharing are prolonged individually by prayer, which punctuates the life of each member like the recital of the hours of the breviary. 'More and more, we went back to the sacraments, to mass and communion every day, just as the opposite was happening in the traditional Catholic associations.'[30]

On the intellectual and doctrinal level, the theologians whose work inspired the movement – especially Henri de Lubac and Hans Urs von Balthasar – were studied very thoroughly.[31] Members were particularly helped to get good grades at school and university, by means of collective revision and the distribution of duplicated sheets 'to develop knowledge taught in class, or if necessary correct it.'[32] This of course meant that while members were assisted towards social and intellectual progress, they had to keep a wary eye on the 'dominant culture', propagated by the secular university, which obscured the presence of God in history, barred the way to truly Christian inspiration in what the human mind created, and so on and so on.

Outings, excursions and holiday camps meant that long periods could be spent together in a truly Christian atmosphere,[33] as close

---

29   In communist parlance, the organizational unit next above the 'cell'. – Translator.
30   Ibid., p. 36.
31   Henri de Lubac, a French theologian who was made a cardinal by John Paul II, and Hans Urs von Balthasar, his Swiss disciple, were the masters of a contemporary Catholic school of thought which was also joined by Father Giussani and Cardinals Lustiger and Ratzinger. In opposition to an 'anthropological theology' which advocated that 'the Church should be [. . .] immersed in the world, the bearer of a project of freedom in full sympathy with projects that men are building concretely in history' and which considers that 'man, in order to accept God, no longer has to accept any break', von Balthasar thinks that 'man and the world do not have a meaning apart from Revelation; without it, they remain in error or indeterminacy' (after Abruzzese, op. cit., pp. 89–91). This meaning is the 'religious meaning', one of Father Giussani's concepts, and the title of one of his best-known works (*Le Sens religieux* [Paris: Fayard, 1988]).
32   Luigi Giussani, *Le Mouvement*, op. cit., p. 37.
33   Compare this with the method employed by the Islamist movements in socializing Egyptian students (chap. 1, p. 25)

as possible to the ideal, which some of the most enthusiastic members described as a foretaste of 'heaven on earth'.[34]

The strength and attractiveness of the ideal, which, in contrast to the sparse ranks of Catholic Action, brought a great number of young people into the movement, also made nonsense of the punctilious moralism dispensed by parish priests at the time. Student Youth did not segregate the sexes at all, convinced that its members, fully aware of their Catholic identity, did not need to have their sexuality kept under surveillance. This refusal to segregate also reflected the command to live together in communion, like the mystical body of Christ; but the institutional Church found it shocking and suspicious, and Father Giussani became the butt of censure and the recipient of warnings. This did not make him alter the way in which his 'honeycombs' and camps were run, and he subsequently used it as an argument, especially in combating the '*intégriste*' and retrograde label which his opponents tried to fasten on him.

Student Youth adopted a threefold aim: culture, charity, mission. The first was targeted particularly at redefining the place of an authentic Christian culture in society over against the 'dominant values'. 'Charity' was first practised in the poverty-stricken suburbs of Milan, where Father Giussani's followers offered help with survival, literacy and health, always with religious instruction attached. 'Mission' meant sending out members to Brazil, then to Uganda and Zaire, beginning in 1962. Moreover, Father Giussani took care to emphasize that these lines of action 'betokened criteria and concerns that should have been of interest to an observer capable of drawing a parallel between these and similar experiments carried out by Castro or Mao'.[35]

Student Youth achieved successes which aroused the envy of Catholic Action (then going through a very difficult period) and was closely watched by the Church authorities; but it had not yet reached the mass-movement proportions that Communion and Liberation attained during the 1980s. It saw itself as the regenerator of Catholicism, which it sensed was losing its hold on society, and the champion of a regenerate Christian presence in opposition

34 Luigi Giussani, op. cit., p. 38.
35 ibid.; pp. 42–3.

to secularized culture and Marxist militancy, offering itself as an alternative social resource. But, from the mid-1960s onwards, the cultural, religious, social and political environment to which Student Youth was reacting was rudely shaken by two events in particular: Vatican II, and the anti-establishment riots of 1968.

Trouble with Vatican II – and the storms of '68

During this period the movement went through a severe crisis, and many members left it. Father Giussani and his followers were wrong-footed by the atmosphere and the dynamic of Vatican II. Paul VI, who closed the council and implemented it, was none other than the ex-archbishop of Milan, the former Cardinal Montini. There, in the Lombard capital, he (like Giussani himself) had measured the gulf between Church and society: Milan, the showcase of Italy's secular modernism, where the successful marched on and left the rest by the wayside. Though the two men agreed on the urgent necessity of a drastic shake-up in the Church, they advocated completely opposite ways of going about it.

The council, in making its *aggiornamento*, had realized how archaic, even incomprehensible, its discourse now seemed to society. To remedy this, they looked in the language of secular society for ideas which were similar to, or identical with, Christian aims – whether secular society knew it or not. The Church would take part in any battle in which its message was involved – especially by campaigning for the dignity of mankind whenever this seemed threatened – in labour relations or in the Third World or under oppressive regimes. Thus it became involved in struggles, not usually starting them, but eager to participate because it saw in them the message of Christ, even if this was not apparent to those conducting the fight. This was (it hoped) the way to break out of the vicious circle of splendid isolation which was increasingly distancing it from the real life of society, and so find its place in the modern world.

Father Giussani and his followers had a completely different approach. They were not out to modernize Christianity, but to Christianize modernism. Not for them to bring their humble little Christian stone to a building founded upon the rock of Enlightenment culture; they would do their own building, integrating their actions in society into a total architecture of uncompromisingly Catholic identity, breaking with the motivations and outlook of the 'dominant secularism'.

Before the council, Student Youth had developed a Catholic discourse and praxis which were almost alone in thrusting aside the archaism of the institutional Church and taking direct social action. But after Vatican II it was faced by a challenge of a very different order. No longer was it a case of wrangling with a decrepit Catholic Action over segregation of the sexes. Now the whole institution of the Church was being 'updated', and Father Giussani's followers had to rethink their strategy. Their rivals within the Catholic world no longer had the obsolete look of the 1950s. They handled the language of the human sciences as adroitly as any members of Student Youth, and many of them, loudly proclaiming their 'progressivism', had plunged into social struggle.

During the years immediately following the council, these progressive Catholics appeared to get on well with the movement of '68, even though some of them eventually lost their Christian faith in the process. In Italy, society was unsettled more deeply and for longer than anywhere else in Europe. 'Rampant May' in Italy lasted from 1967 until the mid-1970s, and some of those who took part turned to terrorism, which spread like a gangrene through the political system. Furthermore, while politics and culture were still feeling the shock waves of 1968, Italy received the full blast of the economic depression and social turmoil which followed the oil price rise in the autumn of 1973. The country adapted to inflation and unemployment by an unprecedented development of unofficial networking and the 'black' economy, which exposed the millions of young people arriving on the labour market to insecurity of a new order.

These social upheavals hit Student Youth in two opposite ways in quick succession. First it found itself deprived of its traditional enemy, 'secularism', the scapegoat of re-Christianization and a convenient stereotype for secular society. For the violent clashes within society resulting from the ideological backwash of '68 entirely put paid to this line of argument. According to the then fashionable mythology, 'students and the proletariat united against the bourgeoisie' were working via the revolutionary alternative towards an ideal communist society. The boundaries were sufficiently ill-defined to beguile some Catholics into seeing the face of the Redeemer in the working class. The partial similarity of approach (which Father Giussani himself stressed) between Student Youth and the left-wing groups helped to confuse many of his followers, who went over bag and baggage to the 'extra-parliamentary struggle' of the extreme left.

By the end of the 1970s it looked as if May '68, on top of Vatican II, had emptied Giussani's movement of much of its substance. On the one hand, the Church had taken the contemporary world to its bosom; on the other, the left had made a radical and spectacular break with the values of the 'dominant culture'. Neither posture was that favoured by the militants of Student Youth, and it looked as if the tempestuous end of the 1960s had put some very stony ground under the seeds of their preaching. But in fact it had only stopped them sprouting for a while – in the fertile soil of the social crisis of the mid-1970s.

Catholic 'communion' versus social crisis

It was in 1970 that Father Giussani's enterprise found its second wind with the creation of the Communion and Liberation movement proper. The founder gathered the faithful core of his followers into a group endeavouring to live in Christian communion here and now, at a time when the left-wing organizations were pinning their hopes on a distant future and meanwhile engaging in an increasingly violent struggle against the 'bourgeois state'. 'The important thing for Communion and Liberation is to make visible the unity that Another, the Christ, has already created among all Christians through baptism. And we aim to do our utmost to make that apparent and manifest in our life. It is this unity bringing us together in the mystery of Christ that we try to live out just as we are, which gives us the right approach to the world and justifies the action we are taking for its liberation.'[36]

Members of the group saw this lived Christian communion as

36   Ibid., p. 81.

their way of putting into practice the leitmotif of the time, 'change your life'. They were fighting many of the same battles as the militants of '68, but with a different motivation and using different methods. 'There was one theme that we developed increasingly from 1965 onwards and which proved to be one of the fundamental values of '68: we said loud and clear that every community or people has a right to express itself despite all pressures from conformist societies and the organs of state.'[37]

Those on the left interpreted affirmations of this kind as an attack on the capitalist and bourgeois state or on the domination of the Third World by Western imperialism. As for the *ciellini*,[38] they saw it in terms of a 'fight against conformity and the false wisdom born of Enlightenment rationalism'[39] – which had, among other things, banished God from the history taught in schools. Another of Father Giussani's arguments was: 'There is another subject on which we can claim to have anticipated '68, clearly evident from documents written between 1965 and 1967, namely the urgent need to change the face of society by instituting new and more human relationships.'

Despite the evident parallelism between these two points of view, the 1970s were to witness an increasing divergence between the social strategies of the two movements. The Italian left was drifting inexorably towards violence, which led certain groups into physical clashes with government in the form of terrorism and political assassination. These were the 'years of lead', which have no real parallel outside Italy, where violence was in effect a mass phenomenon. Communion and Liberation, diametrically opposed to the strategy of confrontation adopted by most left-wing groups, opted for a tactic of Catholic 'presence' within a society in deep crisis. This policy paid off handsomely from the end of the decade, while the Italian left went into irreversible decline.

The economic crisis that hit Western Europe following the steep rise in the oil price in autumn 1973 had dramatic repercussions in Italy. It led to the failure of the welfare state and of social security, and to the development of a huge informal economy in

---

37 Ibid.
38 From the initials of 'Communione e Liberazione', pronounced 'chi-ell' in Italian.
39 Luigi Giussani, op. cit., p. 82.

which there was virtually no job security. This situation was compounded by the traditional imbalances between the impoverished south and the industrialized north. The large cities such as Milan were besieged by people from the south in ever-increasing numbers.

Just at this time the swollen universities were disgorging on to the labour market a mass of young *disoccupati*, unable to find work after graduating, who formed a large new underclass of marginalized intellectuals. The prospect of unemployment or work in the black market deepened a profound disillusionment with the values passed on to the young graduates by the educational system, unable to reconcile their education and ambitions with the actual requirements of the market. This led tens of thousands of young people to drop out of university after the first couple of years, and many were the schemes hatched by individuals in order to survive. At the same time, organized student opposition, which traditionally absorbed these frustrations and acted as a mouthpiece for students' demands, disappeared as such. Its officers dispersed among the galaxy of increasingly radical left-wing groups, out of touch with day-to-day problems and postponing the need for a change in society to a shining, and ever-receding, future.[40]

From social action to political militancy

It was by occupying this niche that Communion and Liberation made its breakthrough and took a firm hold among youth. Between 1974 and 1989 the movement went on to gain a foothold in the Italian political system and in Pope John Paul II's entourage. At first it concentrated on re-Christianization 'from below', through social work; nevertheless its ambition was to take on the state in order to roll back 'secularism', and to play a leading part in the redefinition of Catholicism under this pontificate. But by 1990 the difficulties of implementing a strategy 'from above' had forced it back to its mission at the grass roots. These flexible tactics of advance and withdrawal drew upon the versatile potential of the

---

40   For a well-documented analysis of the crisis of the 1970s in Italy as the context for the emergence of Communion and Liberation, see Abbruzzese, op. cit., pp. 135–52.

organization's numerous contacts, enabling it to occupy the space to best advantage.

The 'presence' of Communion and Liberation in society operated through a large number of organizations each having a specific object. Each of them was based on the 'local communities' of Communion and Liberation, a place for discussions, sharing and mutual deepening of Christian faith. At these centres members shared in ritual and worship, and lived out a 'total Christian life' that broke with the motivations of secularized society. Around this community there were two kinds of association: those that took direct action 'in the world' by 'works' or political action, and those in which the best-trained and most highly motivated members were gathered for a specific purpose.

Action 'in the world' was channelled through the Company of Deeds (*Compagnia delle Opere*) and the People's Movement (*Movimento Popolare*). The Company, which was legally constituted in 1986 by merging and rationalizing existing charitable activities, was intended to be a mutual support network that would permit 'better utilization of the resources and energies for promoting the integration of young people and the unemployed into the world of work'. It put firms – more than 3,500 in 1990 – in touch with potential employees, and also promoted training and apprenticeship courses, the founding of businesses in the impoverished areas of the Mezzogiorno, help and rehabilitation programmes for social drop-outs, delinquents and drug addicts, etc.

These activities took place 'as part of the ongoing presence of Catholics in society and in the light of the official teachings of the Church'.[41] To an extent they stood in for the welfare state, riddled with bureaucratic muddle and nepotism, but their motives and criteria were very different. The Company was the 'social showcase' of re-Christianization 'from below', and a prototype of the 'new and more human relationships' that the ideal Catholic society should offer to individuals. Its success has made it an economic and financial power in the land, and its opponents have not scrupled to accuse Communion and Liberation of being a

41 Statutes, art. 4.

Catholic holding company aiming to control the markets in order to attain influence and wealth.

In the task of re-Christianization, the Company of Deeds creates the linkage between the bottom and the top, between charitable works and social entrepreneurs, whereas the People's Movement acts directly in the world of politics. Although it is not officially affiliated to the Christian Democrats, it is a valuable back-up resource for that party, while reserving the right to work with other parties as circumstances dictate and to campaign against any Christian Democrat leader suspected of cherishing 'secularist' sympathies. It takes part in the cut-and-thrust of politics, but does not feel bound by its rules; it is '*in* politics' but not '*of* politics'. It uses politics to promote the break with secularism and to build up a Christian society. Its main leader, Roberto Formigoni, has been elected a Christian Democrat deputy and Vice-President of the European Parliament; and yet Communion and Liberation can choose to withdraw from the political scene if it considers that politics is proving a hindrance to its mission.

Father Giussani's followers first entered the political arena in 1974, when there was a referendum on divorce. They said they had done so at the express request of the highest officials of the Church, who were worried about the possible outcome of the referendum (which did indeed favour divorce). The *ciellini* mobilized from one end of the country to the other – even though they thought the contest to be ill-advised and lost in advance. The People's Movement was created on the hoof. Although Paul VI's ideas on religion differed considerably from those of Father Giussani, he appreciated the help received from the latter's supporters, and said so. From then on, the movement was once more viewed favourably from the Vatican; this favour reached dizzying heights under John Paul II.

Each year since 1979 the People's Movement has organized a huge 'meeting of friendship among the nations' at the end of August, at the seaside resort of Rimini. For a whole week it stages what is in effect a show of strength – like the political parties with their annual conventions. Over ten years the numbers attending constantly increased, as did media coverage of the event, while the numbers attending the festival of *Unità* (*Unità* being the daily paper of the Italian communist party) were falling year by year. The meeting is also the showcase of the movement and a platform for popularizing whatever action it currently wishes to advocate. The most sophisticated means of communication are employed to ensure the success of the operation; this is just one more way of showing that a religious message can make enthusiastic use of the most sophisticated technical and scientific languages without thereby conceding that reason is superior to faith.

Through the Company of Deeds and the People's Movement, re-Christianization was able to occupy the whole field from below and from above, from finding work for the unemployed to taking part in the internecine struggles of the Christian Democratic Party. But Communion and Liberation had other satellites as well. A team of journalists in sympathy with its aims published the weekly *Il Sabato* [*Saturday*], which fulminated against all 'secularized' Christians, stigmatizing them as 'Catho-communists'. The monthlies *Thirty Days in the Church and in the World*, published in 1989 in six languages, and *Literae Communionis*, the internal organ of Communion and Liberation, presented theological issues and Church policy to a more informed readership. The publishers Editoriale Jaca popularized the writings of the leaders of the movement and of theologians sympathetic to them, and any writing – however seemingly remote from the intellectual outlook of the movement – that could be turned to account by a Catholic culture making the break with secularism.

The great flexibility of the Communion and Liberation organizations operating in the world was due to a 'hard core' of elite organizations, demanding intense personal commitment, in which all the leaders were to be found: the Fraternity of Communion and Liberation and the Memores Domini association. The latter consisted of laypeople who had consecrated themselves to God in chastity, and who bore exemplary witness to the Christian message 'in the world'. Living alone or in communities, they were the strongest link between the movement as such and its fields of social action. The Fraternity consisted of adults with solid professional careers, selected by the group of leaders, with Father Giussani as life president. That too was a very strong network, which set the guidelines for all the associations operating in and around

Communion and Liberation; it was also, in the eyes of canon law, a religious movement of laypeople, and was recognized as such by the Vatican in 1982.

Communion and Liberation inevitably made many enemies because it touched Italian society at so many points and because of the coherence, vigour and attractiveness of its message to many disoriented Italian Catholics; and not least because of its special connections, including ideological ones, with such close associates of the Pope as Cardinals Ratzinger and Lustiger, who directly represented the papal desire for a 'new evangelization'. Italian Catholics who did not believe in re-Christianization by a break with the secularized foundations of society, some of whom also had contacts in the Vatican, were outraged by the intellectual terrorism deployed against them, especially in the columns of *Il Sabato*.

Moreover, many Italian bishops were ill at ease with a movement which appealed directly to the laity and bypassed diocesan and parish channels, and which often voiced 'anti-clerical' sentiments. Father Giussani, in a booklet published in six languages and entitled *Layman, meaning Christian*, described the Church (unless revived by charisma) as being in a state of *rigor mortis*, and accused certain bishops of 'stifling charisma'.[42] The religious establishment faced these attacks with angelic patience: the movement did, after all, have the ear of the Vatican. But during the 'meeting for friendship among nations' in August 1989, a very violent dispute revived the conflicts between the religious establishment and the militants of Communion and Liberation in an extension of internecine battles among the Christian Democrats. Communion and Liberation was the loser, and had to make a tactical retreat.

The dispute began with a university catering cooperative called La Cascina,[43] which had been formed in Rome by the Company of Deeds. Communion and Liberation considered it to be an excellent social work project. It met an urgent and large-scale need by supplying cheap meals to students while at the same time giving employment to many young people. But political adversaries

42   Luigi Giussani, *Layman* (1988), p. 25. The text reproduces an interview that appeared in no. 8 (1987) of *Thirty Days in the Church and in the World*.
43   A word describing farms in northern Italy in which several families live.

of the People's Movement had accused it of having received illegal aid and subsidies from the mayor of Rome, a Christian Democrat who was a supporter of Giulio Andreotti, President of the Council. Andreotti was the idol of young Communion and Liberation members and was the guest star at the 1989 meeting.

Ranged against Communion and Liberation were not only its traditional enemies such as the Communist Party, but also the whole of the left wing of the Christian Democrats, supported by some elements in the Vatican, and in particular by the editor of the *Osservatore Romano*, the official daily newspaper of the Holy See. The Rome branch of the People's Movement made a heated reply, in the form of a white paper[44] distributed at the meeting at the very time when Sgr Andreotti was addressing it. This leaflet contained such accusations, and hurled so much abuse at some sections of the clergy, that the Vatican had publicly to scold its star pupils, who had been a bit too sure of themselves and sorely lacking in Christian charity towards the episcopal hierarchy. The weekly *Il Sabato* retorted by publishing its next issue with completely blank pages, and the internal crisis led to several resignations. During the next few months the movement systematically withdrew from the political field and renewed its activity in the social sphere. Re-Christianization 'from above' had met with unlooked-for setbacks, and priority was once more given to resourcing 'from below'.

Communion and Liberation was and is an enterprise unique in Western European Catholicism during the last quarter-century. Its size, its ability to carry on re-Christianization first from below, then from above, and finally to go back to its individual and social grassroots after coming up against an immovable obstacle, have never been equalled. Born in Milan (with all that that implies), inheriting and renewing an 'Ambrosian'[45] tradition of social Catholicism, the movement has only a few small offshoots abroad, despite its energetic proselytising. Whatever hopes its leaders may

---

44 Entitled *Il gigante e la Cascina (The Giant and the Cascina)*. The 'giant' was a kind of Goliath made up of the enemies of Communion and Liberation, rich and powerful, doing battle against David, i.e., the university restaurant 'La Cascina'.
45 Luigi Giussani, *Le Mouvement...*, op. cit., pp. 218–19, and Salvatore Abruzzese, op. cit., p. 192.

have of Slovakia, Poland or Belgium, France is still a 'mission field' – a fact that exercised Father Giussani considerably.[46]

Meanwhile in France: charisma, and trouble in the schools

Since the mid-1970s France has been the theatre of a significant re-Christianization movement. But this movement has operated almost entirely 'from below', through a burgeoning of 'charismatic renewal' groups; they have not wished, nor been able, to undertake extensive social action or to enter the realm of politics.

The origins of the 'charismatic renewal' in contemporary European Catholicism are to be found in the United States, among certain groups of American Catholics who had been influenced by the (Protestant) Pentecostals.[47] It was to these groups that the future founders of the European movement looked, in the 1970s, for inspiration and a model. All believers who are committed to 'renewal' begin by experiencing, or desiring, a personal relationship with God, expressed through the Holy Spirit, in the form of an emotional shock beyond human understanding. The Holy Spirit 'descends' upon those whom He chooses, irrespective of their status, lay or clerical, their educational level or their social standing. He bestows upon them 'spiritual gifts' (charisma), of which the most spectacular are 'speaking with tongues' and miraculous healing powers.

In France, this renewed and intense conception of the Catholic faith has enjoyed a significant success since the late 1970s. In 1987 the sociologist Danièle Hervieu-Léger estimated that 200,000 people were involved in the charismatic renewal, either on a regular basis or by way of occasional meetings or retreats.[48] This large number of adherents is spread over a great many prayer groups (nearly a thousand), some of them structured around larger communities. The modes of awareness, forms of vocation and manner of life of the faithful are extremely varied. Members of some of the groups live under the same roof, in town or country

46   Luigi Giussani, op. cit., p. 192.
47   This phenomenon is described in more detail later on (see chapter 3).
48   Danièle Hervieu-Léger, 'Charismatisme catholique et institution', in *Le Retour des certitudes*, op. cit., p. 223.

(some in former monastic buildings left vacant by a shortage of monks), while others meet regularly but otherwise live what is to all appearances an ordinary life 'in the world'. Some of the communities, like the 'Lion of Judah', have 'specialized' in miraculous healings, and others in caring for mentally handicapped people (L'Arche), dropouts (Berdine) or the destitute (the Bread of Life).[49] In France most of the converts are young educated adults, often graduates, who are 'both most directly imbued with the ideals of progress and the most directly affected, economically and socially, by the disappearance of the certainty of growth that was taken for granted in the 1960s.'[50]

In these cases Catholic identity is affirmed only within the framework of re-Christianization 'from below'. What the charismatic movement wants is to reshape individuals, bring about their inner conversion to Christ. The disciples model their lives on the gospel 'like the early Christians', trying to put the words of Jesus literally into practice. When some of them undertake intensive charitable work, they are not thereby becoming social entrepreneurs after the fashion of the Company of Deeds of Communion and Liberation. Neither has the 'renewal' produced anything equivalent to what the People's Movement represents in Italy, although some of the most powerful communities are beginning to build up networks of friendship and support in political and financial circles.

Nevertheless there are people in France who want re-Christianization 'from below' to lead into a renegotiation of the secular state, as codified by the law of 1905 on the separation of Church and state. The bishops, led by the archbishops of Lyon and Paris, Cardinals Decourtray and Lustiger, want to bring

---

49 There are two well documented books on the charismatic movement as a whole: Monique Hébrard's report, very expressive and revised and updated several times, *Les Nouveaux disciples: dix ans après* (Paris: Centurion, 1987) and Frédéric Lenoir's collection of interviews, *Les Communautés nouvelles: interviews des fondateurs* (Paris: Fayard, 1988). These two authors were insiders who were converted to charismatic Christianity by one of the communities about which they write. For an analysis of the charismatic groups in terms of religious sociology, see the articles by Martine Cohen, 'Figures de l'individualisme moderne: essai sur deux communautés charismatiques', *Esprit* (April 1986); 'Vers de nouveaux rapports avec l'institution ecclésiastique: l'exemple du renouveau charismatique en France', *Archives de sciences sociales des religions*, 62, 1 (1986) and 'Le renouveau charismatique en France ou l'affirmation des catholicismes', *Christus* (July 1986).
50 Danièle Hervieu-Léger, op. cit., pp. 227–8.

Catholicism out of the private sphere to which the state has confined it, and to give it the 'public legal status' it now demands.[51] From this point of view, the experience of the most vigorous charismatic communities constitutes a French version of the challenge to secularism (*laïcité*). For these communities are making a complete break with the imperatives of *laïcité* and laying the foundations of a 'Christian' social order. But, up to 1990 at least, the charismatic groups had not followed the bishops very far into this battle, preferring to devote themselves to their own particular mode of individual and community mission and not seek contacts among the organs of state.

If the bishops have had some success, it is chiefly in relation to schooling. In 1984 there was a demonstration in defence of private schools which forced the government of the day to withdraw a bill directed against them. Schools, as the place where children's family values came up against social acculturation, were a domain which the Church could never wholly abandon to the secular state. The success of the demonstration, the largest since May 1968, also showed that, in the field of education, the policy of re-Christianization could bring thousands of Catholics on to the streets, indifferent though they might be to other areas of contention such as birth control.

A further episode in the struggle of Christianity to regain 'public legal status' was the 'Islamic veil' affair of autumn 1989. Both the bishops and the chief rabbis expressed active support for the re-Islamization movements, which wanted Muslim girls to be allowed to wear the veil in secondary schools. As schools in France are rigidly secular, holding that religious affiliation belongs to the private sphere and is not to be expressed in school, the supporters of re-Christianization, re-Islamization and re-Judaization made common cause to negotiate a 'new *laïcité*' that would enable them to occupy the public domain, even if initially only in certain institutions – such as schools.

Compared with Italy, where Communion and Liberation and its satellites have pursued a coherent and successful strategy of re-Christianization simultaneously 'from below' and 'from above',

51 See above, pp. 66–7.

France presents a much more fragmented picture. The myriad of prayer groups and charismatic communities, whose members break with the surrounding 'secular' society in their daily living, have no other aim 'in the world' than to expand their communities by dint of active proselytization. This, then, is a very long-term programme of re-Christianization from below, not complemented by groups taking 'positive social action' comparable to the Company of Deeds. And the 'children of light' cannot as such be mobilized on a command from an episcopate whose leaders wish gradually to re-Christianize the areas and institutions of society.

Such successes as have been achieved by this policy were due to temporary mobilizations of Catholics who then faded away again (as in 1984), or to alliances with other movements, Muslim or Jewish, working for the same ends (as in autumn 1989). Such bases are infinitely more fragile and less dependable than the networks of hundreds of thousands of sympathizers who support Father Giussani's mission. Yet notwithstanding the differences of social structure, political culture and Catholic tradition between France and her neighbours across the Alps, the many facets of their respective re-Christianizations belong to a similar historical sequence. It derives from the crisis that changed the face of European capitalism in the 1970s; from the consternation produced by social upheaval and the disappearance of the old alliances, the old values of the optimistic 'Thirty Glorious Years' which, to Catholics, were incarnate in Vatican II.

On the ruins of communism

It is not only in Western Europe that re-Christianization has appeared. It has also lived alongside Eastern communism during the last two decades – and helped to bring about its collapse.

To the Catholic Church the elevation of the Polish cardinal Karol Wojtyla to the pontificate in the autumn of 1978 seems in retrospect like a kind of 'gift of prophecy'. In 1979, during his first visit to his native country after his enthronement, he proclaimed: 'This pope comes to speak, before the whole Church, Europe and the world, of these often forgotten nations and peoples.

He comes to shout aloud.'[52] That in itself was a considerable turnaround for what was then known as 'the church of silence'. But very few imagined that the Pope would see the hopes expressed in his sermon fulfilled, with the collapse of the communist system in Poland, the demolition of the Iron Curtain and reincorporation into the European concert of nations which since 1945 had constituted 'the other Europe'.

In Czechoslovakia, where the Church suffered real persecution through the four decades of communism, the first official invitation issued by President Havel after the 'velvet revolution' was to John Paul II. In spring 1990 he went, by government invitation, to visit a country where six months earlier most dioceses had not even had a bishop. It was almost unbelievable. On 21 April 1990 he was in Prague, addressing the people and hearing their hymns from a promontory formerly occupied by a towering statue of Stalin, while the service was broadcast through loudspeakers that had originally been installed at every crossroads to grind out communist propaganda.

In the Letna Park, where once the 'masses of the People' had been bussed in to applaud heads of state of 'fraternal countries', a crowd of the faithful was celebrating mass in the rain. But just as many were there simply out of curiosity. The newly reconstituted Christian Democrats, backed by a pastoral letter from the Cardinal Primate, had counted on victory in the parliamentary elections of June 1990. But it did not happen. On the contrary, the 'Catholic party' suffered the humiliation of winning fewer votes than the communists, while the Civic Forum, for which many Catholics had voted, won by a large margin.

Nevertheless, it looked as though the passing of communism might open the way to a significant surge of re-Christianization in societies emerging from forty years of totalitarianism. In Poland, after all, the Church had been the last recourse against the party state; in Czechoslovakia, it had suffered a persecution that gave it moral legitimacy. Furthermore, the ideological content of re-Christianization – as set forth by Cardinal Ratzinger, for example

52   Address at Gniezno in June 1979, cited by Patrick Michel, *La Société retrouvée* (Paris: Fayard, 1988), trans. Alan Braley, *Politics and Religion in Eastern Europe* (Cambridge: Polity Press, 1991), p. 135.

– openly claims to supersede communism. It is no longer simply anathematized, as formerly, but is seen through Christian eyes as the very manifestation of totalitarianism, the negation of freedom and human rights, because it denies the existence of God. Indeed, communism, as the inevitable culmination of the process of the Enlightenment and the supreme argument against it, provided negative proof of the necessity of re-Christianization.

In Western Europe re-Christianization was first deployed amid the social crisis of the mid-1970s, taking over as a practical source of the inspiration and solidarity which the secular utopias of the industrial age no longer had the power to provide. In the 'other Europe' things turned out somewhat differently. Even before communism collapsed in 1989, the Polish church had succeeded in reorganizing a fragmented society in defiance of the state; and some types of re-Christianization from below had appeared in Bohemia, and even more in Slovakia, before the 'velvet revolution'.

But when free elections were held and as a market economy was progressively introduced, democratic aspirations proved stronger than the thirst for transcendence; the wish to express differing opinions proved stronger than acceptance of revealed truths – understandably so after forty years of subscribing to other truths said to be just as unassailable. Even in ultra-Catholic Slovakia the rumour that, if the Christian Democrat party won, crucifixes would have to be put up in all schools and workplaces (a replacement for portraits of Stalin?) helped to take many good Christian voters out of that particular lobby.

And in Poland, before communism ended, some people were wondering whether, if the country were to recover 'freedom of political life', its 'marvellous spiritual tension' would endure, whether 'what is born in response to the dangerous challenge of totalitarianism [. . .] would cease to exist as soon as that challenge disappeared.'[53] This hypothesis came true in 1989; the prime minister, Tadeusz Mazowiecki, was a Catholic intellectual, but he certainly could not be made the instrument of a policy of re-Christianizing society from above. Some of his friends were elected to the Diet despite the hostility of the episcopate, which had

53 Adam Zagajewski, op. cit., p. 233.

sponsored rival candidates. And in the conflict that arose in the summer of 1990 between the prime minister and his recent ally Lech Walesa, the latter accused the government of carrying out a 'leftist' policy, meaning that it was following principles that he did not consider to be very Catholic.

To understand what is at stake for re-Christianization as the basically Catholic countries of Eastern and Central Europe emerge from communism, we must first remind ourselves how the Polish 'model' was constructed. We shall then compare that model with the particular way in which Catholicism performed its socializing task in Bohemia.

The Polish model and its ambiguities

Throughout history, membership of the Catholic Church has been one of the most important components in the identity of a Pole. Between Protestant Prussia in the West and Orthodox Russia in the East, which have twice dismembered it, Poland has succeeded in surviving as a nation by making its Catholic faith into a cultural rampart. The conquest by Nazi Germany in 1939, followed by Soviet domination after the war, were simply two more episodes in this long geopolitical heritage. But they were more than just examples of territorial expansion; they resulted in the imposition of the totalitarian model brought in by the invader.

Nazism was accompanied by the systematic annihilation of Poland's cultural elites – in addition to the planned extermination of the Jews. Thus communism was imposed upon a country deprived of its intelligentsia, and it promoted 'new men' to the seats of knowledge, men who would be its vassals. Only one organized group was left to oppose it and to perpetuate values alien to socialism – the Catholic clergy. After a first decade in which the government seemed set on liquidating the Catholic Church, and which culminated in the imprisonment of the primate, Cardinal Wyszynski, from 1953 to 1956, the government had to seek a *modus vivendi* with the Church. The political and social crisis which shook the communist order in 1956 had made the party leaders anxious to find compromises with civil society, and the Church was an indispensable partner for obtaining a modicum of social peace not based solely on repression.

The Church speaks for society

It was in the context of this first victory over totalitarianism that the Church, as the spokesman for civil society, began to think of Poland as a laboratory for re-Christianization. Its sights were now on the future, on post-communist society; Catholicism must cease to embody only the resistances of a past 'condemned by history'. This conception gained credibility because, at the time, there was virtually no other organized source of values opposed to totalitarianism.

This new Catholic outlook found a symbol in the Nowa-Huta affair. Nowa-Huta was an industrial town of about a hundred thousand people built during the 1950s; as its name ('the new steelworks') indicates, it was the archetypal proletarian city, New Man writ large. It had no church, excepting a small chapel that had existed previously and been allowed to survive. Yet around this single place of worship sometimes as many as ten thousand people gathered for Sunday mass. In 1957 the government made land available for building a church; but three years later it had a school established there. Not until 1968, after repeated pressure and conflicts, accompanied by clashes in the city, did the building of the church begin. Undertaken by the faithful themselves, it was finished in 1977 and was inaugurated by Karol Wojtyla, at that time Archbishop of Cracow.[54] So, when he became Pope the next year, he had just witnessed a stubborn and successful fight for the affirmation of Catholic identity in an atheistic state.

Poland's experience of re-Christianization from below was first and foremost an alternative view of society, a reaction to the shoddiness of everyday life, the penury and despair engendered by the Soviet system. The Church found a way to counter the religious indifference of young people educated in Marxism-Leninism: it set up a vast network of 'catechism points', which by the end of the 1970s numbered more than twenty thousand. Even more important, it showed enterprise and initiative, giving the young a taste of communal living which would induce them to break with socialist mores in their daily life – a socialism that

---

54 See Patrick Michel, *L'Eglise polonaise et l'avenir de la nation* (Paris: Centurion, 1981), pp. 21–4.

by the 1970s had been veneered with a poor man's consumerism, financed by massive borrowings from Western banks. Patrick Michel[55] notes that, 'in trying to invent a new way of living out the faith, the Church created the Oasis movement which [in 1980] brought together nearly 30,000 young people in holiday camps dotted all over Poland, where they lived in a communal atmosphere of reflection, prayer and sharing. These camps usually lasted for two weeks, and the groups continued to meet after they had returned home.'

Unlike Italy, where Communion and Liberation had come into being outside – and, to a certain extent, in opposition to – the Church hierarchy, in communist Poland Catholicism, Church and episcopate were united. Even though, as in Czechoslovakia and Hungary, the government had conjured up associations of priests 'for peace',[56] manipulated by the government, these only involved small minorities and had no credibility in the eyes of the faithful. So there is a continuum, running from the structures of re-Christianization from below – anything from Catholic communities socializing the young to believers building their own churches – right up to the Cardinal Primate. He became the chief spokesman for civil society over against the state, and negotiated re-Christianization 'from above', demanding and obtaining many concessions including a *de facto* public law status for the Church, in return for a modicum of social peace.

Competition from Solidarnosc

The high point of this Catholic version of reconquest of 'the world' came with the 'kneeling revolution' at the end of the 1970s, while John Paul II was taking up his duties in Rome. The workers in the Gdansk shipyards, on strike against 'the party of the working class', processed, rosary in hand and a hymn on their lips, behind

---

55   Ibid., p. 51.
56   In Poland *Pax*, in Czechoslovakia *Pacem in Terris*, in Hungary *Opus Pacis*. These titles imitated Vatican terminology by using Latin, and seemed to refer – even by direct imitation in the case of Czechoslovakia – to the encyclical *Pacem in Terris* with which John XXIII had inaugurated the Church's *Ostpolitik* in April 1963. They were also in harmony with the 'peace' line taken in communist propaganda after the war, culminating in the 'peace movement' aimed at disarmament (of the West).

banners representing the Holy Virgin, and celebrated mass in their workplaces;[57] it seemed at the time to be concrete evidence of the success of re-Christianization 'from below'. They became the government's chief political interlocutor, and gained a victory without precedent in the communist world in August 1980 when Solidarnosc, their independent trade union with ten million members, was legalized.

And yet during the eighteen months of Solidarnosc's legal existence, before General Jaruzelski introduced martial law on 13 December 1981, it became evident that even the smallest opening up of the political system encroached upon the Church's claim to be the chief spokesman for civil society. The leaders of the trade union very quickly went for the highest political profile they could manage, and tried to limit the Church to a 'spiritual force'.[58] Only after 13 December, when Solidarnosc had been declared illegal, was the Church able to regain its position as interlocutor with the communist government – until that government in turn disappeared in 1989.

And yet things were no longer as they had been before 1980, for during the sixteen months in which Solidarnosc led a legal existence re-Christianization from above had ceased to seem the only credible future after the disappearance of communism. And the 'relative secularization of Polish society'[59] that occurred during this period prefigured a more thoroughgoing secularization after 1989, when the totalitarian regime collapsed and was replaced by a democratic one.

From then onwards the Church turned its attention to succouring those who were being left by the wayside in the transition to a market economy. It deployed re-Christianization from below, and focused on to unemployment, inflation and the likely increase in poverty, hoping thereby to become the interlocutor with the

---

57 At exactly the same time as, in Europe, mosques were opened in factories where immigrant Muslims were working. They were to play a major role in the social movements of the early 1980s, but did not move into politics at that stage (see Gilles Kepel, *Les Banlieues de l'Islam*, op. cit., chap. 3).
58 See Krzystof Pomian,'Religion et politique en Pologne (1945–1984)', *XXe Siècle*, 10 (April–June 1986), pp. 83–101.
59 Patrick Michel, *Politics and Religion* . . . , trans. A. Braley (Cambridge: Polity Press, 1991), p. 43, and note 55, p. 210.

democratic regime on behalf of civil society, just as it had been *vis-à-vis* the former totalitarian government.

Poland in the 1970s was a textbook example of re-Christianization controlled by the Church hierarchy and moving upwards from below. But this situation, so ideal for the Church, came about only because two factors coincided: the importance of Catholicism in defining the national identity, and the Church's monopoly as representative of civil society over against the totalitarian state. When these two conditions were not both present, re-Christianization could take place only partially, from below, and had to yield, even within the Church, to those – and they were powerful – who thought that Catholicism should take another direction as it emerged from forty years in the frozen wastes of a totalitarian state.

Bohemia: the counter-model

From many points of view the situation of the Church in Bohemia was the reverse of that in Poland. Though there were superficial similarities, and although the Church hierarchy thought that re-Christianization from above would be possible after communism had crumbled, Catholicism in Bohemia allowed the democratic convictions of its adherents to take precedence over confessional identity. In order to retrace this process and analyse its implications, we must first remind ourselves of the unprecedented persecution to which the Church was subjected between 1948 and 1989.

The downside of forced re-Catholicization

Czechoslovakia is the only country in the former Soviet bloc in which the communist party has ever received more than one-third of the votes in free elections. This result, which was obtained in 1946, enabled the communists to take part in a coalition government, after which it was easy to seize power in the 'Prague coup' of February 1948.[60] In the second half of that year, 'The general

---

60 Jacques Rupnik's book, *The other Europe* (London: Weidenfeld & Nicolson, 1988), contains a detailed description of these events.

secretary of the CP, R. Slansky, announced the priority of the "ideological, political and administrative struggle" against the forces of reaction, chief among which he included the hierarchy of the Catholic Church.'[61]

And yet, contrary to the situation in neighbouring Poland, the Catholic Church did not embody the national identity, and was scarcely in a position to become the spokesman for civil society. In Slovakia the church bore the recent stigma of Nazi collaboration by one of its members, Bishop Tiso, who had been head of the 'Independent' Slovak puppet state during the war. One of Bishop Tiso's chief claims to notoriety was the deportation of the large Jewish population of Slovakia to the death camps from autumn of 1941 onwards. Even though the Slovak bishops had protested against the deportations,[62] the Church had to maintain a rather low political profile during the years that followed the defeat of the Third Reich.

But in Bohemia and Moravia the Catholic Church had been savagely persecuted by the Nazis. The Archbishop of Prague, Joseph Beran, had been in Dachau before he took office in 1946. But even this unblemished record could not entirely dissipate the ancestral suspicion of the Catholic Church that was endemic in the land of John Hus, excommunicated and burnt at the stake in 1415. Among Czechs, institutional Catholicism symbolized the destruction of the nation and its forced incorporation into the Austrian empire, after the defeat at the White Mountain.[63] Because of the 're-Catholicization' that was carried out during the Counter-Reformation so as to extirpate the Hussite spirit, and in which fanatical German-speaking Jesuits, addicted to autos-da-fé, played a prominent part, the Church was regarded by the common people as an instrument of foreign domination.[64]

---

61 Jacques Rupnik, 'Tchécoslovaquie: des églises dans la tourmente', *Etudes* (September 1986), p. 231.
62 Karel Skalicky, 'The Vicissitudes of the Catholic Church in Czechoslovakia, 1918 to 1988', in *Czechoslovakia Crossroads and Crisis, 1918–1988*, ed. Norman Stone and Eduard Strouhal (London: Macmillan/BBC, 1989), p. 310.
63 On 8 November 1620, at the battle of the White Mountain (*Bila Hora*), a hill to the West of Prague, the Czech troops were crushed by a coalition of Catholic armies. Bohemia lost its independence and was incorporated into the Habsburg empire.
64 On Catholicism in Czech historiography, see the critical approach of Zdenek Kalista, 'Le catholicisme dans l'histoire tchèque', *Istina*, 28, 1 (1983), pp. 5–30.

Just after the end of the First World War, when the Czechoslovak Republic was proclaimed, anti-Catholic feeling was very widespread in Bohemia. It was expressed in spoliation of a number of churches, and by the creation of a 'Czechoslovak church' which left Rome in 1920, together with more than 300 priests; ten years later it numbered some 800,000 members.[65] As will be seen, relationships between the Catholic Church and the Czech national identity were the exact opposite of those in Poland. In Slovakia, however, a 'Polish type' Catholicism prevailed, conjoined with nationalism, as opposed to Bohemia which was the dominant and 'miscreant' partner to which Slovakia had been joined upon the break-up of the Austro-Hungarian empire.

The anti-church policy conducted by the communists from 1948 onwards was in some ways a continuation of the course already taken by the state before the war. But although Masaryk[66] and his friends adopted an attitude of defiance going well beyond the anti-clericalism of the self-styled French 'radicals' at that time, he observed the democratic rules of a legally constituted state; the Communist Party, on the other hand, organized a systematic persecution of Catholicism without parallel in the Soviet bloc.

In 1948 all church property was nationalized and religious instruction was made illegal. In 1949, the state created a 'Catholic Action Organization' subservient to it; Cardinal Beran, in a pastoral letter, declared the movement 'schismatic'. He was immediately placed under house arrest in the archbishop's palace, from which he emerged only fourteen years later, to go into exile in Rome. In March 1950 most of the superiors and provincials of the religious congregations were arraigned for 'espionage and treason' and given long prison sentences. During the night of 13–14 April, 'police broke into all Catholic convents in the Republic, took away the nuns, priests and laypeople and herded them into a number of "concentration convents" [. . .] The monasteries were ransacked in the search for documents to provide proof of the

---

65 In addition to Skalicky, op. cit., p. 300, see Marie-Elisabeth Ducreux, 'Entre catholicisme et protestantisme'. *Le débat*, 59 (April 1990), p. 106ff.
66 Thomas Garrigue Masaryk (1850–1937) was the founder and president of the first Czechoslovak republic.

anti-revolutionary propaganda of which the religious were accused; nothing was found, but everything was turned over and pillaged.'[67]

All the religious orders were proscribed, and the bishops were arrested and given sentences of up to twenty years in prison – while a 'Peace movement of the Catholic clergy', run by an excommunicated priest, did duty as a 'spokesman' for Catholics with the government.

Under Satan's sun

The destruction of the external, visible structure of the Czech Church had disastrous personal consequences for the thousands of priests, nuns and monks who were sent to labour camps or to high-security prisons. Even those who were given a 'permit to exercise' their priestly functions were under close police surveillance. The persecution greatly hampered contacts between the lower clergy and the hierarchy – whose members were in prison or under house arrest – and between the hierarchy and the Vatican. But this persecution, which brought home to its victims the true reality of Christian martyrdom, enabled an 'inner structure' of the Church to be formed. In sharp contrast to the arrogance of earlier re-Catholicization, the pomp and the gilded baroque of the Counter-Reformation, far from the bishop's palaces, in cells or stone-breaking on the roads, there arose theologians of human distress for whom Catholicism took on a new meaning. At the Vatican II Council Cardinal Beran, in exile after his fourteen years of house arrest, was to say: 'In my country the Catholic Church seems to be expiating its faults and the sins committed in its name against freedom of religion in times past: the burning of the priest Jan Hus in the fifteenth century and, in the seventeenth century, the forced reconversion to Catholicism of a large part of the Czech people.'[68]

Father Joseph Zverina, who was incarcerated from 1952 to 1964, noted that, in these conditions, when it was impossible not

67 Andrea Rebichini, *Chiesa, società e stato in Cecoslovachia, 1948–1968* (Padua: Ceseo-Liviana, n.d.), p. 52.
68 Quoted by Jacques Rupnik, op. cit., p. 234, after T. Beeson, *Discretion and Valour: Religious Conditions in Russia and Eastern Europe* (London, 1981), p. 238.

merely to celebrate mass but even to practise charity, the only possible expression of Catholic faith remaining was 'the inner practice of the spiritual life. This was not escapism, but a matter of life and death, the basis of our opposition.' This church that lived within him and his imprisoned colleagues was not a 'silent' church but a church 'in silence', not 'underground' but 'exposed to the sun...of Satan'! In the evenings he devoted his energies to tapping out dogmatic theology in morse code to the prisoner in the next cell.[69] But besides preserving in their inmost hearts this faith that was the mark of their identity as Catholics, the imprisoned priests and religious got to know the mass of political prisoners of all opinions – many of them non-believers – and even communists who had fallen foul of the party line at one time or another. This dawning awareness that all kinds of people were suffering under the heel of totalitarianism led several of them to speak up, as Christians, on behalf of all, including atheists. Other Catholics took a different route by setting up small networks of re-Christianization from below, aimed initially at creating a fellowship for believers marginalized by the communist system.

At first these groups were formed by laypeople, who were less harassed by the police than the priests. During the 1950s some Catholics who, in accordance with the Church's teaching, had large families, began to make contacts so as to obtain religious instruction for their children. They met together to pray and renew their Catholic identity, breaking with the communist social order that blanketed the country. The initial aim was to find answers to the problems of large families in a socialist society: but, as one of the women founders of this movement said: 'Large families were either Catholic or gypsy . . .'[70] As the gypsies had a different outlook on the world, the criterion for recognizing the Christian family was that it should contain at least four children. But in building a 'large families club' which established a network of 'horizontal' mutual aid in daily life, its founders reconstituted an embryo 'Christian society'. Despite the difficulties of organizing all these activities in secret, summer camps for children were

69   Interview with Josef Zverina, Prague, 20 June 1990. Father Zverina died in August 1990.
70   Interview with Maria Kaplanova, Prague, 21 June 1990.

started, and then some simple leaflets were home-produced for circulation in the network. This first Catholic *samizdat* for children was designed as an antidote to the dominant values of dialectical materialism, and they presented a 'Christian view of the world'. Funds received from Germany via international contacts with the ecumenical prayer community at Taizé in France helped to keep the movement going during the 1960s.

At the time of the 'Prague Spring', from the beginning of 1968 until the Soviet invasion in the night of August 20–1, the Catholic Church briefly recovered the freedom which it had been denied for twenty years. Religious and priests who had not yet served the whole of their sentences were released from prison, the underground networks were able to coordinate with one another and information could be passed around.[71] Catholics were 'passive' beneficiaries of the spring rather than active contributors to the revolution, which was initiated by the 'Dubcek' communists, devotees of 'socialism with a human face'.

Re-Christianization 'from below' or democratic opposition?

When normalization descended upon Czechoslovakia after August 1968, the government resumed its previous hostility to the Church. This was evidenced by the return of Karel Hruza (whose name, in Czech, means 'terror') to the Secretariat of Religious Affairs, whence he had been evicted during the spring. But whereas the first twenty years had been characterized by violent persecution aimed at breaking individuals, during the second half of the communist era the government followed a policy of blackmail, threats and intimidation against an aging clergy, some of whom had been worn out by persecution.

Pacem in Terris,[72] the new association of 'fellow-traveller' priests set up by the government in 1970, managed to bring in nearly a third of all churchmen, including all the bishops with the exception of Cardinal Tomasek, who had succeeded Bishop Beran. Meanwhile the Vatican pursued its *Ostpolitik* (which sought to preserve

71   See Karel Skalicky, 'Vent'anni dalla Primavera di Praga: la chiesa tra primavera e perestrojka', *L'altra Europa*, 3 (1988), pp. 37–8, and Andrea Rebichini, op. cit., pp. 71–92.
72   See above, p. 84.

what remained of the structures of the 'visible Church' in the East and to reconstitute the ecclesiastical hierarchy) to the point of negotiating with the communist government, and these talks resulted in the implicit tolerance of *Pacem in Terris* by Rome. 'Instead of preserving the Church', remarks Jacques Rupnik, 'this policy helped to break it up spiritually and morally, leading to a rift between the clergy and the faithful.'[73]

From the mid-1970s onwards two attitudes emerged among those Catholic priests and laypeople, who refused all compromise with the regime and felt that a *modus vivendi* would be in effect a *modus moriendi*. Some concentrated on strengthening the networks of re-Christianization 'from below', and these grew to a much greater size than before 1968; while a minority of the clergy and laypeople committed themselves to dissidence. To some extent these attitudes were complementary, but they proceeded from two different conceptions of the place of Catholicism in society which were to come into collision when communism collapsed.

At that time re-Christianization 'from below' was represented mainly by the *Focolari* ('little hearths'), a movement founded at the end of the Second World War in Trento, Italy, by a Franciscan laywoman, Chiara Lubich. When bombs were falling all around her and people were dying in their thousands, she tried to discover whether there was still a reason for living and hoping in the midst of this cataclysm, this complete submergence of human values. She found it in the will to live out the Gospel to the letter, word for word: these would be the 'words of life' that would set the agenda for each day of a Christian existence.

In the first decade of normalization this movement made headway among young adults in Prague just finishing their studies or starting their working lives, who wanted to live as Catholics and who shunned a captive church structure permeated by *Pacem in Terris*. They 'felt as if they were reliving the experience of the first Christians': they met in the forest to celebrate the mass in secret and to read the Scriptures together. Having neither photocopiers nor printing machines, they copied out the 'words of life' by hand,

---

73   Jacques Rupnik, op. cit., p. 240. On the period 1968–78, see also Andrea Rebichini, *Chiesa, società . . .* , vol. 2, 1968–78 (Padua: Ceseo-Liviana, 1979), *passim*.

like monks in a scriptorium, and passed them around. Performing 'the experiment of spiritual community, of community of goods', giving a Christian meaning to existence outside communist society, they embarked upon proselytism and, according to one of their leaders, numbered some 10,000 'hearths' by the end of the 1980s.[74]

Those who spread this kind of re-Christianization 'from below' did not really encounter repression. 'Mary always covered us with her cloak', said this same leader, who stresses that he never tried 'to fight against the state', unlike the Havels and Zverinas (see below), and who considers that, for believers, 'the greatest revolution is not that of November 1989, but the one that occurs within each person when Jesus Christ has won and you decide to follow God's path.' As will be seen later on, this withdrawal from the political scene held good only as long as communism lasted.

While re-Christianization was adopting this deliberately apolitical stance, other Christians chose a path of resistance to normalization that brought them in touch with the secular dissidents with whom they had forged links in prison. Charter 77 was launched by a group of Czech intellectuals calling for the effective application of the UN Convention on the observance of Civic, Political and Cultural Rights, and of the Final Act of the Helsinki Conference, both ratified by Czechoslovakia in 1976. Over a third of its 1,200 signatories were Catholics, including the philosopher Vaclav Benda and the priests Joseph Zverina and Vaclav Maly. A fresh wave of persecution then broke out against the signatories, who lost their jobs, were threatened and imprisoned, and, if priests, had their 'permit to exercise' revoked and were sent to do various kinds of manual labour. Under intense government pressure, Cardinal Tomasek stated that he was not a signatory to the Charter, and that the Church did not identify with it. In fact, the Charter awakened very little response in deeply Catholic Slovakia.

Father Zverina sent an open letter to the Cardinal bitterly criticizing his attitude: 'Your statement is not inspired by the Gospel but by the shameful needs of propaganda and by the hysterical witchhunt directed against those who have dared to

74 Interview with Petr Eller, Prague, 19 June 1990.

demand respect for the law'. To Christians who held aloof from an initiative taken jointly with unbelievers, atheists and even dissident communists, Zverina answered, in the same letter: 'It is certainly true that the signatories include all sorts of people, and some Catholics may disagree with many of them (but generally those Catholics are the kind who prove incapable of taking action within the law, and who are quick to denounce others). But are not sinners also entitled to demand justice for themselves, for others and even for the Church?'[75]

This stance, which led to Father Zverina's arrest for having 'obstructed the monitoring of the Church by the state', is very different from re-Christianization 'from below' as illustrated by the *Focolari*. What it foregrounds is not the Christian striving to live out the Gospel by following the 'word of life': it is the victim of oppression, any victim, even an atheist. That outlook was very noticeable among priests and religious who had experienced prison or the punishment inflicted upon intellectuals by the Party of the Working Class – relegation to the working class. Father Vaclav Maly, who was one of the spokesmen for Charter 77, and the Provincial of the Dominicans in Czechoslovakia, Father Dominique Duka, are other eloquent examples. The latter, who was secretly a novice in 1966 and was ordained in 1970, is a member of the younger generation of ecclesiastics; a country priest, he was deprived of his 'permit to exercise' in 1975 and put to work on the assembly line in the Skoda factory at Pilsen. He was a 'worker priest' in a rather different meaning of the term from that of the 1950s in France.[76] For six years, in contact with students, he organized groups on Christian philosophy and theology and prepared other novices.

Arrested in 1981 and sentenced to fifteen months in a secure state prison, he shared a cell with Vaclav Havel and joined the

---

75 'Letter from Father Joseph Zverina to Cardial Tomasek, February 1977', in *Istina* 28, 1 (1983), pp. 94–5. On the situation of the Church in Czechoslovakia and the attitude of Christians towards Charter 77, see the same journal, issues 28, 2 (1983); 24, 2–3 (1979); and 22 (1977).

76 A good many of the clergy underwent this manual labour, including even a (then clandestine) bishop, Mgr. Jan Korec, who now heads the Nitra diocese in Slovakia. See what he said in *Thirty Days in the Church & the World* (March 1989), pp. 56–9.

imprisoned chartists. It was, for him, a 'second novitiate',[77] at least as important as the first one.

He did baptize some prisoners, for whom his cell-mate stood godfather; but he also became convinced of the importance of dialogue with non-Catholics.

The failure of Christian Democracy

When the communist regime collapsed in November 1989 Cardinal Tomasek, who took a much firmer line with the communist regime under John Paul II than under Paul VI, played an important moral role. On 21 November he condemned the violent suppression of a student demonstration a few days after the event; in mid-December he opposed a last-minute manoeuvre of the Communist Party, which proposed that the new president should be elected by referendum, and openly supported Vaclav Havel, tipping the balance in favour of the playwright and his Civic Forum.

But during the months following the establishment of a democratic regime in Czechoslovakia, Catholics were sharply divided in their political allegiances. There were many Catholics in the transitional government, and they had two choices with regard to the elections that were to be held in June 1990; either they could stand as members of the Civic Forum, a course which would have strengthened the alliances that had been formed in initiatives like Charter 77, or they could make a separate 'Christian' list.

The bishops, backed by the Vatican (which had the 'Polish model' much in mind), chose the second course, looking towards the creation of a 'Christian democratic alliance' in which chartist Catholics would work together with a 'Catholic' rump party, which for four decades had been a fellow-traveller of the communists, possessing little in the way of legitimacy but a great many buildings, printing presses and the like. It was hoped that the alliance would win in Slovakia by a large majority and obtain enough additional votes in Bohemia-Moravia to come to power in Prague.

The various movements of re-Christianization 'from below' mob-

---

77   Interview with Father Duka, Prague, 17 April 1990.

ilized their networks to vote Christian Democrat – even including groups, like the *Focolari*, which had declined to take any part in politics under the communist regime. The bishops were in favour of this move 'upwards' and in a pastoral letter they called on the faithful to vote Christian Democrat. According to one of the leaders of the *Focolari*, a Christian Democrat government would have represented 'an unusual opportunity to promote the Christian education of children, to found more moral Catholic schools, and to encourage the formation of Christian families in order to change society which had undergone totalitarian pressure against the faith.'

But there were other Catholics, both clerical and lay, who had fought against communism side by side with unbelievers and had shared their prison cells; these made no secret of their refusal to take part in a strategy of re-Christianization 'from above' by leaving their erstwhile comrades-in-prison and joining up with Catholics who had adapted very well to four decades of totalitarian rule, during which they had shown themselves 'ready to denounce the others'.[78] It was actually alleged a few days before the elections that the leader of the Christian Democrat alliance, a former fellow-traveller of the communists, had been paid a monthly retainer by the police to keep an eye on Catholic chartists who were now sharing the candidates' list with him, and that his pious zeal had even induced him to recommend some of them for 'severe punishment'. This scandal created such a furore that the 'Christian' party – whose campaign had not really been able to make headway – suffered a serious reverse, receiving only 10 per cent of the vote, and finishing in a humiliating third place behind the 'reconstructed' Communist Party!

Some members of the 're-Christianization from below' groups, whose sudden foray into politics had been snubbed by the electorate, thought that the scandal was a manoeuvre by Jews and freemasons with influence in Civic Forum. For them, the 10 per cent who voted for the alliance were the 'true believers', whose task it would be to build the Christian alternative to the spread of capitalism and the social and moral evils this would

78 See above, p. 94.

bring in its train. The right way to avert this threat was to strengthen re-Christianization 'from below', by utilizing the climate of democracy to give it a mass dimension. In a progression from the individual's encounter with Christ to the social movement, by way of 'Christian families' gathered in communities, the long-term objective was the creation of a society with Catholic foundations. From this point of view, the education of children was of crucial importance, within re-Christianized families who would 'be a sort of oxygen tent'.[79]

On the other hand, many priests and religious thought that 'a link between the Church and a "Christian" party would create problems and bring back memories of the Counter-Reformation'; they estimated that '70 per cent of the faithful voted for parties other[80] than the Christian Democrats',[81] and refused to vote only for this party of 'true believers'. Though the bishops insisted that pastoral activity must be aimed primarily at strengthening the links between Catholics, many of the religious thought that in a city like Prague, where there was a climate of indifference towards the faith, Catholics should in no event cut themselves off from that 'world' but should, on the contrary, make their presence felt strongly within it.

Father Vaclav Maly, who was the spokesman for Charter 77 and one of the most eloquent speakers of the 'velvet revolution' in November 1989, returned in 1990 to his suburban parish in Prague. He too thought that the pastoral letter enjoining the faithful to vote Christian Democrat was a mistake: 'The Church should proclaim Christian values to the whole of society, but allow Catholics to vote as they wish.' He held that, in a society that was emerging morally devastated from forty years of totalitarian rule, the function of his parish was 'to be open to everybody. People must truly communicate, instead of simply going to church. I want the Gospel to be a power for exploration, not a closed system of truth. I want to show that I am searching with them,

79 Interview with Petr Ettler.
80 Besides Civic Forum, the ex-Communist Party and the Christian Democrats, the other parties fielding candidates included those proposing autonomy for Slovakia and Moravia, which were unexpectedly successful, probably at the expense of the Christian Democrats.
81 Interview with Father Duka, Prague, 21 June 1990.

that I don't have all the answers in advance.' In a Czechoslovakia which was opening itself to democracy, the priority was 'to change people's outlook so that they behave as citizens and take responsibility'.[82] Saint-Gabriel of Smihov, where he carried out his priestly duties at the grassroots – baptisms, weddings, the mass, funerals and confessions – was at the same time a 'cultural centre' where the new Czechoslovak democracy was being built in microcosm, with 'some funny parishioners' unassailable in their atheism, for whom Father Vaclav's Gospel was a valuable aid to discussion.

In the mid-1970s the Church began a process of reaffirming Catholic identity, trying to put an end to the uncertainties of the post-conciliar period. But this new theological reflection coincided with a decade of fundamental change in the world, an economic and social crisis which had repercussions in the intellectual and moral sphere. The secular utopias of the 1960s, which Vatican II had translated into the language of the Church, were followed by ten years of confusion, marked by the breakup of traditional solidarities – a decade of what, for lack of a capacity to interpret it, was called 'post-modernism'. And as the 1980s ended, it led on to the collapse of 'scientific socialism'.

In this situation, the Catholic Church and its flock were faced with a dilemma. A number of Catholics joined groups working for re-Christianization either 'from below' or 'from above' on the lines described in this chapter, which can be compared with movements observable in Islam during the same period.

But in the very places which saw the death throes of totalitarian communism, and where believers in re-Christianization hoped that 'Christian society' could come to birth, this strategy clashed with the democratic aspirations of some Catholics. They held that in this world the expression of ultimate Truth, of which the Church is the guardian, is subordinate to men's search for their freedom; no 'Christian party' has the prerogative of establishing a social order modelled on a Truth of which it believes itself to be the sole guardian. This 'constraint by democracy' does not at present

82   Interview with Father Maly, Prague, 21 June 1990.

exist in the field of re-Islamization. But, as we shall see, it is present – though in rather different ways – in the sphere tenanted by the Evangelicals and Fundamentalists of the United States.

3

Saving America

In September 1989 Hurricane Hugo, after devastating the Carib-
bean island of Guadeloupe, spent its remaining fury on the town
of Charlotte in the United States, where the televangelist Jim
Bakker was on trial for financial irregularities, besides facing a
number of charges of immoral conduct. The winds were so violent
that the court hearing had to be suspended for a day, and the
followers of this cathode-ray pastor saw in this a sign of God's
anger against the inhabitants of Charlotte for persecuting His
minister. But even in a country in which the weather is almost
an object of worship, that was not enough to prevent sentence being
passed on a man who had made public credulity and multiple fraud
into the foundations of a veritable empire. The jewel in his crown
was a kind of 'Christian Disneyland' known as Heritage USA
which, despite the large numbers who visited it, went into a much-
publicized bankruptcy and where the preacher who thundered on
television against homosexuality occasionally re-created the orgies
of Sodom with his close associates.

The American press had followed this story avidly for several
years: its episodes seemed indistinguishable from the twists and
turns and fragile suspense of a soap opera whose stars had jumped
out of their usual programme slot and invaded the 8 o'clock news
and the documentaries. No ridiculous trait of Tammy Bakker,
Jim's wife and his screen partner, was spared. Her high-pitched
voice, her incredible false eyelashes, the Rimmel that ran at each
of her televised whingeings, aroused fervent commiseration from
believers equalled only by the sarcasm of sceptics. As for Jim, he
had let himself go with an attractive church-secretary in a room
at a Florida motel; and as the price of her silence and for the

purgation of her sin, this young lady became the recipient of some of the money sent to the Bakkers by the faithful *ad maiorem dei gloriam*. When that source dried up, journalists were fed the story and the repentant Magdalene uncovered for the girly magazines the flesh that had aroused the lust of the televangelist. Any credibility Jim Bakker still retained was fatally damaged, and the Charlotte trial was the last episode in the series. 'THE END' came up on the small screen as the handcuffed preacher was led off to serve a sentence of forty-five years in prison.

But the Bakker story was no soap opera: it was real. Jim and Tammy had been able to build their financial empire because millions of flesh-and-blood Americans had been beguiled, comforted, reassured or healed by their preaching and their presence in the home, to the point of regularly sending them enough money to make this religious enterprise prosper in the country where business is king. Ever since 1976 the *Charlotte Observer*, the leading daily newspaper of North Carolina, had been featuring news about the PTL (Praise the Lord) cable network, which showed up the fraud and breaches of trust involved in its operations; the initials PTL came to mean 'Pass the Loot' and then, after the episode in the Florida motel, 'Pay the Lady!'. But the widespread suspicion of the *bona fides* of this minister had no effect on the generosity of the faithful and the donors; for those who believed it was simply not a problem.

Televangelism as a social phenomenon

In September 1977, among numerous letters that appeared in the *Charlotte Observer* supporting PTL there was one from an unemployed man of sixty who said that his whole income amounted to 162 dollars of public assistance every fortnight. He hadn't a dime, was heavily in debt, had no family and, he added, had bad teeth. And yet every month he sent PTL 7.77 dollars, a figure with magic virtues. This payment, which would be peanuts to an American on the average income, represented a sacrifice for him; but he urged all his brothers and sisters in Christ to do the same, so as to help a minister of God who, he thought, was the only

The Revenge of God

person interested in him in the depths of his distress, and who looked on him as a human being.[1]

Obviously not all the 'PTL faithful' belonged to the poorest of the poor, even though the correspondence columns of the *Charlotte Observer* show that a great many of the gifts came from those who had not shared in the general prosperity. Besides a whole string of small postal orders, PTL used to receive more substantial contributions from reasonably prosperous Americans, such as the cheque for 6,000 dollars sent by a lady who had an unhappy married life, was obese and depressive, and who expected a miracle in return. The miracle did not come; the lady went into hospital and summoned Jim Bakker to return her gift in order to pay for her medical treatment: that did not come either.[2]

This network of millions of regular donors – whose stories and letters showed an astonishingly similar pattern – created for PTL a market, both commercial and ideological, which was bound to attract enterprising spirits of all kinds in the America of the late twentieth century, and they lined up to appear on the Bakkers' chat show. There were to be seen all the supporters of the Evangelical movement, from the humblest pastors to personalities with abundant contacts in politics, such as President Carter's sister – herself a specialist in faith-healing, the salvation of well-known sinners and mass baptisms of adults.[3] Various gurus of the alternative culture of the 1960s, now converted, came on the show to denounce the error of their former ways and to speak for Jesus. Paul Stookey, archetype of the protest singers of the 1960s (when he was a member of the trio Peter, Paul and Mary), stated on PTL: 'At the end of the 60s we looked to leaders to spearhead our movements. The movement that is going on now has an invisible leader. . .it is a kind of culmination of that which we thirsted after in the 60s. . .'[4] As for Eldridge Cleaver, former leader of the Black Panthers and theoretician of the armed struggle in the black ghettos against white America, he related on PTL how he had found God, an event that occurred when he was in political exile

1 *Charlotte Observer* (14 September 1977).
2 Ibid. (3 September 1977).
3 Ibid. (18 December 1978).
4 Ibid. (15 September 1977).

on the French Riviera; gazing out from his balcony at the moon over the Mediterranean, he distinctly saw, etched in succession on the radiant surface of that orb, the features of Malcolm X, Castro, Mao, Che Guevara and, lastly, Jesus. He then realized that that was the way for him: 'Ten years ago, I thought like Marx that religion was the opium of the people. . . but I discovered that, in fact, Jesus Christ was just what the doctor ordered for my life.'[5]

Industrialists, sports and media celebrities and conservative politicians also appeared on the show. At times Bakker strained the format to its limits – as when he invited Larry Flint, king of the pornographic press, whose awakening to repentance (which he attributed to Jimmy Carter's sister) was too much even for Bakker's most hardened fans to swallow.[6] But, more predictably, those who found a ready-made audience on PTL were people like Senator Jesse Helms, who had close links with the Fundamentalist movements of the 'New Christian Right'. He campaigned on PTL against taxation of private schools, in favour of school prayers, against the withdrawal of American troops from South Korea, and on other subjects dear to the movement. All of which caused a lady viewer from Texas to write: 'I do not have an adequate vocabulary to tell you how uplifting it has been to have the cream of the Christian community come in my home each weekday and share their time, talents, philosophies, hopes and faiths – all Bible-based, of course.'[7]

With hindsight the Bakker phenomenon has been reduced to a gigantic fraud, an interpretation supported by the verdict of the court which tried him. And yet, beyond those malpractices and the grotesque or scabrous aspects of the affair, the fact remains that, from the mid-1970s onwards, millions of Americans felt a need for the kind of religious experience afforded by Jim, Tammy and others like them. For they were not the only televangelists on the market. Their colleagues and competitors – Jim Robinson, Jerry Falwell, Oral Roberts, Pat Robertson, Jimmy Swaggart, Robert Schuller and others less well known – all contributed, in

5 Ibid. (18 January 1977).
6 Ibid. (4 February 1978).
7 Ibid. (5 December 1978).

their various ways, to this cultural change over the airwaves, this massive invasion of the TV by evangelical preachers, as the century drew towards its close. Nor is the phenomenon confined to the screen, which is only the most visible indication of a groundswell that led some strata of American society to adopt the language of evangelical or fundamentalist religion to express their rejection of 'secular values' (which they saw as dominant and harmful) and their desire for a profound change in the ethics of society.

Since the mid-1970s many surveys have attempted to describe and quantify 'fundamentalist' or 'evangelical' America, though neither the researchers nor the respondents have always been at pains to define these terms. In 1978, according to a survey carried out for the magazine *Christianity Today*, 22 per cent of Americans stated that they were 'Evangelicals', while 35 per cent said they were 'Liberal Protestants', 30 per cent 'Catholics', 4 per cent 'non-Christians' and 9 per cent 'secularists'.[8] In 1986 a Gallup poll indicated that 33 per cent of the adult population described itself as 'Evangelical', which would give a figure of 58 million persons.[9]

Figures like these, which reveal the size of the phenomenon but not its significance, provided Jerry Falwell, the most politically minded of the televangelists and founder of the Moral Majority and of Liberty University, with a starting point for his crusade to re-Christianize America. In 1980, in the preface to his book *Listen, America!*, he wrote:

> According to recent polls [. . .] there are in America today more than sixty million people who profess to be born-again Christians, sixty million others who consider themselves religious promoralists, and fifty million others who are idealistic moralists, who want their children to grow up in a moral society. [. . .] 84% of the American people believe that the Ten Commandments are still valid for today. And yet, as we look at these statistics, we must admit that we, the American People, have allowed a vocal minority of nongodly men and women to bring America to the brink of death [. . .] It

---

8 Cited in James Davidson Hunter, *American Evangelicalism, Conservative Religion and the Quandary of Modernity* (Newark, NJ: Rutgers University Press, 1983), p. 49.
9 Quoted by (*Inter aliis*) Larry Martz and Ginny Carroll, *Ministry of Greed* (New York: Weidenfeld & Nicolson, 1988), p. 23.

is now time that moral Americans band together to save our beloved nation . . .[10]

Throughout the 1980s the politico-religious movement that Jerry Falwell created in 1979, the Moral Majority, was the concrete expression of this intention. It put forward a number of themes on which its members were to unite and fight, such as the campaigns against abortion and for school prayers, forming an interface between the family and civil society and a starting point for the challenge to the 'nongodly' policies of the state. This movement, and others that shared some of its aims, experienced remarkable growth between the mid-1970s and the end of the 1980s within the larger framework of what is known in the United States as Fundamentalism, Evangelicalism, or the New Christian Right.

All these phenomena, as well as the Charismatic and Pentecostalist renewals that were making great strides at the same time, are the heirs of an essentially American tradition that has come up with particularly vigorous responses to the challenges it has faced, during the past quarter century, from a society apparently so secular that it seemed bound to relegate religion to the private sphere. If we are to take the measure of the 'newly won significance of this movement today, to analyse its paradoxical presence at the heart of post-industrial American culture, we must first go back to the historical origins of all these movements.

From backwoods America to high tech

The word 'fundamentalism' is generally thought to have come into common use in the 1920s, following the publication in the United States, from 1910 onwards, of a series of twelve volumes entitled *The Fundamentals* and containing ninety articles written by various Protestant theologians who were opposed to any compromise with the surrounding modernism. *The Fundamentals* was financed by two brothers, business tycoons, and over three million copies were

---

10 Jerry Falwell, *Listen, America!* (New York: Doubleday, 1980), p. xi.

distributed free of charge.[11] But it was mainly the 'Scopes affair' that brought the term 'fundamentalism' into the current American vocabulary while investing it from the outset with a connotation of controversy. John T. Scopes was a young biology teacher at a school in Tennessee, and he used in class a textbook containing references to the evolution of species. That was an infringement of the state laws which prohibited the teaching of 'any theory that denies the story of the divine creation of man'. He was accordingly put on trial in 1925, but the case turned into the trial of the fundamentalist sub-culture in America; this sub-culture was brought into ridicule by the press reports of the outmoded arguments used by Scopes's opponents, especially as eminent members of the intellectual and scientific elite of the day testified on his behalf.

As contrasted with the 'modernism' or the 'liberalism' professed by the Protestant establishment, Fundamentalism is defined primarily by belief in the *absolute* infallibility of the Bible. The holy scriptures, both the Old and New Testaments, are held to be the literal expression of Divine Truth – especially all the moral or ethical commandments or politico-social injunctions they contain. Secondly, Fundamentalists believe in the divinity of Christ and in the salvation of the soul by the effective action of his life, death and physical resurrection. Fundamentalists must also do their utmost to convert those who have not yet assented to this belief.[12] Beyond the theological controversies, the two camps are coterminous with two opposed Americas which regularly confronted one another between the two world wars: the industrialized, modernized and vigorously expanding North, and the agricultural South with its outdated social organization, which seems to have been in an inexorable spiral of decline ever since its defeat in the Civil War.

It was the South that provided the big battalions of old-time

11 See the reissue of the text with an introduction by George Marsden, *The Fundamentals: a Testimony to Truth* (New York: Garland, 1988), 12 vols. The original edition was published between 1910 and 1915 in Chicago, by the Testimony Publishing Co. Among the essays written on this subject, see especially James Barr, *Fundamentalism* (London: SCM Press, 1977) and George Marsden, *Fundamentalism and American Culture: the Shaping of Twentieth Century Evangelicism, 1870–1925* (New York: Oxford University Press, 1980). In French, the journal *Lumière et vie* devoted its issue no. 186 (March 1988) to Christian fundamentalism.
12 See Hunter, op. cit., p. 57, and Golding, op. cit.

Fundamentalism; it became known as the Bible Belt, the most southerly of the 'belts' – cattle belt, maize belt, cotton belt – which follow one another on the map of the United States. It was the favourite haunt of preachers whose uncouthness, fanaticism, hypocrisy and unscrupulousness inspired a whole literary genre among the East Coast intellectual elite. The archetype of these characters is Elmer Gantry, created by the Nobel prizewinner Sinclair Lewis in 1927.[13] Gantry is a completely amoral individual – cheat, perjurer, womanizer, drunkard – whose traits Lewis synthesized from a number of individuals he had known, but he rapidly became the typical representative of Fundamentalism as portrayed by intellectuals. From Gantry to Bakker, the image of the Fundamentalist charlatan has scarcely varied; it contains undeniable aspects of truth, but has also helped to mask the social phenomenon that gave such preachers their impact.

For even after the verdict in the Scopes case, it would have been a mistake to conclude that this extreme form of American religion represented a culture that was marginal and doomed to defeat. Prohibition, which was legally enacted in 1919 and lasted until 1933, showed the power of a conservative, rigorist Protestant ethic in the American social system. And the country is prone to revert to it in times of stress, in the tradition of the Great Awakenings that have occurred on that continent ever since the Puritans arrived, intent on founding the New Jerusalem. The depression of 1929 and its aftermath deeply undermined the belief in modernism and progress that had been built up in the industrial civilization of the North. And, in the millenarian interpretation placed upon it by the Fundamentalists, 'The Great Depression was [. . .] a sign of God's vindictive punishment on an apostate America as well as a sign of Christ's imminent return.'[14] Everything that happened in the world belonged to a chain of cause and effect, obeying God's plan, which they were uniquely equipped to interpret. It was this conviction which enabled them to seize upon the multifarious crises that have afflicted American society down to our own day, always ready with both a diagnosis and a cure – the cure of redemption.

13 Sinclair Lewis, *Elmer Gantry* (New York: Harcourt, Brace, 1927).
14 James Davison Hunter, op. cit., p. 39.

Political Fundamentalists and social Evangelicals

Throughout the postwar era, Fundamentalism has been associated with the most 'reactionary' trends of opinion in politics, with the virulent anti-communists of the Cold War, and with witch-hunts. Because of this some theologians, who shared the belief in the infallibility of the Bible but were embarrassed by the connections between Fundamentalism and the extreme right, reactivated the term 'Evangelicals'. The Evangelical message claimed at first to be religious and social; only later, with the great movement of the mid-1970s, did it enter the political arena. So within the context of American Protestantism the Evangelicals differ from the so-called liberal or mainline denominations in placing greater emphasis on personal piety and the ethical or moral themes literally drawn from the Scriptures, while their adversaries more explicitly wish to have a say in public affairs.

The postwar developments in mainline Protestantism have reflected the changes in 'enlightened' American opinion. During the 1950s it resembled in many ways a religion of opulence, justifying enjoyment of American prosperity. Membership of the various churches grew, rising from 43 per cent of Americans in 1920 to 62 per cent in 1956; according to the sociologist Martin Marty, these numerous new churchgoers 'needed a means of justifying their complacencies, soothing their anxieties, pronouncing benedictions on their way of life, and organizing the reality around them. Millions turned to religion, and Protestantism benefited from the return of religion.'[15]

From the 1960s onwards, mainline Protestants ceased to be self-satisfied and became concerned for 'the other America'[16] – the America of the poor, the ghettos and the minorities. This was the era of large social programmes initiated by the Kennedy and Johnson governments to 'wage war on poverty' and to bring those Americans who had fallen by the wayside back into the mainstream

---

15   Martin Marty, *Religious Empire* (New York: Dial, 1970), quoted in Hunter, ibid., p. 42.
16   This was the title of a book by Michael Harrington, *The Other America* (Baltimore: Penguin Books, 1961). This work was an event which opened the eyes of rich America to the hidden part of herself, those who lived in the rural areas but also in the run-down suburbs and inner cities.

of universal prosperity. This desire of the churches to be in the 'world', and to bear witness for Christ by stressing the theme of social justice, surfaced at the same time as Catholic efforts towards *aggiornamento* and presence in the 'world' as represented by Vatican II.

In both cases the move aroused opposition; in the United States, Evangelicals expressed considerable distrust of the social leanings of liberal Protestants which were leading some of them to question the validity of capitalism, and which might weaken their search for salvation and their quest for another world. For example, in May 1966, in a widely read article published in the May 1966 *Readers Digest*, J. Howard Pew, a prominent evangelical and board chairman of Sun Oil, advised readers against political activity, citing the example of Christ who 'refused to enmesh himself or his followers in the economic, social and political problems of his day – problems certainly as serious as those we face today.. . .He made it crystal clear that we are to seek "first the kingdom of God and his righteousness" – carefully pointing out that "the kingdom is within you".'[17]

Many observers hold that Liberals and Evangelicals adopted diametrically opposed standpoints regarding social and political commitment throughout the 1960s, and some of them see in retrospect that the decline of the mainline churches and the rise of the Evangelicals during the following decade was due to their excessive leanings towards social involvement:

> Church officials were accused by parishioners of ignoring their primary responsibility to attend to the personal spiritual needs of their congregations, preach the scriptures, and bring converts to Christ. Church members were castigated by their ministers for turning away from Christian concerns for the world and ignoring the cries of suffering humanity at their doorsteps. Both were, of course, partially justified in their claims. The upshot was loss of mainline church membership and, for many, a turn toward the

17 Quoted by Robert Wuthnow, 'Political Rebirth of American Evangelicism', in *The New Christian Right: Mobilization & Legitimation*, ed. Liebman and Wuthnow (New York: Aldine, 1983).

evangelical churches to answer the personal need for spiritual guidance and/or spiritual refuge.[18]

In 1967, for the first time in two centuries, this turning away from the mainline churches was reflected in the statistics. Ten of the largest denominations were affected, including Lutherans, Episcopalians, Methodists, Presbyterians and Congregationalists. In 1970 it was the turn of the Catholic Church in the United States to announce the first drop in membership since the beginning of the century. Dean Kelley, one of the first sociologists to observe this phenomenon, commented: 'while the mainline churches have tried to support the political and economic claims of our society's minorities and outcasts, it is the sectarian groups that have had most success in attracting new members from these very sectors of society.'[19]

Faith healing and social therapy

However, this reverse trend, which the statistics clearly locate between the late 1960s and the early 1970s,[20] cannot be attributed simply to a contrast between the decline of 'worldly' mainline churches and the success of Evangelical churches exclusively focused on personal salvation and the afterlife. Evangelicals too had a very significant social commitment, even if they did not describe it in the same terms as liberal Protestants. This commitment operated at different levels, from the parish to the formation of networks which made use of the national media – first press and radio, later television – to spread their message: a new society, with new communities of true believers. From the mid-1970s onwards, the message – for some – was extended to a political transformation of America by means of re-Christianization.

As the Evangelicals saw it, the way to check and deal with social ills was to unmask sin and redeem it. Their practice was to seek the cause of evil in separation from God; if this separation

18 Jeremy Rifkin (with Ted Howard), *The Emerging Order: God in the Age of Scarcity* (New York: G.P. Putnam's Sons, 1979), p. 102.
19 Dean Kelley, *Why Conservative Churches are Growing: a Study in Sociology of Religion* (New York: Harper & Row, 1986), p. xxv.
20 See the numerous graphs published by Dean Kelley, op. cit., *passim*.

could be overcome, the evil would be banished and health restored. Sin was located in the individual, and it was individual salvation that would effect the salvation of the group. This conviction explains many of the approaches favoured by this religious movement: the need for individual conversion or baptism of 'born-again' adults, the importance attributed to manifestations of the Holy Spirit – in particular glossolalia (speaking in tongues), but also faith healing. Again, prime emphasis was placed on the family and its moral organization, which in the later 1970s formed the basis for the reconquest of civil society and the state.

As we have seen, for twenty years after the war politics was the domain of small Fundamentalist groups who collaborated closely with the extreme right, while the Evangelicals, starting with the individual, were more concerned with the family and civil society. The re-Christianization 'from above' of the former group was highly visible, but had little effect on the mass of the population; whereas although the re-Christianization 'from below' of the latter did have some mass effects, it is generally held to be a phenomenon relating to religious zeal and emotion, while its socio-political dimension usually remains hidden.

At the national level, two outstanding personalities represent this position: Billy Graham and Oral Roberts. In the years following the Second World War, Billy Graham took up the methods of Evangelical preaching that had been featured by Billy Sunday during the first half of the century, but he combined them with extensive use of the mass media – press, radio and later television. With Charles Finney (1792–1875) and Dwight Moody (1837–1899), Billy Sunday (1862–1935) had been one of the pioneers of mass evangelism. These men perfected the technique of itinerant 'revivals', mass services held under canvas, prepared for by a network of local preachers. These 'mass-meeting' services created an extraordinary tension in an audience 'warmed up' by sermons in which descriptions of the torments that awaited sinners were set alongside the supreme hope offered to those who would decide for Christ at the end of the service. And, since gifts helped with forgiveness of sins, Sunday and his colleagues, who were astute businessmen, all left considerable fortunes. Even though they had no explicit political message, these evangelists were well regarded in government circles for their ability to inculcate 'Christian values' in their hearers, who could thus presumably be insulated from any contamination by Marxist or socialist ideas.

After the Second World War Billy Graham, then a young and promising preacher, was noticed by the press magnate William Randolph Hearst, the model for Citizen Kane. In 1949 Hearst gave the order 'puff Graham!', and he immediately acquired national status. One year later, he was preaching on the radio and reaching some fifteen million listeners. In 1951 he went in for television, and as a TV celebrity, in America and later worldwide, he greatly assisted the Evangelical message to break out of the circles to which it had been largely confined, the poorly educated inhabitants of the Southern Bible Belt. It was Billy Graham who 'transformed Evangelical religion into a mainstream cultural phenomenon.'[21] He was on personal terms with several American presidents (especially Richard Nixon), serving them as 'unofficial chaplain'[22] until Ronald Reagan replaced him with Jerry Falwell; but he always took care not to give an explicitly political content to his message, so as to bring out the difference between his worldwide aura and celebrity and the more limited appeal of Fundamentalist circles properly so called.

The same thing happened with another preacher whose career lasted from before the war to the end of the 1980s – Oral Roberts. More than Graham, whose extraordinary fame made him into a personality unique in the Evangelical movement, Oral Roberts symbolized the pastor who set out to re-Christianize society 'from below', who made the individual the starting point for healing the ills of society. Born in 1918 into a family of Pentecostalist preachers, Oral Roberts nearly died of tuberculosis while a teenager, but was 'miraculously'[23] healed. In 1936 he received 'baptism in the Holy Spirit' and began to speak in tongues, pronouncing words in a language unknown to man while in a state of trance. For about ten years he was a preacher in a Pentecostal church, but then gave up his pastorate to devote himself solely to saving souls through faith healing. In 1947 he made his headquarters in Tulsa,

21   Jeffrey K. Hadden and Anson Shupe, *Televangelism, Religion and Politics on God's Frontier* (New York: Holt, 1988), p. 120.
22   Ibid., p. 169.
23   See the copiously documented biography by David Edwin Harrell Jr., *Oral Roberts: an American Life* (Bloomington: Indiana University Press, 1985), *passim*.

Oklahoma, at the geographical centre of the United States, from which his 'crusades for Christ' were to radiate. He perfected the techniques of his forerunners the itinerant preachers, and blew them up to enormous size. Each year the crusade set itself the aim of 'winning a million souls for Christ', a formula that conjoins the traditional concern of the pastor with the quantitative obsession of American-style marketing; while he was saving souls by the million, McDonalds Fast Foods boasted of selling hamburgers – by the million.

A large organization was built up to keep account of the numbers of the 'saved', to canvass for others, and to correspond with all those who sent gifts to finance the campaigns. In 1954 Oral Roberts began to buy time on television, and any viewer could see him live laying hands on sick people and shouting 'Heal!'. The effect was seldom immediate, but the shock produced in some of the 'patients' presenting symptoms of psychosomatic illnesses led to remissions, as sometimes happens in such cases. By the laying on of hands, Roberts ran to earth the devil that had plagued the person and forced it out by the power of his faith in God, whose medium he claimed to be. The howl emitted by the one 'possessed' when the tension was at its peak – usually followed by fainting – became the enraged cry of Satan compelled to release his prey.

Such practices immediately bring to mind a tradition of demonology that smacks more of the Middle Ages than of America in the 1950s. And from 1955 onwards they led to conflicts between Roberts and the Fundamentalists, who did not believe in his miracle cures and accused him of projecting a trivial, damaging image of their common cause. They viewed it in far more political terms. As a matter of fact, in 1956 Roberts's televised healings were denounced at length in the *New York Times* – organ of the detested secular establishment – as a hoax.

But does denunciation of this kind give us the full measure of the social significance of such events? In the case of Oral Roberts (as in that of Jim Bakker) two things were going on simultaneously at different levels.

First, there was their actual activities, which enabled them to amass considerable fortunes by soliciting gifts from believers – to whom they made promises that they were hardly in a position to honour, since these related to the salvation of the soul (or even the health of the body), a chancy matter if ever there was one. And the investments they made with the dollars they accumulated proved to be equally chancy, for both Bakker and Roberts were forced to retire from the public scene by spectacular bankruptcies.

Second, there was the type of 'salvation' they both offered, which met a need confusedly articulated by millions of Americans. These people believed in Bakker's and Roberts's powers of mediation and (in the latter case) healing, and expressed that belief notably by their gifts of money.

This second level of the phenomenon calls for a closer analysis than a mere denunciation of charlatans or swindlers, and cannot be reduced to condescending commiseration with credulous and deluded masses. By claiming to put individuals into direct contact with the beyond, Evangelical preachers enable them to bypass their social or organizational environment and to transcend it without regard to hierarchies of power, knowledge or wealth. Everyone, rich or poor, white or black, farmer or businessman, can be saved. The Spirit bloweth where it listeth – or at any rate whither the preacher sends it. Ethnic or family origin is no longer important. This is particularly evident in the case of baptism: Evangelicals regard as meaningless a rite of community member-ship such as infant baptism; they favour adult baptism, the mean-ing of which is consciously and fully accepted by the candidate. It is in the society of the elect that the 'saved' individual will find his or her true place.

The individual experience of salvation comes in a wide variety of ways, reflecting the differing outlooks represented in contemporary Evangelicalism. In Jim Bakker's 'Christian Disneyland', Heritage USA, adult baptisms were carried out in a heated swimming pool in which candidates were immersed fully clothed. With Pentecos-tals or Charismatics, baptism in the Holy Spirit is generally the occasion for the newly baptised to testify to the presence of the Holy Spirit within them by 'speaking in tongues', i.e., by emitting, in a language unknown to mankind, a series of sounds the meaning of which is known only to God. This practice refers to the story of Pentecost (Acts 1: 2), when the apostles spoke to people from different parts of the ancient Middle East, to each in his own tongue, although the apostles had never learned those languages.

In the case of present-day Pentecostals the 'miracle' does not have the same content: they do not speak in a human language previously unknown to them, but in a divine 'language' incomprehensible to mere mortals. There too, all are equal before the Creator: worldly wisdom is of no avail to pierce a mystery accessible to faith alone, and this faith has as much intensity, or value, in an illiterate Southern farmer as in a university professor or an East Coast capitalist.

Faith healing, ordinarily regarded as the acme of fraud on the part of the practitioner and the nadir of mental backwardness in the patient, is an example of a similar disregard for the social hierarchy of knowledge and ability, taken to a further extreme. When Oral Roberts, laying on his hands, put the individual into direct touch with God, he was trying to re-establish an order that had been disturbed by the irruption of evil caused by a demon. For him the diseased body was no longer the object of impersonal diagnosis and medical operation, but the special channel of communication with the environment beyond, a communication which healing would re-establish by introducing the healed one into the new community of the elect. This process is directly opposite to the social praxis of the mainline churches. What is being attempted here is not primarily to promote access to health and happiness in this world in order to emphasize the concern of Christians for mankind. It is to save individuals by re-establishing their broken relationship with the Creator and reintroducing them into a community entirely motivated by Christian virtue through the inspiration of the Holy Spirit.

The Catholic branch

At the end of the 1960s this movement, which until then had been confined to the Pentecostal Protestants (the most overtly pietist of the Evangelicals), entered American Catholicism. This event was destined to be of great importance, not only in the United States – where it extended the influence of 're-Christianization from below' beyond its original sources – but also among Catholics well beyond the frontiers of America. It spawned many of the charismatic renewals that took place in Europe from 1975 onwards.

It was in the spring of 1967 that some Catholic laymen, lecturers at Duquesne University, began to take an interest in the experiences of the Protestant Pentecostals.[24] They had themselves baptized in the Holy Spirit by these Pentecostals and began to spread the good news, influencing in particular some students and lecturers at Notre Dame University, one of the major intellectual centres of Catholicism in the New World. Between 1971, when *The New Covenant*, the first bulletin of the Catholic Pentecostals (or Charismatics) appeared, and 1978, the prayer groups meeting under the influence of this movement increased to some 600,000 members: the movement had come a long way, and grown very large. The religious outlook is similar to that of the Pentecostals; Catholics belonging to the movement in the first half of the 1970s believed that the official Catholic Church had been weakened and contaminated by the very evils in society it was supposed to combat. Only a new breath of the Holy Spirit would revitalize it to form a community of true Christians within the surrounding secularized society.

A young Catholic couple, interviewed in 1969, replied as follows: 'There has been a remarkable failure on the part of institutional Christianity, Catholic and Protestant alike, to speak a relevant word of salvation to the modern man. [. . .] We believe the baptism in the Holy spirit with these dynamic gifts and fruit speaks radically to the secular man.'[25] Vatican II adopted the world's language by having the mass celebrated in the vernacular instead of Latin; charismatic Catholics took the opposite course: 'speaking in tongues', in a language that men cannot understand, restores the full dimension of the divine mystery.[26] It is when the individual's relationship to the Creator is reactivated that Christians rediscover the organizing principle of their private life and public behaviour, in a secular society that no longer carries meaning for them, since the Church has ceased to teach that society as it ought to do.

But, like their Protestant counterparts, Catholic Pentecostal movements retreated from the idea of transforming and re-Christianizing

---

24   Meredith McGuire, *Pentecostal Catholics: Power, Charisma and Order in a Religious Movement* (Philadelphia: Temple University Press, 1982), p. 5.
25   Ibid., p. 3.
26   Ibid., p. 32.

society as a whole; they did not proclaim any political ambition, and concentrated on creating a new type of community. Until the mid-1970s this was the attitude of most American Evangelicals. When the Southern 'born-again' Baptist Jimmy Carter was elected President of the United States, people woke up to the fact that some of those Evangelicals now had designs on the state itself.

Into politics

The weeklies *Time* and *Newsweek* called 1976 'the year of the Evangelicals'; at any rate, it was the year in which the press took notice of the phenomenon, which became interesting as soon as it broke upon the political scene. Initially this Evangelicalism was associated with moral regeneration. The new president was thought to embody it, after the Watergate affair that brought so much opprobrium on the methods and means used by politicians. At that time Evangelicalism was not exclusively associated with conservatism in politics: Jimmy Carter was the Democratic Party candidate, the archetype of what is known in the United States as a 'Liberal', more or less what Europeans would call a 'social democrat'.

Later on, with Ronald Reagan's election in 1980 and his subsequent re-election, the signs were reversed. The new president received much support from politico-religious movements claiming to be Evangelical or Fundamentalist (since when the two terms have tended to overlap) and located definitely on the right of the political spectrum. Of these, Jerry Falwell's Moral Majority had the highest profile, but it was not the only one: many pressure groups were formed, with the ultimate objective of influencing political decisions in order to re-Christianize America. Some of them had a well-defined aim, such as prayers in schools or the outlawing of abortion, but they viewed these within an overall perspective. They were no longer concerned simply to resocialize born-again Christians within a community of the elect; they aimed to change the political order starting with the school, which is the interface between the family and civil society.[27] As Jerry Falwell

27 Compare chap. 2, the strategy of the Catholic re-Christianization movements in Europe.

wrote in his Action Programme, there are 'five major problems that have political consequences, political implications, that moral Americans should be ready to face: abortion, homosexuality, pornography, humanism, the fractured family.'[28]

For these ills to be healed it was not enough for individuals to be saved, America must be saved as well. A new politico-religious culture was emerging in the United States. Its concern with the political process derived from the postwar Fundamentalist tradition – but its starting point was no longer opposition to communism (as in the Cold War) but the threat to individual morality represented by secular society. It retained the mass mobilization and social restructuring practised by the Evangelicals during the 1950s and 1960s, but it was no longer content to form mini-communities of true believers: its objective was the Capitol.

The question of abortion, which Falwell placed at the head of the 'major problems that have political consequences', is where private and public life intersect. It is a lever which, beginning with the family, enables pressure to be brought to bear on the state by mobilizing civil society. Its starting point in the United States was the verdict of the Supreme Court in 1973 in the case Roe vs Wade which legalized abortion on demand.[29] The Fundamentalists held that this explicitly infringed the most sacred commands of Christianity, and in particular the fifth commandment 'Thou shalt not kill'. And in authorizing this violation of the law of God, the state authorities themselves were on the wrong side of the supreme law, a fact which justified civil disobedience in the name of obedience to Christ. Falwell wrote, 'The only ground for citizens refusing to obey the law would be when human law violates divine law.'[30]

The Fundamentalists combine several strategies in waging the fight against this 'impious' law. The most radical of these are brought together in the association Operation Rescue, which takes its name from a quotation from Proverbs which in its Fundamen-

---

28   Falwell, op. cit., p. 252
29   Text and comments can be read in Marie-France Toinet, *La Cour suprême: les grands arrêts* (Nancy: Presses universitaires, 1989), p. 169 ff.
30   Op. cit., p. 16.

talist version reads: 'Rescue those who are unjustly sentenced to death; don't stand back and let them die.'[31] Militants picketed clinics and hospitals in which abortions were carried out, so that the police had to remove them by force. The media pictures of these events were irrestible reminders of the same police arresting anti-Vietnam protestors ten years earlier. The consciousness-raising tactic was the same, but those claiming to be society's conscience against arbitrary state iniquity had passed from one extreme of the political spectrum to the other.

The White House after the kingdom of Satan

The strategy chosen by Jerry Falwell and his friends, though consciously less spectacular, was no less effective: 'Americans have a grave responsibility to vote in those leaders who will rule America justly, under divine guidance ...'[32] To that end the Moral Majority, created in 1979 when the United States was about to undergo one of its greatest humiliations – the hostage-taking of the embassy staff in Teheran – was to play an important part in the election of the candidate who was expected to restore the laws of God, Ronald Reagan.

From the religious point of view the American electorate did not have much choice at the 1980 presidential election, for each of the three major candidates – Anderson, Carter and Reagan – claimed to be an Evangelical – a sign of the times! But they were not all of the same shade. During the hostage affair, Jimmy Carter seemed above all to embody Christ's command to turn the other cheek; Ronald Reagan stood as champion of the American patriots who identify with the message of the Bible and regard the United States as the New Jerusalem. During the electoral campaign he openly expressed doubt of Darwinian evolution and opined that Creationist theory ought to be taught alongside it in schools; he attacked the 'neutral' school system devoid of ethical teaching,

---

31 Proverbs 24: 11. The version used is that of the Living Bible. See the book by the founder of the Association, Randall A. Terry, *Operation Rescue* (Springdale, PA: Whitaker House, 1988) *passim*. Compare the Jerusalem Bible version, which is harder to use as a text for anti-abortion action: 'Save those being dragged towards death, but can you rescue those on their way to execution?' (London, 1985).
32 Op. cit., p. 15.

blaming it for the growth of crime and drug addiction – all echoing the ideas of the most far-out Fundamentalists.[33] And in 1982, speaking to the National Association of Evangelicals, he said: 'I have always thought that this blessed country has been specially set apart, that a divine plan has placed this great continent here, between the oceans, so that it may be found by all people everywhere in the world who feel a special love for faith and freedom.' He went on to make 1983 the 'year of the Bible'.[34]

The Fundamentalist movements of the 'New Christian Right' (Moral Majority, Christian Voice, Religious Roundtable, etc.)[35] claimed the credit for Reagan's success in both 1980 and 1984 and attributed the overwhelming victory of the Republican Party to the fact that they had for the first time been able to bring to the polls two to four million Evangelicals who had never taken much interest in politics. This statement perhaps needs some qualification, but an analysis of the 1980 voting nevertheless shows that the Evangelicals did turn out, and that, far from being corralled within their traditional rural bastion of the deep South, they were also to be found in the most modern cities of the United States, and were contributing actively to the changing of post-industrial society.

Many more Evangelicals did vote in this than in previous elections: 77 per cent against 61.1 per cent of white Evangelicals in the Southern states, and 74.6 per cent against 60.8 per cent in the rest of the country, whereas the non-Evangelical vote was declining or stable. As for their party preferences, outside the Bible Belt these varied much more widely: in 1976 57.3 per cent of them had voted for Carter, but only 28.7 per cent did so in 1980, while Reagan received 67.8 per cent of the votes (compared with 42.7 per cent in 1976 for Jerry Ford). In the South, support for Carter declined only slightly from 40.8 per cent in 1976 to

33   Hadden and Shupe, op. cit., p. 212.
34   Quoted by Golding, op cit., p. 369. Ronald Reagan repeated these sentiments on several occasions, particularly during the centennial ceremonies on the Statue of Liberty, near the end of his second term of office.
35   James Davidson Hunter, *Evangelicalism: the Coming Generation* (Chicago: University of Chicago Press, 1987), p. 125.

38.8 per cent in 1980, and Reagan received 61.2 per cent of the votes where Ford had gained 59.2 per cent.[36] The great leap forward in the electoral mobilization of the Evangelicals shows the growing influence of those who believed in 're-Christianization from above', now led by the New Christian Right, as against simply resocializing the elect in communities of believers. The massive vote for Reagan by white Evangelicals outside the Bible Belt is all the more noteworthy because it contributed so largely to his success.

This political rebirth of American Evangelicalism since the later part of the 1970s has several dimensions: though it undoubtedly marks a theological turning point, it also illustrates the socio-cultural factors in the new place taken by Evangelicals in society as a whole.

Theologically speaking, the mass of Evangelicals could be described as 'premillenarians', who believe that things can only get worse on the earth until Christ chooses the elect and removes them from this world, before returning with them to build the Kingdom of Heaven on Earth. This belief translates into absolute cultural and political pessimism, and is concerned only with the Christian perfecting of saved individuals, so that they may be among the elect when the time comes. This old tradition, a constant theme throughout Protestant history, is not confined to a few isolated sects in America: Hal Lindsey's book *The Late Great Planet Earth*,[37] an eschatological thriller which predicts a series of cataclysms culminating in the battle of Armageddon between Antichrist and Jesus, sold more than ten million copies when it was published in 1970.

This dim Evangelical view of the capacity of man to work for God and for Good is the religious expression of the marginalization

36 Corwin Smidt, 'Born-again politics: the political behaviour of evangelical Christians in the South and non-South', in *Religion and Politics in the South: Mass and Elite Perspectives*, ed. Tod A. Baker, Robert P. Steed and Laurence W. Moreland (New York: Prager, 1983), pp. 42–6. This analysis used the data gathered by the Center for Political Studies of the University of Michigan. The 'Evangelicals' were identified by three criteria: respondents 1) had to state that religion played an important part in their life; 2) had to acknowledge that they viewed the Bible as 'God's work and all it says is true'; 3) had to report that they had had a born-again experience (p. 31ff.).
37 Hal Lindsey, *The Late Great Planet Earth* (Grand Rapids, MI: Zondervan, 1970). See also, in the same vein, Thomas McCall and Zola Levitt, *Satan in the Sanctuary* (Chicago: Moody, 1973) and *The Coming Russian Invasion of Israel* (rev. edn, Chicago: Moody, 1987).

so many of them suffered between the ending of Prohibition and the mid-1970s. For during the thirteen years of Prohibition Protestants of their ilk succeeded in imposing one of their principal values, temperance, at the very heart of the American legislative apparatus via the Eighteenth Amendment, the prohibition of alcohol. But when this was abrogated in 1933, the Fundamentalist and Evangelical sub-culture emerged vanquished from its twofold confrontation: with the new immigrants from Southern and Eastern Europe, 'lovers of strong drink', in the working-class suburbs, and with the intelligentsia in their luxury apartments, imbued with the high culture of London, Paris and Berlin.

For nearly half a century the movement withdrew to a sort of internal exile in the deep South, feeling powerless to fight the dominant values of 'secular humanism' propagated by the 'Liberals' through the media and the universities, and transmitted by the legislative changes in areas such as education and individual morality. This process culminated in the decision of the Supreme Court legalizing abortion in 1973. But great consternation had been caused as far back as 1962, when the Court had pronounced a judgement forbidding prayers in state schools, even ecumenical prayers such as were used in New York State. The New York wording, which was held to be unconstitutional, went as follows: 'Almighty God, we acknowledge our dependence upon Thee, and pray Thee to bless us and our parents, our teachers and our country.' The Court based its decision on the First Amendment, which provides that 'Congress shall make no law respecting an establishment of religion or prohibiting the free exercise thereof.'[38]

It appeared to the Evangelicals and Fundamentalists that 'secular humanism' was winning hands down because of its ability not only to create and spread dominant values, but also to give them the force of law. This latter dimension was not very noticeable until the 1960s, and it was felt as a serious threat by the Fundamentalists. That prepared the ground for the political awakening that occurred in the following years, as if the transition to the

---

38   For the debates on the meaning of the First Amendment, see especially Leonard W. Levy, *The Establishment Clause: Religion and the First Amendment* (New York: Macmillan, 1986), *passim*.

political sphere was initially a defensive move, a question of survival, and only later an ambition to reconquer.

The massive support given to Reagan's candidature in 1980 was the most striking expression of this, as was noted by Gary North, himself a 'political' Fundamentalist, at a meeting he attended:

> Here were the nation's fundamentalist religious leaders [. . .] telling the crowd that the election of 1980 is only the beginning, that the principles of the Bible can become the law of the land. [. . .] Here was a startling sight to see: thousands of Christians, including pastors, who had believed all their lives in the imminent return of Christ, the rise of Satan's forces, and the inevitable failure of the church to convert the world, now standing up to cheer other pastors, who also have believed this doctrine of earthly defeat all their lives, but who were proclaiming victory, in time and on earth.[39]

Into the universities

This theological shift towards politics was the counterpart to social changes among the Evangelicals. Until the 1970s all the quantitative surveys of this population agreed that it had been sidelined during the twenty years of sustained prosperity that followed the war. Living mainly in rural areas or small towns in the South (including some on the Atlantic seaboard) and the central West (43.7 per cent lived in townships of fewer than 2,500 inhabitants), older and with an above-average proportion of the elderly and of married women, it contained a significant proportion of low-income groups: in 1978, 25.3 per cent of Evangelicals earned less than the average of 4,000 dollars a year. Compared with the population as a whole, more Evangelicals failed to complete the eighth grade (8.9 per cent) or high school (28.9 per cent). As J. D. Hunter noted,

---

39   Gary North, *Christian Reconstruction*, pamphlet published by the Institute for Christian Economics, quoted by Donald Heinz, 'The struggle to reconstruct America', in Liebmann and Wuthnow, op. cit., p. 136.

overall, contemporary Evangelicals are most widely represented among the moderately educated, lower and lower middle-income, working-class occupations. There are indications, however, that Evangelicals are rising in these categories owing to a more highly educated younger population.[40]

It was this young educated generation that was to play a major part in the 'move into politics' by Evangelicals in the last quarter century. A better education enabled these young people to emerge from the sidelines to which many of their parents were confined, and to take their place in post-industrial urban society. But this did not mean that they discarded their old family values in favour of 'secular humanism'; on the contrary, they seized the opportunity to strengthen their inherited beliefs by using the most sophisticated modern technology in order to defend and promote them.

During the 1970s access to education by young Evangelicals improved considerably: between 1971 and 1978 there was a 47 per cent increase in the number of Evangelical primary and secondary schools, and a 95 per cent increase in student enrolment. In 1985 there were 18,000 of these schools and colleges, with 2.5 million children.

This is all the more remarkable seeing that a drop in the birth rate during the 1970s produced a 13.6 per cent fall in the total number of American schoolchildren.[41] The numbers of Evangelicals in higher education also rose: whereas in 1960 only 7 per cent of American Evangelicals went to university, by the mid-1970s the proportion had risen to 23 per cent.

Hadden and Shupe observe that no other religious group experienced such a considerable change in its relation to higher education at that time.[42] Along the same lines, surveys carried out in the late 1970s and early 1980s show that there were more young adults among the Evangelicals and Fundamentalists than any other group of American Protestants, including the 'Liberals': in 1978–9 at national level, 54 per cent of the Evangelicals ques-

40 Hunter, *American Evangelicalism*, op. cit., pp. 49–55.
41 Hunter, *The Coming Generation.* . ., op. cit., p. 6.
42 Hadden and Shupe, op. cit., pp. 82–3, drawing largely on the survey by Stuart Rothenberg and Frank Newport, *The Evangelical Votes* (Institute of Government and Politics, 1984).

tioned were aged between 18 and 50, and in 1984 only 17 per cent of them were more than 65 years old.[43]

These young adults and their numerous offspring (their high birth rate being consonant with their religious beliefs) usually received or had received their education in establishments that they controlled, up to the end of high school, after which the small proportions going on to higher education went either to theological colleges or to universities that were not controlled by Fundamentalists or Evangelicals. In this respect too a significant change took place during the 1970s, with the creation of Fundamentalist universities aiming to teach all disciplines, on the basis of belief in the infallibility of the Bible.

Some Evangelical universities were already functioning during the 1960s, but they were premillenarian, and were not really interested in training elites to go out and conquer society by re-Christianizing it from above. Two of the best known were Bob Jones University and Oral Roberts University, which was established in 1965. The last-named, for example, chiefly aspired to be a locus of 'technical' training for Pentecostals, enabling them both to 'win souls individually or in mass' and to train themselves in 'scientific' worldwide faith healing with the aid of the most sophisticated audiovisual equipment.

The Oral Roberts project culminated in a faculty of medicine, the 'city of faith', accredited in 1979 and designed to combine faith healing with advanced medical research; but people with cancer (for example) were by no means keen to come to a hospital where their disease was said to be caused by demoniac possession, and the project had to be abandoned. In any event, Roberts's real aim from the outset was to withdraw the students' souls from the baneful influence of secular education; he held that every year thousands of young people who had been through Evangelical high schools were 'lost to the full gospel movement by virtue of going to those other universities where God was not supreme.' The only answer, he concluded, was 'to build a major, class A, academic university in addition to the University of Evangelism.'[44] In 1981 the Oral Roberts University at Tulsa, Oklahoma, had

43   Hadden and Shupe, ibid., pp. 83–4.
44   Harrell, op. cit., pp. 209–11.

4,170 students, a teaching staff of 375, a library of a million volumes, and seven departments (arts and sciences, business, dentistry, law, medicine, nursing and theology). Students had to sign a 'code of honor' strictly regulating the length of women's skirts and men's hair, and morality on and off campus, etc.

There is no doubt that the most political and dynamic Evangelical university is the one that Jerry Falwell established in 1971 at Lynchburg, Virginia, first under the name of Liberty Baptist College and then Liberty University. According to Hadden and Shupe,

> The Liberty University complex is the key to understanding Jerry Falwell's plan for expanding his parachurch empire and his influence on American history [. . .] his university will send out literally thousands of graduates who have been trained to think about the world in a manner highly consistent with his own religious beliefs and socioeconomic philosophy. His graduates will enter every walk of life . . .[45]

This institution is at the heart of a whole range of techniques of re-Christianization of American society from above that Falwell established in the 1970s and 1980s. Liberty University represents a long-term political investment, carrying on the work of the short-term pressure provided by the Moral Majority and ensuring a future for his ideals. In order to understand how this complex works we have to place it once more in its overall context.

The chief begetter of the operation, Jerry Falwell, was born in 1933 into a formerly rural family that was not noted for any religious fervour. His father, an unsuccessful businessman, had a very unhappy life. After having killed his own brother in 1931 in what was held to be legitimate self-defence, he took to drink and died of cirrhosis of the liver. Jerry Falwell had hardly any contact with religion before the age of 18. In 1950 he entered a technical school intending to become a mechanical engineer, and it was there that his 'conversion' took place: he gave up engineering and went into training to become a pastor. By 1956 he had founded his own independent church, called the Thomas Road Baptist

45 Hadden and Shupe, op. cit., pp. 137–8.

Church, after the street in which his church (initially with a congregation of 35) was housed, in an empty storehouse belonging to a soda factory. None of his biographers thinks that Fundamentalism held any particular spiritual attractions for him at that stage, and it seems to have been a career choice that led him to organize his own church.[46]

Thanks to his extraordinary organizing ability and his rare talent for employing the latest media techniques in the service of his preaching, he increased his congregation to 864 within a year. Making use of radio, telephone, and all the techniques of canvassing to bring in members and money, he began using television in the early 1960s. In 1968 he created a television unit to film and broadcast his sermons, which drew big audiences as part of a programme entitled 'The Old Time Gospel Hour'.

Throughout the 1960s, when Falwell was still nothing more than a local preacher, his evangelical message was addressed to the socio-cultural changes taking place in Lynchburg, for which he tried to find answers. But this small town of 70,000 inhabitants, situated in the heart of rural Virginia about 250 kilometres from Washington, typified the changes which, in the 1960s, turned the South from a backwater into a modern, post-industrial society. In the words of the essayist Frances Fitzgerald,

> In the early 50s, Lynchburg had a relatively unskilled work force and a very small middle class; today, it has a highly skilled work force and a much larger middle class. Falwell's parishioners stand, as it were, on the cusp of this new middle class. They are clerical workers, technicians, and small businessmen, and skilled and semi-skilled workers in the new factories.[47]

Like Falwell himself, many of his followers are engineers or students of technology.[48] That gives a completely modern, efficient dimension to their relationship with the Holy Scriptures and the way they use those scriptures in the task of re-Christianizing society. But it also poses the problem of reconciling belief in the

---

46 Frances Fitzgerald, *Cities on a Hill: a Journey through Contemporary American Cultures* (New York: Simon & Schuster, 1986) especially p. 143 ff.
47 Ibid., p. 137.
48 Ibid., p. 159.

infallibility of the Bible with contemporary science and engineering. In the 1920s Fundamentalism seemed to be a-scientific or even anti-scientific (as in the Scopes case); but the Fundamentalists of the 1970s and 1980s claimed that science was perfectly compatible with the most uncompromising belief. Oral Roberts University took this claim to the point of making medicine a branch of faith healing, but that was and remains an extreme case, and the teaching was discontinued in the autumn of 1989. They have not ventured along that hazardous path at Liberty University: in addition to the Department of Religious Studies, students are free to attend the School of Commerce and Political Science, the School of Communication Techniques, the Faculty of Education and the Faculty of Arts and Sciences.

The last-mentioned faculty teaches not only the 'neutral' disciplines such as information technology, chemistry, mathematics and music, but also history, philosophy and biology, which clearly reflect Falwell's ideological choices and his intention to break with the dominant values of 'secular humanism'. All students must attend the compulsory course entitled 'Life History', 'which is intended to give them an in-depth understanding of the controversy between creationism and evolutionism', i.e., to represent the theory of divine creation of man as being the expression of the truth, and to provide them with arguments with which to refute Darwinian evolutionism.

On the campus, the Center for Creation Studies and the Museum of Life and Earth History 'illustrate the concepts of the creation theory, describe its research, and glorify the Creator of the earth and of life.'[49] At all events, no one can get a teaching job in the university unless he or she swears to accept its values; they must have turned to Christ and have had a born-again experience; they must believe in the infallibility of the Bible and the theory of the divine creation of man, etc. Students too must testify that they have had a born-again experience. Education at Liberty University is not founded on doubt and the questioning of received ideas, but on becoming a disciple of the intangible Truth in its manifold aspects.

49   Liberty University, *Center for Creation Studies, Museum of Life and Earth History*, folder, undated [1989].

Before turning itself into a university the establishment started more modestly with the founding of Liberty Baptist College in 1971. At that time it was designed mainly for the training of young pastors who shared Falwell's beliefs and wished to found churches affiliated to Thomas Road Baptist Church throughout the United States. However, the television audiences were readier to give money in support of a brick-and-mortar project, such as a college, hospital, cathedral or the like, than simply to contribute to a collection for the propagation of the faith. Not until 1985 did the college become a university – after Falwell's other grand design, the Moral Majority, had gone as far as it seemed likely to go.

'Wholly political' or re-Christianization 'from below'

Yet it was the Moral Majority that had given the 'New Christian Right' its largest audience, galvanizing the hopes of its members with an intensity equalling that of the hostility it aroused in the 'secularists' and the Liberal left in America. Between 1979, when it was founded, and June 1989, when its financial liquidation was announced, the Moral Majority had changed its spots more than once. Beginning as a political lobby at the elections of 1980 and 1984, it had become to some extent the victim of its own controversial success. Its extreme politicization, and the virulence and high media profile of its stands on abortion, homosexuality, pornography, prayers in schools and other causes, had raised obstacles to the dissemination of its ethical and social message except among the Evangelical converted.

Surveys carried out in the early 1980s were unanimous in reporting rather low levels of approval of the movement. In 1981 Gallup noted that 40 per cent of respondents nationally had heard of the Moral Majority, but only 8 per cent had a favourable opinion of it. In 1982, 55 per cent had heard of it and 12 per cent favoured it. In 1985 another national survey indicated 3 per cent very favourable to the movement and 6 per cent sympathizers, but 69 per cent hostile or critical. Falwell took note of these difficulties and in January 1986 announced the creation of a new movement, Liberty Federation, which was to follow on from Moral

Majority and also 'widen its horizons' beyond the strictly political
sphere:

> [. . .] for the last six years the press had dragged the name of
> the Moral Majority through the mud. There are many people
> who are in agreement with everything we say, but who dare not
> publicly express support on this or that question for fear of being
> vilified . . .[50]

The change of organization was in some ways a natural evolution, but it was also a result of strategic choices very closely
connected with that particular politico-religious juncture. It is
significant that the polysemic word 'liberty' was substituted for
'moral', with its more precise connotations, in an attempt to prevent hostile reactions from crystallizing in that large section of
public opinion that had indicated its rejection of the Moral
Majority. But there was also a change from a 'wholly political'
approach to one that favoured activity in the social and educational
spheres – a shift which was also affecting Catholic, Muslim and
Jewish politico-religious movements at that time. For by putting
all their eggs into the basket of politics – legally in the democracies
and illegally in the Third World – these movements risked becoming commonplace and losing their special characteristics, by passing under the Caudine Forks of 'politician's politics'.

For example, in Italy the involvement of Communion and Liberation in the internal conflicts of the Christian Democrats drew it
into violent arguments which tarnished its credibility as a religious
movement and not only led to conflicts with the Vatican but
also gave it an excessively 'reactionary' image: its leaders then
abandoned politics and reverted to re-Christianization 'from
below', articulated around the social service projects of its Company of Deeds. Similarly, the supporters of the 'New Christian
Right' in America had to decide just how far they wanted the
movement to be involved in supporting the Republican Party.
Should it become a mere machine for delivering Evangelical voters,

---

50   Quoted in Jeffrey Hadden, Anson Shupe, James Hawdon and Kenneth Martin, 'Why
Jerry Falwell killed the Moral Majority', in *The God Pumpers: Religion in the Electronic Age*,
ed. Marshall Fishwick and Ray Browne (Bowling Green, OH: Bowling Green State
University Press, 1987), p. 102. See also p. 104.

in exchange for sinecures and perks of various kinds when that party was in power? Could it obtain a secure foothold in politics by getting a leading Evangelical nominated as the Republican presidential candidate?

In the context of the 1988 presidential elections, Jerry Falwell and Pat Robertson represent two different options. Whereas Falwell had withdrawn from politics in the strict sense in favour of the social and educational sphere by changing from the Moral Majority to the Liberty Federation, Robertson sought election as a Republican candidate. This televangelist was a senator's son, a graduate of Yale University and chairman of the Christian Broadcasting Network – a typical representative of White Anglo-Saxon Protestant society. It was a change from self-made preachers like Jim Bakker or Jimmy Swaggart, whose antics, sex scandals and get-rich-quick careers did not exactly single them out as credible candidates for office.

To the surprise of commentators who had rather hastily assumed that all televangelists were like the most highly coloured versions, Robertson led the Republican primaries in some states at the first caucuses, and George Bush had to gain control of the party machine in order to eliminate this rival. But Robertson's final failure, despite his initial successes, is a telling pointer to the difficulties that face a politico-religious movement trying to change into a political party and compelled by that fact to take on board other aims and methods. And even conservatism itself, a blanket notion under which Evangelicals and Republicans lay down together through the 1980s, did not mean the same thing to both parties. The conservatism of Evangelicals is primarily cultural, moral and social, whereas 'secular' conservatives as found in the Republican establishment are interested above all in the economic organization of society.[51] And in point of fact the Evangelicals did not often manage to achieve the changes they desired in the areas that most concerned them, such as abortion, school prayers, homosexuality or pornography, even during the eight years of Reagan's presidency, despite his leanings towards them.

In this context, the long-term investment in social and edu-

---

51 Corwin Smidt, op. cit., p. 51.

cational matters that Jerry Falwell made with Liberty University and the Liberty Federation is aimed at a much more far-reaching revolution than a temporary alliance with the Prince or a hypothetical conquest of executive power. It is on the ground of values and their production that the fight has to be waged. 'Secular humanism' is at the root of all the evils that the Evangelicals and Fundamentalists denounce, and it is at that level that the message must be propagated.

Politics is only an epiphenomenon, an effect, not a cause. According to Falwell, the Moral Majority had a bad press because the 'secular humanists' who control the media, this 'vocal minority of nongodly men and women', manipulated opinion. Real power is not, or not exclusively, within the control of government or in the formation of pressure groups. For that, a cultural victory must be gained over the 'Liberal' intelligentsia, which must be defeated on its own ground.

The way to achieve this is to harry it through all the semantic registers that it penetrates or influences, from the mass culture of amusement parks and downmarket television programmes to the most sophisticated cultural productions, while also mounting public opinion campaigns that express social problems in truly Evangelical categories and language. Here too a similar phenomenon is observable in the Catholic, Jewish and Muslim worlds: Communion and Liberation, for example, aims to unseat the 'secular' Italian intelligentsia from its dominant cultural position and put a 'Christian' alternative in its place. The Lubavitch and the Islamists also oppose, respectively, the culture of the 'assimilated' Jewish intellectuals and the 'Westernized' Muslims – in each case with a system of values drawn from religious dogma and purporting to become an alternative culture. But the American Evangelicals have a much greater panoply of resources for this purpose, ranging from television channels to universities.

The struggle against 'secular humanism'

James Hunter calls the adversary the 'new class – an elite class of workers in the knowledge industries'.[52] This is the American

---

52   Hunter, *Evangelicalism and the Quandary of Modernity*, op. cit., p. 118.

intellectual establishment of the 1970s and 1980s which is in part the heir to the intelligentsia of the 1930s – the Sinclair Lewises and Menckens who belonged to the global high culture and had nothing but disdain for the 'backward' sub-culture of the Fundamentalists – and in part also the child of the 1960s counter-culture, in its Liberal or libertarian variants domesticated by Hollywood scriptwriters and the publicists of Madison Avenue. Such is the face of the detested 'secular humanism'. Its original sin is to have broken the link between man and God, and to favour the emancipation of reason, desires and instincts in opposition to faith and obedience to God's commands.

Fundamentalists believe that 'secular humanism' is two-faced. On the social level, it stifles the individual's freedom of action by trussing him up in a web of legal and bureaucratic constraints the sole purpose of which is to reinforce the power of the state; conversely, on the ethical level it advocates complete freedom which instantly degenerates into licence and amorality. Jerry Falwell holds that the fight against these two faces must be carried on simultaneously.

The welfare state is castigated as follows:

> Today government has become all-powerful as we have exchanged freedom for security. For all too many years, Americans have been educated to dependence rather than to liberty [. . .] Welfarism has grown because Americans have forgotten to tithe and give offerings. Until the early days of this century, it was widely recognized that churches and other private institutions carried the primary responsibility, not merely for education, but also for health and charity. The way to defeat welfarism in America is for those who wish to see God's law restored to our country to tithe fully to organizations that will remove from government those tasks that are more properly addressed by religious and private organizations. Our nation's growing welfare system alone threatens our country with bankruptcy. It is time that we realized the working population of America cannot indefinitely carry on the burden of governmental spending.[53]

---

53 Jerry Falwell, op. cit., p. 12.

This first register of the Fundamentalist ideology strikes the same note as the most traditional social conservativism, from which it differs only in emphasizing that social problems ought to be handled by religious organizations. At the end of the 1970s, which for the United States was a decade of economic and social crisis, inflation and unemployment, the Fundamentalist argument laid the blame for all these evils on the redistributive system built up over the 1960s and 1970s by the Kennedy and Johnson administrations, with the aim of bringing the neglected victims of the 'other America' into the common prosperity by a policy of massive financial transfers.

But it is another 'other America' that Falwell is addressing here, in tones somewhat reminiscent of the Prohibitionists in the early 1920s. This time it is not the blacks, the Hispanics or the underworld ghettos in American cities, but the world of the 'poor whites', who received nothing from the social welfare programmes but had to pay for them through taxes, and who were excluded from the networks of political, cultural and social power, although their children did have access to higher education. For the Fundamentalists, the culprits were the 'Liberals' in the American meaning of the word – those who share an ideology rather like that of Social Democrats in Europe. According to Jeremy Rifkin,

> In the Sixties and Seventies liberals promised they could end poverty, crime and a host of other social blights by tinkering with the system, and they failed. The public watched as liberals ushered in a proliferation of new legislation, government agencies and bureaucratic red tape. After it was over, the sweeping and unrealistic promises went unfulfilled. The American people, in turn, began to equate liberalism with incompetence, naïveté and the squandering of public monies on every social problem in sight.[54]

The second face of Liberalism, just as odious in the eyes of the Fundamentalists, is the licence that it tolerates, nay encourages, in ethical matters. Individual liberty, so valuable in the commercial world, can only lead, in the moral sphere, to abortion, homosexuality or pornography, seen as an excellent way to destroy the

54   Rifkin, op. cit., p. 6.

family. If the family is destroyed, individuals are handed over defenceless to the power of the non-godly state, which then crushes them. Consequently, Fundamentalists are convinced of the need to reconstitute and strengthen intermediary structures between the individual and the state, meaning the family in the first instance, but also the community structure which helps out the family or, if necessary, takes over from it. This happens in a number of difficult social situations, and also at adolescence, when individuals leave the family circle and make their entry into society; at this point the individual's Fundamentalist's world view may be disturbed, and he or she may fall an easy victim to temptation and sin.

Accordingly, Falwell has established a home for pregnant women who are alone or who do not wish to keep their child. They are cared for completely during pregnancy on condition that they do not resort to abortion, but are then given every facility for having their babies adopted. The function of Liberty University is to provide young people from Evangelical families with a social life within a closed and ideologically homogeneous environment before they are 'let loose' into the outside world. The aim is not only to train them, to strengthen their souls before they are subjected to the temptations of the world, but also to encourage students to become engaged so that they will then proceed to found Evangelical families.

To anybody who has spent some time on the Liberty campus, it is a striking spectacle. The dormitories are single-sex, and strict surveillance, a mixture of coercion and self-discipline, is practised. French kissing is forbidden, and any sexual relations between unmarried students are punished by expulsion. (Married couples live in town.) But kissing on the cheek is permitted, and couples are free to hold hands, though not to put an arm round the partner's waist. Students willingly defend this sexual self-discipline when questioned about it by a visiting stranger; they maintain that total repression would be bound to lead to deviant practices, in particular to homosexuality, which (they say) is rife in a rival Fundamentalist university in which all flirting is forbidden. On the other hand, the expression of sexual desire would go against the spirit of the educational aims of the university.

This channelling of sexuality towards marriage between fellow-students and the procreation of future Evangelicals is a leading theme in the Sunday School. One such session I attended in October 1989 made a point of tracking down anything conducive in sin in television broadcasts, and students had to confess whether during the past year they had seen a film in which any characters showed their bare behinds. The meeting had begun with a little sketch in which a man looking at a pornographic video was pulled up short by God and recalled to the Way. And the parents present were informed that when films were shown at Liberty they had first been 'edited', any passage considered as licentious being removed.

But Falwell founded a university, not a monastery: his students are not cutting themselves off from the world, they are changing it, living out the ideal Fundamentalist society in advance. The cinema, television, radio and other media form a most important part of the curriculum, and the students publish a weekly newspaper, *The Liberty Champion*, which is highly professional in style and content. They also produce programmes for the internal television circuit. When later on they become journalists, producers or anchormen in their future professional life, they will be standardbearers for the Fundamentalist idea that the mastery of modern technology does not have to imply secularization.

Robertson thought that the way to re-Christianize society was to get a televangelist elected president of the United States; Falwell holds that the victory over secular humanism will be won on the cultural field, with the weapons of the mass media. The televangelists of his generation have built up a gigantic but peripheral network of religious television; but the media students at Liberty University must tomorrow be in positions of power or influence on the generalist, public or commercial networks. That is the way for the children of the Southern televangelists to conquer the heart of America – by Christianizing modernism.

Among all the movements of religious reaffirmation that have appeared on the world political scene since the mid-1970s, the American Evangelists and Fundamentalists hold a position both singular and central.

Their singularity is due first of all to their extraordinary ability to use the most up-to-date language and technology in propagating their message: nowhere else is there anything to equal televangelism, though imams and cardinals have learnt to make use of television. But, in the American case, this phenomenon is the culmination of a 'native' tradition that began with the itinerant preachers of the great age of the revivals, before the Second World War. It is also in the tradition of the radio sermons from which Billy Graham's name has been inseparable ever since the war. More than anywhere else, it operates within a market for goods and services that dictates the very shape of its message. Unlike countries with a Catholic tradition, in which the Church enjoys a dominant position as an institution, the American preaching market is open to scores of independent small entrepreneurs competing with one another according to classical capitalist criteria. Most of the people who have built up religious 'empires' are self-made men, many of whom have created their own church or denomination. This fierce competition, reminiscent of the 'struggle for existence' described by their *bête noire* Charles Darwin, has led to excesses that have caused several of them to founder in ridicule. Those whose moral scruples – to say nothing of religion – were unable to resist the fascination of dollars too quickly amassed have ended their careers behind bars. Nowhere in contemporary Catholicism, Islam or Judaism can we find these elective analogies between a religious movement and the spirit of capitalism each taken to extremes.

But the re-Christianization movements in American Protestantism do have a number of characteristics in common with Catholic movements in Europe, and also with re-Islamization. In the first place, they appeal to a youthful public which has had access to higher education and whose parents, far less educated, have moved from a rural environment to modern cities. Paradoxically, the parallels between Islam and America appear to be strongest in this respect. The Islamist militants are the children of the *fellahs* who were thrust into the shanty-towns of the Muslim world by the rural exodus. The young militants in the contemporary Fundamentalist movements come not from the townships of the deep South, as did the majority of their parents, but from the large cities in the Southern and Northern United States; many of them have had higher education – though not in the best universities – mainly in the applied sciences, just like the Islamist militants.

In both cases they formed a 'counter-elite', in opposition to the current holders of cultural power, who produced the dominant values and ethical standards of the establishment: in the Muslim countries, these were the Westernized intelligentsia, and in America the 'new class' of cultural entrepreneurs that was formed at the end of the 1960s and raised on secular humanism.

Of course, these two worlds were separated by the social gulf between the Third World and the premier world power, and the young Fundamentalists did not have to endure the generally lamentable social conditions of the Muslim students. But if we leave the universities and turn to the clientele of faith healers like Oral Roberts, or to Jim Bakker's television audience, we shall find that the American poor can scarcely be in a better condition than the poor of the underdeveloped Muslim countries. In the United States, re-Christianization from below takes the form of large-scale social therapy as much as a response to cultural demand. There too is to be found rejection of a modernism felt to be foreign and alienating, destructive of individual and family identity. This accounts for the insistence on imposing strict ethical standards to regulate private life, prohibit abortion, channel sexuality towards marriage alone and ensure the education of children in institutions protected from the influences of the 'world'.

Socially, both re-Christianization and re-Islamization aim to break the link between modern technology and the dominant cultural standards of the civilization which produced it. Though both excel in the use of this technology, their ability to create anything comparable has not yet been proven.

Lastly, the move into politics of the American re-Christianization movements has followed an original path: nowhere else is there a parallel for the postwar separation between the Evangelicals, working from below, and the Fundamentalists, who took the high ground during the Cold War. Paradoxically, the first president of America to proclaim himself an Evangelical, Jimmy Carter, had the image of a 'Liberal' – a term abhorred by Fundamentalists.

Ever since the mid-1970s Fundamentalists have steered the Evangelical movement (in the wider meaning of the term) towards the more 'conservative' parties, working for the election of Ronald Reagan in 1980 and 1984. In 1988 attempts by one of their number to win the Republican presidential nomination ended in failure. During this period there were again similarities to situations observable in Catholicism and in Islam. In Italy Communion and Liberation, and in Poland the episcopate, succeeded in steering movements of re-Christianization 'from below', well grounded in society, towards the fringes of power. But in both cases they failed to cross the political threshold and were forced to retreat to a pastoral function based on practical social work. They aim to re-Christianize specific environments, schools in particular. In the Muslim world, the phenomenon developed in broadly the same way; only the Shi'ites managed to bring the Islamic revolution to a victorious conclusion, and during the later 1980s the movements of re-Islamization 'from below' were moving upwards, trying to gain possession of environments which were already Islamized. There too, the school is a crucial bone of contention. Nevertheless, because these latter movements had no cultural connections with democracy they clashed with the surrounding society in a way that had no parallel in Christian countries.

In order to assess the importance of this democratic variable, to show how it influences the reaffirmation of religious identity on the political scene, we must now examine a phenomenon that belongs neither to Christianity nor to Islam: the re-Judaization movements.

4

The Redemption of Israel

In April 1984 the Israeli police arrested members of a Jewish terrorist group suspected of having murdered several students of the Islamic university of Hebron and perpetrated attempts on the lives of Palestinian mayors. The network was broken up just as some of its activists were preparing to blow up buses crowded with Arabs. Others had drawn up a plan for dynamiting the Dome of the Rock and the Al Aksa mosque – the third most sacred place in Islam – situated on the Temple Mount[1] in Jerusalem, the Jewish people's most holy place.

Many Israelis were profoundly shocked by the discovery of this 'Jewish underground', especially when it was realized that many of the accused belonged to the inner core of Gush Emunim (the Bloc of the Faithful), a politico-religious movement born in the aftermath of the Arab–Israeli war of October 1973, which ended in a psychological defeat for the Jewish state. Amid the disarray that followed the hostilities, and which led to a confusion of values and to a questioning of the certitudes that had been implicitly shared by many Israelis since 1948, Gush Emunim propounded a strongly and uncompromisingly ideological doctrine. It became the self-proclaimed herald of the re-Judaization of Israel, over against a state and a society culturally dominated by a secular and quasi-socialist conception of Zionism.

As it planted more and more settlements in the Occupied Territories (even in defiance of the authorities) and contested every step of the retreat from Sinai that followed the Camp David

---

1   In Arabic, Al Haram al Sharif (the sacred sanctuary), whence the prophet Mohammed is said to have ascended into heaven.

accord, the Gush was replacing the legal concept of the State of Israel by the biblical concept of the Land of Israel (*Eretz Yisrael*), which legitimized the occupation of the territories by virtue of the specific pact that God made with the Chosen People. Although its active membership never rose above twenty thousand, the ideas that the Gush disseminated and the aura surrounding some of its leaders have played a crucial part in the changes that have taken place in Israel since the mid-1970s. In the spring of 1987 a representative selection of Israeli personalities, asked to nominate the most outstanding individuals since 1967 (the date of the Six Day war) bracketed Menachem Begin with Rabbi Moshe Levinger, the figurehead of Gush Emunim, in first place.[2]

But the Gush was only one manifestation of the vastly more extensive re-Judaization movement which throughout this period was constantly growing, both inside Israel and among the Jews of the diaspora. Gush represented the most explicitly political pole of this movement; and, as it wanted to exert influence on the state and went in for violent action – in some cases even for terrorism – it attracted the attention of the media, of the Israeli and American governments, and of many academics in the two countries. In analysing the movement, many observers did no more than transpose the Protestant idea of 'fundamentalism' in the crudest meaning of the term, and called the members of the Gush 'Jewish fundamentalists', locating them somewhere between the Christian and Islamic variants of the phenomenon.

However, at the very time when the Gush was in the ascendant, other forms of return to Judaism were developing. In a very visible paradox, 'ultra-orthodox' groups, recognizable to the least observant by their black robes (inherited from seventeenth-century Lithuanian dress) experienced remarkable growth. They recruited many new members, both university students and Sephardic Jews, immigrants from the Arab countries in which such orthodox groups were quite unknown. In the Israeli parliament, the political parties representing these *haredim* (literally 'quakers' or 'godfearers') grew to such a size that they had to be included in any government

2 Ian S. Lustick, *For the Land and the Lord: Jewish Fundamentalism in Israel* (New York: Council on Foreign Relations, 1988), p. 13.

coalition, and they exacted a very high price for their support of other parties.

In the 1970s the entire Jewish world was affected by a *teshuvah* (or *tshuvah*, a term which signifies 'return to Judaism' and 'repentance', that is to say the return to full observance of the Jewish law, the *Halakah*). The 'penitents' (*baalei teshuvah*) break with the temptations of secular society and reorganize their existence, basing it solely on the commandments and prohibitions derived from the Jewish sacred texts. This break necessitates a strict separation between Jews and *goyim* (non-Jews, gentiles) in order to combat assimilation, the supreme threat to the perpetuation of the Chosen People. *Teshuvah* also means, within the Jewish people itself, a redefinition of identity. Merely to be a Jew is not enough: one must observe all the 613 religious prohibitions and obligations (*mitsvot*) that regulate Jewish existence, from the most trivial daily bodily functions to the organization of life in society.

The 'return movement' spread, to differing degrees, in countries as different as the United States, the Soviet Union, France and Israel, affecting Jews of many different persuasions: 'assimilated Jews', communists and Zionists, Jews only vaguely aware of their Jewishness and militant supporters of the secular Zionism embodied in the Jewish state.

It was in the mid-1970s that the phenomenon surfaced in various guises: the creation of movements like Gush Emunim (1974); the opening of the great *yeshivot* (talmudic colleges) in Jerusalem for 'penitents' such as Machon Meir or Ohr Hahayim (1974);[3] the coming to power of the religious conservative coalition led by Menachem Begin (1977); and the conversion to orthodoxy of former militants who had made a name for themselves in the counter-culture or the left-wing movements of 1968.

From repentance to proselytism: life histories

For it was at that time that accounts began to appear, written by Jews who previously had been non-religious, secularized or even atheists, celebrating their discovery of religion and calling on their

3   Janet O'Dea Aviad, *Return to Judaism: Religious Renewal in Israel* (Chicago: University of Chicago Press, 1983), p. 22.

readers to follow the commandments of the Law. They claimed that their move had been prompted by contemporary 'post-modernism', which was characterized by a crisis of values showing that secularism was at a dead end. As with Protestant Fundamentalism in America, and the Islamist movements or Communion and Liberation, these enthusiastically religious autobiographers took great care to emphasize that there was absolutely no incompatibility between their zeal for their faith, their minute observance of ritual and their command of the latest and most sophisticated knowledge or technology.

In 1968 two American *baalei teshuvah* (penitents) published such autobiographies, the first examples of a literary genre that was to become quite extensive. In *Being Jewish*, Shimon Hurwitz introduces himself as 'a Jew, a product of mid-twentieth-century American culture. He did not know what it meant to be truly Jewish. . .' He discovered the latter by enrolling in a *yeshiva* (talmudic college) which showed him the dead-end nature of Western society and its system of values, and he judged that 'authentic Jewish culture and Western culture and society are 180° apart'. Western culture is utterly empty and pointless, aiming only to satisfy the desires of the individual in a context of unfettered materialism. Without knowledge of God, the assimilated Jew is left to his own devices in a total ethical indifference. Only the rediscovery of the Torah and observance of the commandments will restore meaning to his life.[4]

Mayer Schiller's *The Road Back*, published in the same year, starts out from a similar discovery: the author, borrowing from Durkheim, calls the modern era an 'age of anomie'. This can be traced back to the Enlightenment, when 'man cut himself adrift from his firm moorings in a theocentric universe, and was inextricably swept out by the current of secular ideology into the bizarre and hostile sea of doubt where he now flounders . . .'[5] Here the Enlightenment represents the supreme expression of human pride, which tries to emancipate reason from faith; and reason left to

---

4 Shimon Hurwitz, *Being Jewish* (Jerusalem and New York: Feldheim, 1978), quoted in Aviad, op. cit., pp. 155–6
5 Mayer Schiller, *The Road Back: a Discovery of Judaism without Embellishments* (Jerusalem and New York: Feldheim, 1978), p. 25.

itself cannot but engender totalitarianism, of which the French Revolution was the first significant manifestation and Nazism the end result.[6]

This is reminiscent of Hannah Arendt, and it echoes a line of reasoning that appears in the writings of Cardinal Ratzinger and Cardinal Lustiger, who trace the 'pagan' manifestations of Nazi and Stalinist totalitarianism back to the Enlightenment and its French offspring. The Italian Catholics of Communion and Liberation took a similar line, regarding the Enlightenment world view as the source of secularism, the enemy in chief.

The Jewish world also had its Enlightenment, the *Haskalah*, in which the intelligentsia emancipated itself from the tutelage of the rabbis and set about shedding the ghetto mentality. This way of thinking had been violently condemned by orthodox Jews, who regarded it as culpable departure from the Law. But the rise of Zionism, offspring of the *Haskalah*, had rendered that polemic obsolete. Now, however, with the *teshuvah* – return and repentance – it recovered its force and relevance.

Mayer Schiller belongs to this orthodox strain, but he represents its most modern conceivable expression: his book is intended as a critique of secularized society from a dual standpoint, sacred and profane. Unlike the traditional *haredim* (ultra-orthodox), who cultivate a pious ignorance of worldly knowledge, the author has taken the trouble to acquire such knowledge in order to find therein arguments likely to appeal to the assimilated Jews, his intended audience, whom he wants to bring back to the *teshuvah* road. Moreover, the textbook nature of his progress is revealed for the edification of the reader in the preface to the book, written by the President of Yeshiva High School, New York: 'Mayer Schiller was born in Brooklyn to a family non-observant of Jewish law. Among his parents and grand-parents were socialists, agnostics and atheists.'

Touched by divine revelation at about the age of eleven, he began by observing the commandments, and then his family allowed him to leave high school and go to an institute specializing in the Torah; this absorbed all his working hours, and in his spare

6   Ibid., p. 67ff.

time he studied secular subjects. Having finished his apprentice-ship, 'The young autodidact has now undertaken to teach, both professionally in the Yeshiva High School in Queens, and by means of writing.'[7]

For Schiller as for Hurwitz, the modern secularized world, cut off from God since the Enlightenment, is a world of 'anxiety, depression and various other neurotic symptoms [. . .] Suicide, violent crime, divorce and a huge amount of other social ills appear to be far more prevalent in the present age than in the "age of faith".'[8] The 'young autodidact' here applies sociological jargon ('anomie', 'neurotic symptoms', 'ills of society') to an argument couched in the register of the strictest belief and observance, and which states as a principle that 'For the Jew, to accept or reject the validity of the Torah is the *most important decision* to be reached in his lifetime. If the faith of Israel is true, then the Jew automatically becomes obligated to observe the ordinances of the Divine revel-ation.'[9] To observe all these ordinances – and to escape perdition – penitents must break with world society:

> Valuing the relevance of our sinaitic contract with God, the believ-ing Jew cannot take up residence in the 'secular city', where so many *real* 'fools'[10] are reaping their well-deserved 'harvest'. For the Jew seeking to retrace his way back to the faith for which his ancestors endured so much, it is imperative that he seeks out a community of Jews who adhere to the doctrines of their faith, and takes part in their endeavors.[11]

Mayer Schiller's sort of *teshuvah* can flourish only by reconstituting enclosed communities sheltered from materialistic, corrupting American society.

Herman Branover, author of *Return*, is a prestigious recruit to the movement, for he is 'one of the world's authorities in the recondite field of magnetohydrodynamics'. And Branover did not

---

7   Schiller, op. cit., p. 7.
8   Ibid., p. 67.
9   Ibid., p. 40.
10   This refers to Psalm 92, vv. 6–7: 'How great are thy deeds, O Lord! How fathomless thy thoughts! He who does not know this is a brute, a fool is he who does not understand this' (NEB).
11   Schiller, op. cit., pp. 206–7.

merely break with the gross temptations of a materialist or con-
sumerist society: he was born and brought up in the Soviet Union,
yet he successfully cast off Marxist-Leninist doctrine and its social
ideal. Written in Russian in 1976 and published in English six
years later, *Return* is the autobiographical record of a *teshuvah* that
began in Riga, Latvia, and (says the author) was pursued in
complete harmony with a career as a leading scientist. Branover
describes himself as 'a godfearing Jew, who observes the *mitsvot*
from the strictest to the easiest, and who is also a great scientist'
– *not* 'a great scientist and, by the way, a believing Jew who lives
by the *mitsvot* of the Torah'.[12] However, if the book is edifying it
is because it elucidates a paradox – the great scientist who nonethe-
less made his *teshuvah*.

Marxist ideology is his first target. At the beginning of the 1950s
Branover, at that time a member of *Komsomol* (the communist youth
organization), entered the polytechnic institute in Leningrad. He
was refused admission to the department of his choice, despite his
brilliant examination results, because he was a Jew. This led him
to question the supposed universalism of the Marxist-Leninist
intellectuals around him, according to whom (we have Ilya Ehrenburg's word for it in a contemporary issue of *Pravda*) there was
no Jewish problem in the USSR. For, said Ehrenburg, the peculiar
nature of Judaism came from the oppression to which Jews were
subjected, and there was no such oppression in the socialist state.

Having experienced anti-semitism, Branover began to doubt the
Marxist credo. Then, pondering his own Jewishness, he developed
an interest in its religious dimension, from which he had been
distanced by his atheist education and his scientific training: 'I
still remained a materialist atheist, believing that science and
modernity themselves negate religion.' [13] But although he looked,
he was unable to find arguments against religion, even in the
most recent scientific theories. On the contrary: 'It was becoming
clear to me that there is a difference between science, which deals
only with the interrelationships of phenomena, and religion, which
reveals the essence and purpose of things.'[14]

12   Herman Branover, *Return* (Jerusalem and New York: Feldheim, 1982), p. 163.
13   Ibid., p. 41.
14   Ibid., p. 42.

Branover's journey began with an affirmation of Jewishness intensified by anti-semitism; he gradually worked backwards from a rejection of Marxism to rejection of its atheist, scientific and secular substrate, which he traced back – again! – to the Jewish Enlightenment of the eighteenth century, the *Haskalah*, 'a monstrous experiment to substitute the treasures of the Jewish soul with "universal humanism".'[15] He ended by making religion the very principle of Jewishness. From this point of view Zionism, founded on a secular conception of Judaism, seemed to Branover to be an unforgivable deviation, although he very soon resolved to emigrate to Israel (which he did in 1972). Until leaving the USSR he was active in organizing, both in Russia and in the non-Russian republics (especially in the Caucasus), communities of strict obedience who observed the *kosheruth* and the *shabbat* and wore the yarmulka, etc.; and he devoted his evenings to the Torah, after a day spent on magnetohydrodynamics.

Israel dazzled him for a moment, but after that he could not find words harsh enough to condemn its secularized society, seeing the 'heirs of the Chosen People – who for more than three thousand years were the bearers and guardians of holiness, justice and human wisdom – turned into such a philistine race, whose heathen cult of the body, pleasure and success is not very modestly covered by the fig-leaf of "progress" and "service to the ideals of all mankind".'[16]

Travelling all over the world to attend conferences on magnetohydrodynamics, he never failed to stop off in Brooklyn to consult the Lubavitcher rebbe,[17] who gave him valuable moral and religious counsels which he endeavoured to apply in order to put the Chosen People back on the road to redemption.

This movement of 'return' and repentance helped to change the character of world Judaism from the mid-1960s onwards. Until then the orthodox and ultra-orthodox – *haredim* – were confined to very few families, who lived largely cut off from the society around them; their children were increasingly inclined to desert them for other, less cramping forms of Judaism. For example, a

15   Ibid., p. 145.
16   Ibid.
17   See below, p. 183ff.

survey of Jewish high-school pupils in America at the end of the 1950s revealed that only one in five children of such orthodox families wanted to continue the tradition. For the social scientists of the time, that was reason enough for thinking that the *haredim* were dead and buried.[18]

In the New World, most Jews adopted one of two expressions of Jewishness. One was 'reform' Judaism, which first arose at the end of the nineteenth century, modelled on Protestant and Catholic modernism. Its adherents practised criticism of the Bible and rejected ritual. In 1883, at the first annual prizegiving of Hebrew Union College – the intellectual citadel of reform Judaism – they actually served non-kosher food.

'Conservative Judaism' was a reaction against this radical break with ritual and observance. Conservative Jews meticulously obeyed the *mitsvot* (ritual injunctions and prohibitions), but sought to reconcile them with the rules of life in the non-Jewish secular city by seeking specific ways of enabling Jews living and working among Gentiles to follow the *kosheruth* and keep the *shabbat*. By opting for this via media they were able to escape the dilemma between orthodoxy and assimilation and, while rejecting a ghetto existence, to preserve an identity based on observance. Conservative Jews were not in favour of breaking with the surrounding society – quite the reverse. They tried to negotiate a place within society that in fact suited the majority of Jewish immigrants from Central Europe, and their children, from the inter-war period until the end of the 1950s.

In other countries that had a strong tradition of radicalism and assimilation, such as France, simply being Jewish became more important than differing forms of observance, and the term 'Israelite' was preferred to 'Jew'[19] – at least until the huge influx of Jews from North Africa which began in the late 1950s. That did not mean that orthodoxy was non-existent, but it continued to be practised only within a small number of families.

18   M. Herbert Danzger, *Returning to Tradition: the Contemporary Revival of Orthodox Judaism* (New Haven and London: Yale University Press, 1989), p. 25.
19   See Dominique Schnapper's survey and typology, *Juifs et Israélites* (Paris: Gallimard, 'Idées' series, 1980), *passim*.

The Jewish 1960s revisited

The 1960s brought considerable social, cultural and political changes in societies in which Jews were strongly represented. They were inimical to the ideals of merely nominal Judaism, which dilute the qualities specific to the Chosen People in a universalist humanism. They were the first signs of the many-faceted 'return' movement that really got into its stride in the following decade.

In the United States, two great problems impressed themselves on Jewish consciousness during the decade: conflicts with the Blacks, and the emergence of the counter-culture.

Until the mid-1960s Jews and Blacks were content to think of themselves as allies against the White Anglo-Saxon Protestant establishment; they fought, alongside the other 'ethnic' groups, to obtain equal civic rights for all and against racial discrimination. Both communities were present in the same large cities and the Jews, who were generally better educated, often acted as spokemen for the demands of the Blacks. But the rise of Black power, which glorified the specific identity of Blacks and was deployed particularly by the Black Muslims (American Blacks who had converted to Islam) resulted in the expulsion of the

> whites – among whom were substantial numbers of Jews – from positions of leadership in the black civil rights movement. [. . .] For the first time ideological differences, exacerbated by economic and status differences, drove Jews and blacks apart. Jews were teachers in schools where students were black, Jews were social workers serving a heavily black clientele, Jews owned retail stores in black neighborhoods.[20]

The Black riots in the mid-1960s, in which Jewish property was more, rather than less, at risk, reminded some among them of the pogroms by Russian or German mobs. This forceful affirmation of identity, strongly ritualistic and ostentatiously exclusive of the Other, was a brusque rejection of the universalist conception of the oneness and cohesion of society as a whole. This atmosphere of exacerbated differences between ethnic groups, be they racial

20 Danzger, op. cit., p. 73.

or religious, was an ideal opportunity for those who wished to make uninhibited observance and separation from the *goyim* the mainspring of Jewish identity; just like the Black Muslims, the ultra-orthodox Jews suddenly found themselves in tune with the spirit of the times.

Even more paradoxically, the 'counter-culture' that was rife among students the world over at the end of the 1960s, and which came to a head in 1968, also prepared the ground for re-Judaization. For both the hippies of the United States and their left-wing counterparts in Europe and the Third World rejected the moral foundations of the established order and denied the legitimacy of democracy, which they decried as a front for the exploitation of the masses by the bourgeoisie or as a repressive, alienating conformism that muzzled self-development. The 'over-throw of all values' attempted by the students of the 'counter-culture' led to the widespread diffusion of social experiments and breakaway communities. Many young American Jews either took to communal living (sometimes coupled with drugs) or joined revolutionary organizations pledged to overthrow the established order and to build a new the society on its ruins – though few agreed on what form this new society should take. And because young Jews had three times the average representation in higher education, they played an important part in the counter-culture.

Even after these movements had gone out of fashion the feeling persisted that rejection of the established order and its values, on which the revolt had been based, still had some validity. Very often the return to Judaism was experienced as a continuation of these movements of the expiring 1960s. The most obvious example would be the Jewish ex-hippies who shed their threadbare jeans, their cadogan and their LSD, entered *yeshivoth* in the United States or Israel and took to black coats, curl-papers and *kosheruth*.[21] In the early 1970s talmudic colleges began to be founded in Jerusalem especially for these people, and recruiting rabbis were to be seen day after day leading young American Jews 'bearded, long haired,

21   Ibid., pp. 79–80.

with guitar in hand and packs slung on their backs, entering the *yeshiva* . . .'[22]

In France, Judaism wore a left-wing aspect in the 1960s, though with some specifically European features that distinguished it from the counter-culture in America. Moreover, the internal balance of the Jewish population tipped in favour of the Sephardim and away from the Ashkenazim.

When the twentieth anniversary of May 1968 was celebrated, many commentators pondered the 'Jewish nature' of that event – a topic which, some years earlier, would have been dubbed far right anti-semitic propaganda. But in essence such questions show that the discovery of Jewish identity by certain '68 militants was actually retrospective. It was common knowledge that many of the leaders in those uprisings were Jewish. Indeed, there was a joke (one among many) which said that the only reason why Yiddish was not spoken at the politbureau of the largest Trotskyite organization in France was that one of the committee members was a Sephardic Jew. And although some studies have linked the revolutionary commitment of the May '68 Jews with the fact that their families had been in the immigrant communist movement, the Resistance or the fight against Hitler,[23] the 'Jewish nature' of this commitment was sublimated by the strictly atheistic revolutionary messianism with which left-wing militants were imbued at that time.

From that point of view the state of Israel was simply the bridgehead of imperialism in the Middle East; it had to be destroyed and replaced by a secular Palestine in which Jews and Arabs would live together in perfect socialist harmony. Between supporting the Vietnamese FLN and confronting the French police, the Jewish left-wingers shouted 'Victory to Palestine!' as loudly as their *goyim* comrades – until the Palestinian massacre of Israeli athletes at the 1972 Munich Olympics made them really uneasy. It was then that they began to distance themselves from the battles of the left, and that many of them rediscovered their identity as

---

22   Aviad, op. cit., p. 29ff. Several examples also in Shalom Cohen, *Dieu est un baril de poudre: Israel et ses intégristes* (Paris: Calmann-Lévy, 1989), in particular pp. 75–92.
23   See H. Hamon and P. Rotman, *Génération*, ii: *Les Années de poudre* (Paris: Seuil, 1987), pp. 645–7.

Jews. For this, among other reasons, the 'Proletarian Left' – the 'Spontanist' wing of the French Maoists – dissolved itself. Some years later the most prominent of its leaders, once a fanatical Marxist-Leninist, returned with equal enthusiasm to his Jewish roots, and founded an ultra-orthodox *yeshiva* in Strasbourg where he was joined by many of his former comrades, including some non-Jews who had converted to Judaism.

The other reason for the profound change in the aspect of French Judaism during the 1960s was the massive influx of Jews from Algeria, Tunisia and Morocco. These people had been nurtured in a different tradition and were rather looked down upon by their Ashkenazi co-religionists. Most of them had remained faithful to various forms of observance of the Law, though they also contained some secularized elites whose Jewishness was nominal. From the 1970s onwards, leadership of the French Jewish community, in both religious and secular matters, passed steadily into the hands of Sephardic Jews. They became the spokesmen for fresh immigrants, who looked to communal solidarity and continued religious observance when trying to negotiate a place for themselves in French society, and to reaffirm an identity that would survive uprooting from North Africa and transplanting on to French soil.

The identity problem took a different form for most of the Ashkenazim, who had been settled in France for several decades. The young Jews, mostly of European origin, who contributed to (or directed) the events of 1968 did not act as representatives of a community, but as individuals working alongside their comrades of all shades of belief, in the great revolutionary utopia. During the 1970s and 1980s the movements for communal re-Judaization consisted mainly of young Sephardim, though a small number of re-Judaized Ashkenazi intellectuals did attract the attention of the media.

In Israel too, structural changes occurred during the 1960s which prepared the way for the burgeoning of religious movements during the following decade. As in France, the growing numbers of Sephardic Jews altered the balance of society. And the 1967 war, in which the Israelis gained control of the most important Bible lands, allowed a redefinition of the ideological frontiers between the State of Israel and the Land of Israel, bringing religious groups and parties into greater prominence.

Generally speaking, Jews from the Arab countries (mainly Morocco, the Yemen and Iraq) were much less in tune with late twentieth-century secular modernism than their compatriots from Europe or America. This divide affected Jews from Morocco, whose elites tended to settle in France or Canada, whereas most of those who emigrated to Israel came from rural villages or from the *mellahs*, traditional Jewish quarters in the medinas in which the poorer Jewish inhabitants lived, hardly touched by French culture.

On arrival in Israel these immigrants would be sent mainly to the 'development towns', cheap settlements scattered around in areas where the state wanted to establish a Jewish presence for reasons of national defence, and to spread the population evenly over the country and relieve the pressure on Jerusalem, Tel-Aviv and Haifa. These settlements had little to recommend them, and only Israelis too poor to move on stayed in them; from the early 1960s onwards they contained 'a high proportion of Jews who had come from Arab countries and were in a low socio-economic category.'[24]

The disparity between the residents in these towns and the dominant Ashkenazi society was also reflected in their respective world views. The Ashkenazi religious leaders, heirs and guardians of sophisticated doctrinal elaborations and scriptural traditions, looked askance at this Judaism with its antiquated dry observance, encrusted with 'superstitions' and beliefs that struck them as suspect or heterodox. Set against it was a culturally very secularized society with interspersed nuclei of orthodox *haredim*, who carried on without making any great political impact on society at large, but controlled a large network of religious education.

---

24   Eyal Ben-Ari and Yoram Bilu, 'Saints' sanctuaries in Israeli development towns: on a mechanism of urban transformation', *Urban Anthropology*, 16, 2 (1987), p. 249. This article contains a critical bibliography of published works on Israeli development towns.

154   *The Revenge of God*

Year One of the Redemption

The war of June 1967 severely disrupted this cultural equilibrium, even though its effects did not become apparent until the following decade. At the beginning Israel was insecure and riven with anxiety: the Arab states and the PLO were vying with one another to predict her imminent destruction, and the blue helmets of the UN had been withdrawn from her frontiers. Only six days later she was gazing with astonished euphoria at the extent of her military success. The West Bank, Sinai and the Golan Heights were occupied and the Arab armies were routed. Even though it was the armed forces of a secular state that had won the victory, it brought out a spectrum of religious values that had been obscured by Zionist nationalism.

In the first place, the frontiers of the territories controlled by the state of Israel now more or less coincided with those of the biblical Promised Land. 'The symbolism of returning to "the land" existed on the plane of the tangible, physical return to treasured landmarks and longed-for vistas as well as the conceptual – re-establishing the connection with the spiritual and cultural associations of the land. [. . .] The Six Day War seemed, then, to be the pivotal moment in the path that led from Israeliness to Jewishness.'[25] Observers did not at first fully grasp the extent of this change, even though there were many symbolic signs of its importance, such as the photographs of Israeli airborne troops in tears before the Wailing Wall that they had just recaptured, or Ben Gurion wearing a *kippa* (skullcap) at the same place, or the statement by Moshe Dayan, then Defence Minister: 'Whoever was not religious became religious today.'[26] It was a feeling of shock, which progressively changed ideas of what it was to be Jewish, both in Israel and in the diaspora. But only one group began straight away to make it explicit and turn it into an ideological model. They were the disciples of Rav Kook.

Rav (rabbi) Avraham Yitzhak Hacohen Kook (1865–1935), the

25   Gideon Aran, 'A mystico-messianic interpretation of modern Israeli history: the Six-Day War as a key event in the development of the original religious culture of Gush Emunim', *Studies in Contemporary Jewry*, 4 (1988), pp. 263–4.
26   Quoted in Danzger, op. cit., pp. 78–9.

first Ashkenazi Chief Rabbi of Palestine at the time of the British mandate, was the first 'master trained in the orthodox tradition of the *yeshivoth* of Central Europe to turn away from the rejection of political Zionism espoused by that tradition.'[27] Rav Kook went against the dominant orthodoxy, which abhorred Zionism as a Jewish version of the secular nationalism born of Enlightenment thought and the French Revolution. In an original work he set out to marry 'divine idea and national sentiment', aspiring 'to make this union exist not only in the illumination of the wilderness but also in political structures and in history.'[28] This union, which was dubbed 'religious Zionism', was to find its ideal embodiment in the State of Israel, which the rav was destined never to see, for he died thirteen years before it was established.

It fell to his son, Rav Zvi Yehuda Kook (who died in 1982), to become the interpreter of his father's ideas in the context of the new state. He held that, however irreligious the Zionists might be, they were the unwitting bearers of a messianic redemption, and that the state of Israel was the unconscious instrument of the divine will. Before the Six Day War the influence of this idiosyncratic political eschatology was slight. But it did provide a framework for a 'transcendent' interpretation of the victory of June 1967 and of the territorial gains that had brought the new frontiers of the Israeli state more or less into line with those of the biblical Promised Land. In mid-May 1967 Rav Zvi Yehuda Kook had indeed spoken the following words, which were later held to be prophetic: '"They divided up my land." Yes – this is true. Where is our Hebron? Do we let it be forgotten? And where are our Shechem [Nablus] and our Jericho? Where are they? Can we ever forsake them? All of Transjordan – it is ours. Every single inch, every square foot . . . belongs to the Land of Israel. Do we have the right to give up even one millimeter?'[29]

Three weeks later those cities had been conquered, together with the Old City of Jerusalem and most of biblical Israel. For Rav Zvi Yehuda Kook and his disciples the army of the secular

---

27 Henri Atlan, 'Etat et religion dans la pensée politique du Rav Kook', in *Colloque des intellectuels juifs de langue française: Israel, le Judaisme et l'Europe, données et débats* (Paris: Gallimard, 'Idées' series, 1984) p. 32.
28 Ibid., pp. 43 and 45.
29 Quoted by Aran, op. cit., p. 268.

Zionist state, while pursuing its own purely military objectives, had unknowingly been carrying out a divine plan to bring the frontiers of the state into line with those of the Promised Land. Kook's followers decided that 1967 was Year One of the era of Redemption. But they had to wait until the aftermath of the war of October 1973, which plunged Israel into trauma and confusion, before their world view broke out of the restricted circle of the rav's disciples and achieved a high profile in society. For 1973 saw the birth of Gush Emunim.

The strategy of faith

In the Jewish world, just as in Islam and Christendom, the 1960s gave birth to the ideology of the movements of religious reaffirmation that were to take organizational shape during the following decade. Rav Kook made his prophecy shortly after Sayyid Qutb, in an Egyptian concentration camp, had elaborated a view of the contemporary world dominated by the *jahiliyya* (barbarism), which should be destroyed by Islamist militants. In Italy Father Giussani's followers were trying to delineate the 'communion' of Catholics that would lead to Christian 'liberation'. But it seemed that everywhere these newborn doctrinal constructions were destined to be swept away by the upheavals of 1968 and their multifarious repercussions among student youth the world over. Everyone wanted to change society, but nothing could have seemed more antiquated or reactionary than to seek inspiration for doing so in a hard-line interpretation of the Holy Scriptures. After 1973 it was a different story.

The Arab–Israeli war which broke out in October of that year did a good deal to bring down the 'progressive' utopias and encourage politico-religious movements. Naturally its first direct impact was on the combatants, but then, by pushing up the price of oil, it started the upward spiral in the prices of raw materials that was to continue for the rest of the decade. And widespread inflation, coupled with a massive rise in unemployment, forced industries worldwide to restructure in a way that disrupted the economic equilibrium set up during the booming 1960s.

That led to unexpected social traumas, putting strains on social security systems and on working-class self-help networks. In Italy this decay in the social fabric favoured the growth of a movement such as Communion and Liberation, with its mission to create new systems of mutual help and charity, based on a renewal of Catholic observance. In the Muslim world the oil dividends induced inflation and brought people crowding from the country-side into the city suburbs, fit breeding grounds for re-Islamization movements. In Israel the consequences of psychological defeat by the Arabs were felt before the longer-term economic effects; it was not long before they brought out re-Judaization movements that had worked out or adapted their doctrinal bases at the end of the 1960s.

Ten years of Gush Emunim (1974–84)

On 6 October 1973 the Egyptian army effected a surprise crossing of the Suez Canal, broke through the Israeli defences on the Bar-Lev line and penetrated into occupied Sinai, while the Syrian army did the same on the Golan Heights. It was some days before the Jewish state, whose inhabitants were celebrating the feast of Yom Kippur, was able to react. Israeli pride was wounded, even though militarily the counter-offensive was a success. Israeli troops recrossed the Suez Canal and did not halt their advance until they were within 101 kilometres of Cairo. The pro-Israeli Western powers had to exert decisive pressure to impose a cease-fire.

In Israel the postwar sagging of morale led to radical criticism of the Labour government that had held power since the state was founded in 1948, against a background of constant pressure by the United States to make territorial concessions to the Arabs in exchange for peace. Out of this lamentable confusion came Gush Emunim, with a vision of the future of Israel that claimed to supersede secular Zionism by substituting the biblical concept of the Land of Israel (*Eretz Yisrael*) for the State of Israel.

Evidently Gush Emunim would not countenance the exchange of one inalienable inch of this land (which belonged to the Jews for all eternity by virtue of the covenant made between God and the Chosen People) for a treaty that was bound to be valueless in any case, since it was made with non-Jews. In pursuit of its own ends, Gush began to establish wildcat settlements in the occupied territories: a policy of *fait accompli*. It was trying to put direct pressure on the goverment, compelling it to pursue a policy of 're-Judaization from above'. They could start immediately by annexing the Occupied Territories and turning Israel into a state well and truly governed by the *Halakah* (Jewish law). That would lead by degrees to Redemption.

Gush was formed in February 1974, a few months after the October war. A group of Rav Zvi Yehuda Kook's disciples met together south of Bethlehem, at Kfar Etzion on the Jerusalem–Hebron road. This place is highly symbolic; it is a Jewish settlement dating from the Palestinian Yishuv, conquered by the Arab Legion in 1948 and then retaken by Israel in 1967; thus it symbolizes both the fragility of the Jewish presence, at the mercy of the Arab armies, and the will to resist them. For the founders of Gush, as for the average Israeli, Kfar Etzion is 'not negotiable'. As far as Gush is concerned the same applies to all the Occupied Territories.

The founders of Gush shared in a larger common culture, of which their movement was the most radical expression. They had their being within that wider culture, and it was to ensure them support, sympathy and even tacit assistance from various parts of the state political machine and the higher reaches of goverment, especially after the victory of Menachem Begin's Likud Party at the 1977 elections. Ashkenazis almost to a man, many of the first Gush militants were Sabras (native-born Israelis), educated in the network of schools controlled by the National Religious Party. This party, an indispensable member of every coalition since the state was founded, had succeeded in preserving a system of independent education which 'created very demanding standards of living and conduct for a quarter of the school population [. . .] Around this system was built an all-embracing life ethic, the effects of which were felt not only in the synagogue and the home, but also in nursery school, in the *ulpanah* or the *yeshiva* [the religious college for girls, or boys].'[30]

For the secular Zionists, in power under a Labour prime minister from 1948 to 1977, independent religious education was the price

---

30   Ehud Sprinzak, 'The iceberg model of political extremism', in *The Impact of Gush Emunim: Politics and Settlement in the West Bank*, ed. David Newman (London: Croom Helm, 1985), p. 37.

that had to be paid, under proportional representation, for the electoral alliance with the National Religious Party, though the latter was quite flexible in its other political demands. This flexibility, and the involvement of the party in the political manoeuvres inseparable from coalition governments, proved distasteful to many young people, educated in the religious schools, who belonged to a faction of the NRP called the *tzeirim* (the young ones). 'Though they favoured a more open affirmation of the identity of Zionism and religion, they were also "in favour" of the greater involvement of religion in social and political life.'[31] These were the founders of Gush, and in Rav Kook they found an intellectual leader who had no ties with the political establishment.

Also at that time, and in order to consummate the marriage between 'divine idea and national sentiment' proposed by Rav Kook senior, they prevailed upon the army to set up the system of *yeshivoth hesder*, under which young religious zionists were able to divide their period of military service between the barracks and the *yeshiva*. Hence the emblem of Israel in the 1970s: a soldier in battledress, with a *kippa* on his head and *tefillin* (rolled bands) around his arms, in the act of saying his prayers.

There was an equivalent way of dressing in civilian life, the 'knitted skullcap culture'. Unlike secular Jews who went bareheaded, and the ultra-orthodox who wore the black coat, Lithuanian fashion, and black hats, fur bonnets or *yarmulka* of black fabric, the Knitted Skullcap People adopted a mixed 'pioneer/religious' look. They wore sneakers, jeans or shorts, a T-shirt or heavy pullover from which the *tzizit*, the fringes of the prayer shawl, dangled ostentatiously, and their head-dress was a multicoloured knitted *kippa* reminiscent of the 'baba cool' look of the 1970s.

This hybrid outfit (paralleled by a language which was a rich mixture of the pious and the trivial) had a dual connotation. Firstly, it assigned its wearers to the pioneer tradition of the founding Zionists (now grown old and respectable), whose torch they handed on in their own fashion. But also, beyond the specifically Israeli reference, the juxtaposition of jeans and skullcap was their way of saying what Iranian and Sunni Islamists were also

---

31 Alain Dieckhoff, 'Le Goush Emounim: esquisse d'ethnographie politique', *Pardès* (November 1990), p. 95.

saying: that stern religious observance is entirely compatible with full membership of the modern world.

The creation of Gush in February 1974 was the sign that the most radical wing of this singular culture had embarked on independent political activism. Without ever claiming to be a political party in the full sense of the word, or even a structured organization with card-carrying militants, Gush got some of its leaders into the Knesset, representing parties whose ideology was compatible; it made astute use of Israeli politicians while being careful not to sully its 'ideological purity' in the alliances and compromises of government coalitions. Its explicit aim, proclaimed from the outset, was to assert full Israeli sovereignty over the whole of the Land of Israel (*Eretz Yisrael*), which meant first and foremost opposing any retreat by Israel from the Occupied Territories and colonizing them so as to ensure that Jews would dominate them for ever.

Gush appeared in the political arena at a time when Israeli society was in profound disarray. The ruling Labour Party had been caught unawares by the Arab offensive, thus forfeiting the legitimacy it had enjoyed since 1948; it could no longer claim to be the infallible champion of Israel's future. This disarray and confusion encouraged the floating of alternatives to the plans of a government which seemed to have lost the initiative and was under strong international pressure to make territorial concessions.

The founders of Gush reacted against this apparent political defeatism by going on the offensive. They staged a great number of marches and demonstrations in the Occupied Territories, thereby attracting to their movement some of the students in the Zionist religious schools. They played an active part in the Jewish coloniz-ation of 'Judaea-Samaria', concentrating particularly on the Elon Moreh settlement near Nablus, from which they were expelled eight times by the army before being left to settle there for good in December 1976.

The first attempts at colonization by Jews in the Occupied Territories had begun just after the 1967 war, in Hebron. Militants led by Rabbi Moshe Levinger occupied a hotel in order to stake the claim of Jews to this city, once home to a Jewish community which was massacred in 1929.[32] In 1970 a new Jewish city,

32   For a partisan account of the occupation of the Park Hotel at Hebron and the settlement attempts at Elon Moreh, see in particular Haggai Segal, *Dear Brothers: the West Bank Jewish Underground* (Jerusalem: Beit-Shamai, 1988), chaps 2 and 3.

Kiriath Arba, arose nearby, and its settlers gave strong support to Gush and to other ultra-nationalist and annexationist parties and movements. But before Menachem Begin's Likud Party won the May 1977 elections there were very few such settlements, and the Labour government put as many obstacles in their way as it could.

After that date, it was the prime minister himself who came to confer state legitimation on Gush's settlement policy. One of Begin's first actions after coming to power was solemnly to declare: 'We shall have many more Elon Morehs.' He said it at Elon Moreh.

Even though Likud's policy proved far more inconsistent than that declaration implied,[33] nevertheless Gush had succeeded, barely three years after its foundation, in achieving one of the aims of its strategy of 're-Judaization from above'. Pressure on the government had induced the state to ratify the colonization of 'Judaea-Samaria', and to the disciples of Rav Kook this was part of a process of annexation which was the prelude to the Redemption of Israel. But the honeymoon between Gush and Begin did not last. The militants saw the visit by Sadat to Jerusalem in the autumn of 1977, followed by the Camp David accord and then by the 1979 peace treaty, as capitulation to the demands of the *goyim*.

They regarded the withdrawal from Sinai, which was returned to Egypt under the terms of the treaty, as a negation of the plan to establish Jewish domination over the whole of *Eretz Yisrael*; according to their reading of the biblical text, its frontier should be 'the river of Egypt' – though it was not clear whether this meant the Nile or the Wadi al Arish, a coastal wadi nearer to Israel. Gush, together with other radical ultra-nationalist groups, took part in the 'Movement to halt the retreat from Sinai'. The high noon of opposition to the Israeli withdrawal came in April 1982, when thousands of militants gathered in the town of Yamit as a deliberate provocation to the army, who expelled them.

---

33 For settlement of the Occupied Territories on the West Bank and the part played by Gush Emunim, see especially Meron Benvenisti, *The West Bank Data Project: a Survey of Israel's Policy* (American Enterprise Institute, 1984, 1986) *passim*, and David Newman, op. cit., chaps 3 and 8 to 14.

Pressure on the state and attempts to stir up Israeli public opinion against the withdrawal from Sinai were both unavailing, and marked the practical limits to the strategy of 're-Judaization from above'.

It was at this time that Rav Zvi Yehuda Kook, the spiritual leader of Gush, died, depriving the movement of its leader at a critical time when it had suffered reverses and was uncertain of its future policy.

Transition to terrorism

Such uncertainties were ominous – the more so as Gush's lack of a strong central organization made it vulnerable to ill-coordinated action by individuals. In 1980 some of its leaders did indeed turn to violent activism, taking the law into their own hands because they thought the government was too 'soft' in dealing with the Palestinian problem.

At Hebron, for instance, the Jewish settlers planted by Gush in the centre of the Arab town were a provocation to many Palestinians, and armed settlers in the streets were a perfect target for terrorists. On 2 May 1980 a group of militants leaving the synagogue were attacked with grenades and sub-machine guns, leaving six of them dead. The authorities reacted by deporting three Arab leaders to Lebanon; but this did not satisfy some Gush activists, who decided to booby-trap cars belonging to the Palestinian mayors whom they held responsible for anti-Israeli agitation. One month after the Hebron murders, the mayor of Nablus, Bassam Chak'a, and his colleague from Ramallah, Karim Halaf, were seriously injured when their vehicles were blown up.

These Gush extremists fought terror with terror, rather like the OAS in Algeria. In substituting their own violence for that of a state which they held to be failing in its duty, they claimed to be expressing the will of Israeli society – as was emphasized in an apologia by one of the members of this nascent 'Jewish underground'. The author was at pains to show the approval with which, he claimed, counter-terror was regarded both by the average Israeli and in government circles. When news of the attack on the mayors was broadcast on the radio, he had heard an ordinary housewife crying: 'I would kiss their [the bombers'] hands.' As for the military governor of the Occupied Territories, he was alleged to have regretted that the victims had been only hurt, not killed. And at Nablus the Arab population had lived in fear since the bombings – which was the result intended. Begin, on the other hand, reacted with the caution of a true politician: he deplored the resort to violence and ordered an enquiry, which led nowhere.[34]

The fact that those involved were not punished and that the operation was a practical success helped to lift the taboo on armed violence. From then onwards some of the leaders of Gush had no further hesitation in taking direct action when they judged it to be necessary.

The counter-terrorists stepped up their operations in 1983, amid the tension caused by the Israeli invasion of Lebanon. They even struck at the heart of Israel itself with the assassination of Emile Gruenzweig, a young Jew demonstrating against the war under the banners of the left-wing group Peace Now, who was killed by a hand-grenade. But this spilling of Jewish blood led to furious arguments between two founder members: Yoel Bin-Nun complained that Gush had opened the door to indiscriminate political killings, but Rabbi Moshe Levinger, leader of the Hebron settlers, was all for counter-terrorism.

After that, armed violence was used only against Palestinians. The murder of a young settler, a *yeshiva* student, who was stabbed to death by Arabs in the Hebron market in July 1983, provided a fresh opportunity for using it. A few days later three people were killed and several dozen injured in an attack carried out at the Islamic university in Hebron by underground Jewish militants. In early 1984 there were a number of attacks on Israeli buses; Gush mounted a large-scale operation to plant bombs on five Arab buses, timed to explode when the vehicles would be crammed full. A massacre was averted by the Israeli secret service, who arrested the Jewish terrorists just as they were planting the charges.

Fireworks for the Messiah

The breakup of the underground network and the interrogation of the suspects alerted the public to the existence of a different

34 Segal, op. cit., pp. 114–17.

kind of conspiracy, the plan to dynamite the mosques on the Temple Mount in Jerusalem. Some experts at the Harvard Center for International Affairs believe that, if executed, it might have started a third world war. In fact, Gideon Aran, an Israeli academic with an incomparable inside knowledge of Gush, remarked that the conspirators had actually envisaged such an outcome:

> The heads of the Underground estimated that the bombing of the 'abomination' would arouse hundreds of millions of Muslims to a *Jihad*, sweeping all mankind into an ultimate confrontation. This they interpreted as the War of Gog and Magog, with cosmic implications. Israel's victorious emergence from this longed-for trial by fire would then pave the way for the coming of the Messiah.[35]

This operation took the logic of re-Judaization 'from above' beyond counter-terrorism into a new dimension. It was no longer a question of pre-empting a government over-eager to compromise the principle of Jewish domination over the whole of *Eretz Yisrael*; now the objective was to hasten the transmutation of this secular Zionist state into the Kingdom of Israel, bearer of the redemption of mankind.

The idea of blowing up the mosques on the Temple Mount had been canvassed in certain restricted religious circles ever since the Israelis had retaken the Old City of Jerusalem in 1967. The chief rabbi of the Israeli army had called for the 'cleansing' of the area but Moshe Dayan, at that time Minister of Defence, would not hear of it.[36] Nearly all the orthodox *yeshivoth* and the leading Israeli rabbis took the view that the *halakah*, the Jewish law, forbade Jews to go on to the Temple Mount before the return of the Messiah. Therefore they felt no urgency about getting rid of the mosques that had been built on it. Nor did the founders of Gush in 1974 pay much attention to this objective; they were obsessed with settling the Occupied Territories. Only when peace talks were begun with Egypt, in 1977, did bitter disillusionment with the State of Israel and the Begin government begin to fester among

---

35 Gideon Aran, 'Jewish Zionist fundamentalism: the bloc of the faithful in Israel (Gush Emunim)', unpublished communication, fol. 5.
36 Segal, op. cit., p. 52.

them. It engendered the idea of taking more radical measures, giving an irreversible thrust to the process of re-Judaization.

Rav Kook had thought that the secular Zionist state, despite its impiety, was unconsciously fulfilling God's purpose. Was it still carrying out that mission now that it was preparing to sign a peace treaty with Egypt involving withdrawal from Sinai, part of the land promised to the Chosen People? Should it not be stopped from signing that treaty, at all costs? Perhaps it was time to do something much more spectacular than establishing more or less illegal settlements on the West Bank, something which would make peace with the Arabs, and territorial concessions, forever impossible.

There was one man who had come to this view by himself, in prison: Shabtai Ben-Dov. A veteran of the Palestinian Yishuv, this self-taught soldier had made use of his six years spent in British prisons to slake an insatiable thirst for knowledge and to learn the principal European languages. Devouring works on history, psychology and political economy as well as the classics, he boasted of having 'integrated the contradictory influences of Freud, Nietzsche and Marx into a unitary world view that conformed with my basic conception of the complete redemption of Israel as an absolute imperative implanted in my soul from the very beginning.'

After his release he studied law, but became convinced of the vanity of worldly knowledge when, one day, he met an eight-year-old child carrying his Talmud back home from school. He commented: 'I – erudite by my own definition – was unable to read even a single page of the Talmud alone. Then and there I decided to take action and catch up with that boy.' He immersed himself in the Torah; later, after his day's work as a government clerk, he would spend his evenings composing long articles which circulated only among his close associates. In them he described the ways of redemption for the Jewish people, a redemption which would be realized when the Kingdom of Israel was reborn, sovereign over the whole of the Promised Land.

Though he read the works of Rav Kook senior, he differed from the latter in believing that the Zionist state would have to be confronted before it could be superseded: 'It will not be the laws of the State themselves that determine for us what we may and may not do in our revolutionary struggle against the State, but rather the Torah of Israel and the consciousness of national responsibility which devolves on us. This will determine the extent to which we recognize the laws of the State.'[37]

When peace negotiations were started between Israel and Egypt, Ben-Dov thought it was more necessary than ever to find a catalyst for the dynamics of redemption, even if this involved a head-on collision with the Zionist state.

During this period some Gush activists, caught unprepared by the negotiations, were looking for a form of action more radical than simply continuing to create settlements in the Occupied Territories. One of them, Yehuda Etzion, came across Ben-Dov's writings and, in conversation with the author, reached the conclusion that the catalyst they were looking for was to 'cleanse the abominations' on the Temple Mount. It seems that when Ben-Dov died, in 1979, he had given his approval to this action.

Etzion soon co-opted an army officer and a mechanical engineer, both well versed in the Torah, and they formed a small group of conspirators; before going into action, they tried to win the backing of a leading rabbi. When Rav Zvi Yehuda Kook was consulted on the principle of the plan he would not commit himself, and the conspirators interpreted this as 'not disapproving'. But no well-known rabbi, either in the Kook movement or among the orthodox, was found who would give his blessing to the project; most of them held that the building of the Third Temple was not to be a human undertaking, but would happen of itself with the Redemption of the Chosen People and the return of the Messiah; there was therefore no need to 'cleanse' the Temple Mount beforehand. The conspirators did not share this eschatological outlook; as they saw it, blowing up the mosques would reopen hostilities with the Arabs and put a stop to the peace process, and that would set the Zionist state once more on the path that would lead inevitably to its transformation into the Kingdom of Israel and to Redemption.

The project was temporarily shelved when two of its originators took part in the attempt on the lives of the Palestinian mayors.

---

37   Ibid., pp. 47–9. The quotations from Ben-Dov are as given in that book.

Then the conspirators were joined by others, among them a French intellectual called Dan Be'eri, a former Protestant who had converted to Judaism. His life story throws considerable light upon the process whereby the strategy of re-Judaization 'from above' can be carried to extremes.

In his youth Dan Be'eri, whose parents were teachers, was in contact with ministers of the Reformed (Calvinist) Church in the Cevennes, and they made a deep impression on him. As an adolescent in the early 1960s he wanted to become a pastor, but his concern for social justice also led him to join the communist students' union. He developed an interest in the history of religion. His academic brilliance earned him a place at the prestigious Lycée Louis-le Grand in Paris, the nursery for top university students and the royal road to the Ecole Normale Supérieure.

He arrived at Louis-le-Grand with the 1964 intake, which also included a high proportion of the future Maoist leaders of May '68. But what most bewildered the young Protestant was the remorselessly competitive atmosphere, among both those who were 'agin the system' and those who wanted to get to the top no matter how; and he found nobody with whom to share his spiritual quest. He dropped out in mid-term and, with a view to learning biblical Hebrew, registered with the Jewish Agency to go to Israel, intending to gain access to the ancient tongue via a mastery of modern Hebrew. The Israelis looked on him somewhat askance, wondering what on earth this non-Jew was up to; eventually he joined a kibbutz, learnt Hebrew, and felt at home in the Holy Land. When he returned to France a year later he was quite out of his element, for he felt that his identity was Israeli, even though he was still a Christian by religion. But, even in his search for primitive Christianity, he was disillusioned: for it seemed to him that when Saint Paul had rejected the idea of the Chosen People and tried to abolish the differences between Israel and other nations, Christianity had become anti-semitic. At that point he renounced Christianity, and he returned to Israel after the June 1967 war.

In 1969, as a 26-year-old student at the Hebrew University in Jerusalem, he decided to convert to Judaism. He was rejected so unceremoniously that he was quite upset. But he persisted with his intention and was guided to Rav Kook's *yeshiva*, Markaz Ha-

Rav, through the good offices of Leon Ashkenazi – 'Manitou' – a French Jew who did a lot to turn Jewish left-wingers back to their roots. Immersing himself in the Torah, which he studied in the *yeshiva* while earning his living by writing out scrolls (of the Torah), Dan Be'eri married and started a family which grew to nine children. In the evenings he studied the Kabbalah and the Zohar under a master, and he completed his studies at the *yeshiva* at the time of the October 1973 war.

After that he devoted himself to teaching; he founded a *talmud-torah* – a religious school for children – in 1978 at Kiriath Arba, a Jewish settlement near Hebron. He joined Gush Emunim as soon as it started trying to form a settlement at Elon Moreh, in 1976. When he was contacted by the small group of conspirators who were planning to blow up the mosques on the Temple Mount, he joined in the plot with gusto. He dismissed the scruples of those who had been vainly trying to secure the approval of a rabbi, having reached his own conclusions after studying sacred texts which he considered himself to know sufficiently well.[38]

The conspirators shared out the preparatory work; they carried out surveys of the places to be dynamited, noted how and when they were occupied, tried to disable the security systems, and got together the explosives to be planted on D-day. But some of them had qualms about actually perpetrating the act: the evacuation of Yamit in 1982, forerunner of the withdrawal from Sinai, aroused no protest, and this made them doubt whether public opinion would support their action. So the project was shelved despite the advanced state it had reached. The conspirators were discovered and arrested, but not until April 1984, after the enquiry into the murder of Palestinians by the network of Jewish counter-terrorists – some of whom were also in the Temple plot.

Teach yourself the Scriptures

There are some striking ideological and socio-cultural similarities between those Jewish conspirators and the group that assassinated Sadat in October 1981. Both were part of a process of re-Judaization

---

38   Interview with Dan Be'eri at Kiriath Arba on March 1990, and Segal, op. cit., pp. 70–3 and 136.

or re-Islamization from above taken to extremes – violence against a symbolic target with the object of precipitating a change in the state. The Jews were trying to get back on the road to Redemption and the Kingdom of Israel, while the Muslims wanted to build the Islamic state on the ruins of the ungodly society, the *jahiliyya*. In both cases those who master-minded the operation were hybrid intellectuals who had first had a secular education, in many cases a technical one, and had then acquired a smattering of religious knowledge, while retaining the conceptual tools they had already acquired. The manifesto of the group that assassinated Sadat, a collage of quotations from medieval Muslim authors and the sacred books of Islam calling for the execution of the 'apostate' ruler, was produced by an electrical engineer. The essays of Shabtai Ben-Dov, looking for a 'catalyst' for the process of Redemption, also come from the pen of an autodidact who boasted that he had made his personal synthesis of the major twentieth-century authors before 'immersing himself in the Torah'.

The conspirators who thought that blowing up the Temple Mount would be a sufficient 'catalyst' had all received a secular education which gave them the assurance to look in Scripture for the justification of their actions. But it was Dan Be'eri, the ex-Protestant and product of an elite French education, who was most confident about by-passing the rabbis.

The Muslim and Jewish religious authorities reacted in the same way to the discovery of the plots: they dissociated themselves, as doctors of the law, the authentic, qualified exegetes of the sacred texts, from the conspirators. They explained that the plotters had perverted the scriptures and their canonical exegesis by manipulating them improperly in order to justify their crimes; the plotters had no right to make their own interpretations of the word of God and the corpus of law derived from it. In Cairo Sheikh Kishk, a ulema with Islamist sympathies, lashed out *ex cathedra* against the 'intellectual fledgelings' who had gone to the Book without professor or sheikh and pronounced final judgements after reading three pages of some medieval author.[39] In Jerusalem Yonatan Blass, one of the rabbis connected with Rav Kook's *yeshiva*, spoke

---

39 See above, chap. 1, and Gilles Kepel, *The Prophet and Pharaoh*, op. cit., chap. 4.

in the same vein, castigating the arrogance of conspirators who imagined that 'the truth has been revealed only to us, and not to the great scholars of Jewish law and thought in this and previous generations'.[40]

The discovery and foiling of the Temple Mount conspiracy was a setback for the movement for 're-Judaization from above' which centred on Gush Emunim – although the actual conspirators were almost negligible in number compared with the whole movement, whose membership is estimated at 50,000, most of them resident in the Occupied Territories.[41] Subjected to violent attacks both from the left and from secular milieux, and reprobated by the orthodox, the Gush militants for a time fell back on social activity among their supporters, and to some extent resumed tactics of re-Judaization 'from below' which had been relegated to the background at the height of their political activities.

Gush sympathizers tended to have large families, much larger than those of secular Israelis; and the need to educate this new and prolific generation of Emunists turned the attention of many militants towards the creation of educational establishments designed to perpetuate their unique culture.

Year: 1990; scene: Beit Hadassa, the most 'hard-line' of the Gush settlements, in the heart of the Arab town of Hebron. A block of houses surrounded by barbed wire and patrolled by guards armed with sub-machine guns. The cries of children at play in the kindergarten. In the settlement leader's apartment, between the shelves holding scrolls of the Torah and the photographs of Rav Kook senior and Rav Kook junior, the youngest child's romper suit has been hung up to dry. Gush, now in a phase of weakness, is tightening the cohesion of its supporters while awaiting the right moment to put the chariot of the Zionist state back on the road to Redemption.

The revival of orthodox Judaism

From the foundation of Gush at Kfar Etzion in 1974 to the arrest of the underground conspirators in 1984, the political and religious

---

40 Segal, op cit., p. 249.
41 Estimate by Dieckhoff, 'Le Goush', op. cit., p. 92.

outlook of the movement was one element of certainty amid the confusion of Israeli society. After the discovery of the Temple Mount conspiracy, which appalled Israelis, even including some Gush sympathizers, the movement went into neutral and other re-Judaization movements were able to occupy the foreground: these were the *haredim* (orthodox) sects and parties.

Unlike Gush, the *haredim* at first followed a strategy of 're-Judaization from below', which led their followers, in Israel and in the diaspora, to break with the surrounding society in daily living and to live in communal ghettos. But after going their own way for a time, some of them began to flex their muscles, and burst into the political arena. They were to exercise a decisive influence in the State of Israel in 1990, controlling government coalitions and forcing acceptance of their demands for the application of Jewish law in public affairs (not to mention cash in hand).

At the beginning of the 1980s the *haredim* came out of the wilderness, and many of their supporters, old and new, regarded the resurrection as miraculous. For the Nazi extermination of Jews in Europe had destroyed the traditional centres of orthodox Judaism, from Lithuania and Poland to Bessarabia. In the aftermath of the Second World War the Zionists pointed an accusing finger at the anti-Zionist orthodox rabbis of Central Europe, to whom they attributed a heavy responsibility for the holocaust. The Zionists claimed that, by forbidding their flocks to emigrate to Palestine and by failing to organize them to resist Hitler's 'final solution', they had made things easy for their executioners, who had only to lead them to the gas chambers 'like lambs to the slaughter'.[42] The Zionists also maintained that this attitude of submission to the Nazis was the inevitable result of the diaspora, which had robbed Jews of their pride and led them into the most humiliating compromises with the non-Jewish society around them.

The symbol of this humiliation was the 'mahyofis Yid', Epinal's image of the 'boot-licking Jew', the buffoon of a Polish aristocrat,

---

42 On the controversy between *haredim* and Zionists with regard to the holocaust, see the article by Menachem Friedmann, 'The haredim and the holocaust', *Jerusalem Quarterly*, 53 (1990), pp. 87–144.

singing sabbath hymns to amuse him and his boon companions. It was in opposition to this image of the grovelling, toadying Jew of the diaspora, fair game for the gas-chambers, that the Zionists created their ideal – the victorious fighter of Israel.

Thus, after the Second World War, the extermination of European Jewry took its place in the Zionist chain of argument that discredited the *haredim* and justified the creation of the State of Israel. This argument had some force at the time, and it was instrumental in marginalizing the *haredim* both in Israel and in the diaspora.

The holocaust as a punishment for Zionism

But from the 1950s onwards a different interpretation of the extermination arose in orthodox circles, in reaction against the Zionist case. According to this argument it was the Zionists who had caused the catastrophe by departing from the traditional attitude of the Jew in exile, which involved seeking compromise with non-Jews. If this attitude had often led Jews to humble themselves before the *goyim* or to buy their goodwill, this did not call for criticism since it had enabled Judaism to survive after the diaspora. It was the enthusiasm of 'emancipated' post-Enlightenment Jews for assimilation, the resentment provoked by their sometimes ostentatious success, and the virulently vocal Zionist opposition to Nazism that had precipitated the backlash of the 'final solution'.

One of the most extreme ultra-orthodox rabbis wrote:

> The Torah warned the Jews to remain totally isolated from the whole way of life of the surrounding peoples [. . .] But the enlightened insist on doing things their own way: only to be like all the gentiles. [. . .] We find that in countries where the Jews have assimilated almost completely among their neighbors [i.e., Germany], they also sustained a terrible blow at their hands.[43]

From this point of view, the extermination was God's punishment of those who transgressed the commandments of the Torah and

---

43 Rabbi Elchanan Wasserman, quoted by Friedmann, op. cit., pp. 108–9.

sought to be like the 'nations', first by assimilation and then by trying to create a Jewish state like all other modern states.

In this way the orthodox ideology turned the Zionist reasoning on its head. Any political initiative by Jews that was not solely motivated by strict observation of the Torah led inevitably to Auschwitz.

Until the end of the 1960s, while the Zionist ideology was in the ascendant and religious movements had little real influence, the orthodox view was definitely out of favour; but in the 1970s the anti-Zionist interpretation began to gain ground as the number of *yeshivoth* and the influence of the *haredim* increased, both inside and outside Israel.

By constructing their own interpretation of the Nazi holocaust, the *haredim* returned to the stage of history. They also wrote the fate of contemporary Jewry into a sacred history guided by God, who relentlessly punishes those who offend against His Law. It was this reading of history that enabled them to forge a link with the younger Jews immersed in a secularized culture. From the 1970s onwards, some of these young Jews began to pass over to orthodoxy by way of *teshuvah* (repentance).

From sect to universal

The world of the *haredim* is a complex one, riddled with internal divisions among rabbis which often prevent them from forming a united front against the various secularized forms of contemporary Judaism. These differences are mirrored in the multiplicity of 'ultra-religious' political parties that have arisen in Israel since the 1980s, and in their differing attitudes to such major questions as the future of the Occupied Territories.

And yet all these movements have a common starting point: they are trying to ensure that the commandments derived from the sacred books, which guarantee the perpetuation of a true Jewish identity and which at so many points distinguish practising Jews from non-practising, or non-Jewish, society, are observed in daily life. In the 1950s this kind of grassroots social monitoring, at the level of the individual, lost its vitality and significance. By seeking to reconstitute it the orthodox are trying to end an interregnum in history, to provide a new basis on which the Judaism of the future can fulfil its destiny.

In the eighteenth century the system of the *kehillot*, the traditional Jewish communities in the diaspora, in which the rabbi was the focus of social and religious control, began to disintegrate under the influence of two opposing forces. On the one hand, the *Haskalah* – the Jewish Enlightenment – brought many European Jews out of the ghetto to become integrated, or even assimilated, with the non-Jewish society around them. This process continued throughout the nineteenth century. But during this same period an extremely vigorous pietist movement, hasidism, began to spread out from among the Polish Jews.

Initiated by Israel Baal Shem Tov (1698–1740), hasidism aimed to renew the relationship between uneducated Jews and the Law and doctrine. It was a reaction to outbreaks of Jewish messianism which had weakened the doctrinal coherence of the Chosen People. Baal Shem Tov's movement was designed to appeal to pious but uneducated Jews through an approach to sacred things that owed more to emotion than to erudition. By bringing the main themes of the Kabbalah up to date and simplifying them, hasidism emphasizes total self-giving to God in a mystical elevation in which expressions of joy, such as singing and dancing, play an essential part.

In contrast to the community rabbi, who is chosen by leading community representatives, selected on account of his learning, and exercises authority over a given geographical area, the hasidic *rebbe*, or 'master', is the charismatic leader of an emotional community of believers brought together by the particular form of their religious expression, regardless of where they live.[44] He acts as mediator between his disciples and God, transmits blessings, treats spiritual and bodily illnesses and gives his disciples the inspired advice that comes to him because of his closeness to God.

In the words of an apologetic history of hasidism: 'There is no evidence that Baal Shem Tov ever received rabbinical ordination. Nature, however, endowed him with qualities that more than compensated for the lack of formal qualifications. He also acquired

---

44   See Menachem Friedmann, 'The changing role of the community rabbinate', *Jerusalem Quarterly*, 25 (1982) pp. 81–2.

a useful knowledge of the healing qualities of various herbs, and people began to come to him for medical advice.'[45]

The hagiographies of the great masters of hasidism, and of other heroes of contemporary Jewish pietism, are litanies of miracles caused by the intercession of the *rebbe*, who can save situations which any rational person would consider irredeemable. Whether in matters of health, employment or money the master's advice, if accompanied by scrupulous observance of the Torah, leads to great blessings for the faithful.[46]

Hasidism is still a very important part of present-day orthodoxy, even though its exaggerated pietism and its unfailing belief in the *rebbe*'s supposedly miraculous links with the divine have caused some adverse reactions. Opposition, founded on a more rigorous scholarly approach to the sacred books, is embodied in the *Mitnaggedim* movement, the other constituent of the orthodox tendency and of opposition to the various Jewish heirs of the Enlightenment.

At the beginning of the twentieth century some of the *haredi* groups set up a federation that enabled them to speak with one voice on the major political questions affecting Jews in the modern world. This organization, founded in 1912, adopted the name Agudat Israel and featured a 'Council of Torah Sages'. It was the first time that hasidic *rebbe* and *yeshiva* masters had worked together to combat Jewish nationalist or socialist ideologies on a 'modern basis' and with their own weapons, the media then available (the press, international conferences, and so on). While continuing with traditional observance, they aimed to break out of the confined space occupied by each sect in Central Europe and work towards a broad formulation of the orthodox position – one that would appeal to young people who at that time were largely uninfluenced by the *haredim*.

Although most of the orthodox rabbis disapproved of emigration to Palestine, fearing that they would be swamped by the well-organized Zionism that was dominant there, some of them went to live either in the Mea Shearim district of Jerusalem or in

---

45   Harry M. Rabinowicz, *Hasidism: the Movement and its Masters* (London: J. Aronson, 1988), p. 32.
46   See, for example, *Le Rabbi de Loubavitch et sa génération*, vols. I and II (Paris: Beth Loubavitch, 1989) or *Baba Salé: la vie du Tsaddik racontée par son serviteur Rav Eliahou Elfassi* (Jerusalem: Gallia, 1986).

settlements they created as enclosed communities in which the Torah would hold undisputed sway. One well-known example was Bnei Brak, near Tel Aviv, founded in 1924 by religious immigrants from Poland. Designed from the outset as an agricultural settlement, in which the land lay fallow every seven years (*shemita*) in accordance with Mosaic law, Bnei Brak rapidly became a showcase for orthodoxy.

Even before the Second World War some very prominent rabbis from Central Europe had gone to live there. One of these was Avraham Karelitz, known as the 'the Hazon Ich', who settled there in 1934; he was followed by some heads of *yeshivot* that had been destroyed by the Nazis, who – unlike most of their disciples – had contrived to escape extermination. Thus the famous *yeshiva* of Poniewitz, in Lithuania, was reconstituted at Bnei Brak; this is the largest of the numerous religious teaching centres in the town, where by 1990 tens of thousands of full-time students were learning the Torah. The most prominent figure is Rav Eliezer Shakh, born in Lithuania in 1898, who arrived in Palestine in 1940 and entered the Poniewitz *yeshiva* in the early 1950s; he subsequently became its head. Shakh is the leading spiritual authority of orthodoxy; his advice is sought on public and private matters from all over the world: 'according to his disciples, there is a growing consensus on his pre-eminence; he is the last witness of a lost generation, the last link with an ancient tradition regarding the destiny of the Jewish people, and it is he who must proclaim the true message of the Torah regarding the great problems of our time.'[47]

The development of Bnei Brak typifies the strategy of the *haredim* since the immediate postwar period, and their ability to adapt to changes in their political environment. During the first twenty years of the state of Israel, from its foundation in 1958 until the Six Day War of June 1967, secular Zionism seemed to hold undisputed sway, and the orthodox rabbis were on the defensive, fighting to preserve their educational system and their community from incursions by the secular state. Thus from 1948 to 1953

---

47   Binyamin Tagger, 'Le Rav Chakh, le "vieil homme" et son mystère' *Kountrass* (*Revue de pensée juive et d'information conçue et pensée à Jerusalem*), 3, 13, p. 33. This issue contains a file on Bnei Brak, from which the information given above is taken.

Agudat Israel belonged to the majority that kept the Ben Gurion government in power, and tried to save what it could. When the prime minister attempted to introduce a uniform system of secular, compulsory education (which would have undermined the *talmud-torahs* and the *yeshivot*), or to bring in conscription (even for girls and *yeshivah* students) the Hazon Ich fought him tooth and nail. The fight continued until Ben Gurion paid a conciliatory visit to the rav at Bnei Brak in 1952. But Agudat left the government majority in the following year, refusing to approve the drafting of girls for military service.

For three decades Agudat had very little influence in the Knesset. On average the religious parties, taken together, obtained between 12 and 15 per cent of the vote at the first eleven elections, held between 1949 and 1984; the religious Zionists of the National Religious Party received the lion's share, leaving only about a third of the total for the anti-Zionists of the Agudat. Throughout this period the *haredim* were struggling to survive, fighting to protect what little space they had and to erect barricades, both symbolic and physical, between themselves and the world outside.

For example, the Neturei Karta, one of the most radical groups within this movement and one which always refused to take part in elections, significantly called its periodical *The Wall*. More concretely, barriers were erected every Friday evening around the Mea Shearim district of Jerusalem, to exclude any vehicular traffic which would violate the *shabbat*. Behind the barriers the process of re-Judaization from below – of a complete break with the customs of the secularized society outside and of strict observance of the *halakah*, the Jewish Law – proceeded at full strength. The orthodox camp was in no hurry to cross them, the more so since the *halakah*, a product of the centuries of diaspora during which Jews had no state, was not really equipped to resolve many questions concerning the organization of a modern state.[48]

---

48 There is a detailed discussion of the opposing views on this subject in Menachem Friedmann, 'L'Etat d'Israel comme dilemme théologique', *Pardès* (November 1990), pp. 15–65, particularly p. 25 and pp. 45–7.

The metastasis of haredism

In the mid-1980s the *haredim* made a triumphal entry on to the
political scene in Israel. Re-Judaization from below had begun to
influence such large communities that it had acquired enough
electoral clout to make the orthodox parties indispensable partners
in any government coalition, given the prevailing system of proportional representation. One such community was the Sephardic
population of Israel, for which it acted as spokesman, giving them
for the first time a voice in institutional politics.

Whereas from 1974 to 1984 Gush Emunim had been the main
champion of the re-Judaization of Israel, it was now the turn of
the *haredim* to be its most highly visible advocates. And while most
followers of Gush were Ashkenazi or Sabra ex-members of the
youth movements in the National Religious Party, and its main
power centres were settlements in the Occupied Territories, the
orthodox drew most of their supporters (including a large contin-
gent of Sephardic Jews) from within the pre-1967 borders.

At the 1988 elections, at which the three *haredi* parties made
their first breakthrough, they drew support not only from the
traditional bastions of orthodoxy such as Bnei Brak, but also from
large development towns such as Netivot, inhabited by impoverished Sephardim. There is a demographic basis for this phenomenon, for it was due to the natural increase of the orthodox
population with its large families closely integrated by the network
of schools: in 1990 Bnei Brak had about 120,000 inhabitants, all
haredim, including some 40,000 schoolchildren in the *talmud-torah*
schools and more than 10,000 students in *yeshivot* and *kolellim*
(training colleges for married men).[49]

In Jerusalem, 'black' Judaism continued its steady growth, both
in the older districts and in the new dormitory suburbs on the
outskirts of the city: one out of every four Jewish inhabitants in
these places was orthodox, and in 1988 the religious parties
received more than 30 per cent of the vote there. Says the historian
Zeev Sternhell: 'That population is growing. Here in Jerusalem
we can see it in everyday life. This means that the orthodox

49   Information taken from *Kountrass*, op. cit., p 16.

require more services, more accommodation, more schools and more public baths. When they come to settle in a district, they completely change its appearance. Some districts which twenty years ago were secular, are now ghettos.'[50]

The success of the *haredim* is also of socio-political significance, for it enables strata of the population that had hitherto remained on the sidelines of the political system to take part in it – or even twist it and try to manipulate its rules to their sole advantage.

It was the elections to the twelfth Knesset on 1 November 1988 that brought the newly won power of orthodoxy from civil society over into parliament. Yet a glance at the figures did not suggest a landslide: 15.3 per cent of the vote and 18 seats out of 120 – a result that had already been obtained several times during the 1960s. But these totals masked a far-reaching change in the religious landscape: the Zionists of the National Religious Party, who had been receiving two-thirds of these votes until the beginning of the 1980s, now had only 26.8 per cent, while the *haredi* share had risen from one-third to 73.2 per cent of the total.[51] And as neither of the two big coalitions – the left, led by Labour, and the right, led by Likud – had an absolute majority, they had to seek support from the *haredim* in order to govern. And the *haredim* drove an extremely hard bargain. Without recognizing the legitimacy of the Zionist state of Israel they traded their support against very substantial government commitments, which enabled them first of all to strengthen their hold over the constantly increasing numbers of their adherents: many subsidies for religious education establishments, a policy on accommodation for 'religious tenants', to name but two. But this process of re-Judaization from below could now be extended to the whole of society, by obliging the secular Zionist government to institute creeping Judaization measures affecting all Jews in Israel. For example, in a draft agreement submitted to the Council of Torah Sages on 4 December 1988 at Bnei Brak, Likud said it 'was prepared to take action against anti-religious propaganda in the media', to accept the

---

50   'Israël: l'isolement ou la paix', debate organized by *Le Journal des élections*, 5 (November/December 1988), p. 48.
51   According to calculations by Menachem Friedmann which he kindly made available to the present author.

definition of Jewish identity 'in accordance with the *halakah*' when establishing the nationality of Jewish converts coming from abroad, and so on.[52]

The orthodox parties were not anxious to wield effective power in a state whose legitimacy they did not recognize; but by controlling parliamentary committees and the private offices of ministers and by getting some of their members into the cabinet they could pursue the process of Judaization from below with enormously increased resources. They had the process financed by the Israeli taxpayer, and set up a plethora of legal safeguards to make it irreversible.

The war of the rabbis

That was the only aim on which all three of the *haredi* parties were in agreement. Their conceptions of orthodoxy, their attitudes with regard to the Arab–Israeli peace process, and the training and origin of the rabbis who were to lead them were all subjects of controversy between them. In November 1988 they drew support from somewhat different sectors of the electorate, thus maximizing the benefits of their disunity. In the lead was the ultra-orthodox Sephardi Shas party which gained six seats, topping up its votes from the Eastern Jews in the development towns; they were followed by Agudat Israel with five seats, mostly Ashkenazi and hasidic; then, with two seats, by Degel Ha Torah, heir to the spirit of the *Mitnaggedim* who were hostile to the intense pietism of the hasidic Jews.

Shas – an acronym for 'Sephardi guardians of the Torah' and a Hebrew term for the six orders of the Mishnah (the oral tradition based on the Torah, the written law) – had already won four seats in 1984. It was formed as the result of a long struggle by Jewish immigrants from Islamic countries to obtain their 'rightful' place in Israeli society, after several attempts at creating a political presence which had systematically stressed the religious aspect, and most of which had ended in failure. Looked down upon by an Ashkenazi Labour establishment that had shaped Zionism to

---

52   See text quoted in Shalom Cohen, *Dieu est un baril de poudre: Israel et ses intégristes*, op. cit., pp. 28–30.

suit its own ends, Sephardim often simply had not bothered to vote. This attitude was punctuated with attempts at rebellion, such as the uprising in the slums of Haifa in 1959, or the creation in 1971 of the Black Panthers, concerned to establish a parallel between their situation and that of the Blacks in the United States. But then many of them had turned to Menachem Begin, ensuring his victory at the polls in 1977; they renewed their confidence in the right-wing parties in 1981 and 1984.[53]

At the same time, these underdogs in secular, socialist Zionist society turned fervently to religion for communal organization, self-help, solidarity, social betterment and a defence of their battered identity. This religious feeling took two main forms. First, there was a symbolic transfer of tombs of the saints, in particular Moroccan ones, to Israel, where they became centres of pilgrimage. Secondly, the faithful gathered around sages (*Hakham*), who were already venerated in the diaspora and who now recovered their role as intercessors with God on behalf of the Sephardim in Israel, who sometimes wondered whether He had abandoned them. The most influential of these 'Masters' was Rav Israel Abuhatzera, known as Baba Salé. He was born in 1890 at Rissani in the Tafilalet (Morocco),[54] chief rabbi of Erfoud since the time of the French protectorate, and his charisma was widely acknowledged in his own country. According to his disciples, he had performed innumerable miracles of the usual type, including last-resort healings when medicine was of no avail. In 1964, when he was sailing from Casablanca to Israel, the raging seas threatened to engulf the ship and everything in it; Baba Salé, who was in his cabin,

> had not noticed anything. He had not even felt the movements of the vessel. The captain begged him to do something. Our master took up his cup [. . .] filled it with wine, blessed it, and then asked his assistant to go up on deck and pour it into the sea in three goes, saying each time 'By the merits of the holy Rabbi Yaacov'.

---

53 See Maurice M. Roumani, 'The Sephardi factor in Israeli politics', *Middle East Journal*, 42, 3 (summer 1988), pp. 423–35. The analyses were made before the 1988 elections.
54 For an 'official' hagiography of Baba Salé, see *Le Saba Kadicha Israel Abihssira*, I, published by his son Rabbi Barukh Abihssira (Netivoth, 1988).

The rav's assistant did exactly as he was told, the miracle took place, and the sea became quite calm.[55]

Although he arrived in the Holy Land with such impressive credentials, it took him some time to consolidate his charismatic following; in 1970 he finally settled in a modest government-subsidized flat in the development town of Netivot, where many immigrants from Morocco lived. His reputation as a miracle-worker made Netivot into a magnet for fervent Jews, so much so that even senior Ashkenazi *rebbe* made the journey to visit Baba Salé and were not ashamed to be photographed in the company of this Sephardi colleague, though his miracle-working pharmacology consisted only of some phials of holy water.[56]

But although Baba Salé continued to dress like a holy man from the Atlas Mountains, in flowing white gandourah and with Turkish slippers, his followers, younger Moroccan Jews who had passed through religious schools in Israel run by Ashkenazi rabbis, adopted the black dress of the latter. If it was paradoxical that the sons of Casablanca and Tunis should adopt the Lithuanian immigré look, it was even more remarkable that status and universality in modern Judaism should be cast in one particular mould, that of Central European orthodoxy – even to learning Yiddish and eating stuffed carp instead of couscous. But though the Sephardi orthodox gave up the gandourah for the black suit and fedora, that did not cause their Ashkenazi fellow students to regard them as equals. It would be a come-down for a religious family of Polish origin to give a daughter, in one of those arranged marriages that were obligatory for *yeshiva* students, to a Bensussan or an Abitbol, one of the despised 'Frenks' – however dazzling his command of the Torah.

The discrimination sensed by Sephardi religious, and their frustration with a party like Agudat Israel that used government subsidies almost exclusively for the benefit of Ashkenazim, provoked the formation of the Eastern, orthodox Shas party in 1984. Together with a Council of Sages of the Torah, all of whose members were Sephardim (a riposte to the Council of Torah Sages,

---

55   Rav Eliahu Elfassi, *Baba Salé: la vie du Tsaddik racontée par son serviteur*, op. cit., p. 34.
56   Ibid., in particular pp. 239–50.

to which only Lithuanians and Poles had ever been admitted), it was placed under the spiritual authority of the Sephardi Grand Rabbi of Israel, Ovadia Yossef. On the conclusion of the campaign full of symbolic gestures, during which Rav Yossef arrived at meetings by helicopter like a messenger from heaven and promised his blessing on all who would vote for Shas, the party made significant gains in the symbolically important town of Netivot, where it received more than a quarter of the votes cast.

But another charismatic rav entered the fray at full tilt, and he too promised a special blessing – for anybody who would vote for Agudat Israel. This was Menachem Mendel Schneerson, known as Rabbi Shlita, grand master of the hasidic movement of Lubavitch. Notwithstanding the reservations expressed by Rav Eliezer Shakh, the strong man of Degel Ha Torah, who denounced this hail of blessings and miracles as a resurgence of heterodox messianism, Agudat won five seats – three more than in 1984.

The entry of the master of the Lubavitch into the Israeli political arena was paradoxical on more than one account. For he was still such an implacable anti-Zionist that he had never set foot in Israel, and it might have seemed that his disciples, who were practising re-Judaization from below with great success all over the world, would not want to get involved in political action. Nevertheless, this recent development in the most dynamic re-Judaization movement of the late twentieth century is symptomatic of the powerful position orthodoxy has now achieved, and of the means it is prepared to use in furthering its ambitions.

'We want Mashiah now!'

The Lubavitch are named after a small village in Russia not far from Smolensk, in which Rabbi Dov Ber, the son and successor of Rabbi Shneor Zalman (1745–1812), went to live in 1813 during the Napoleonic Wars. Like other *rebbe* of the period, Zalman had claimed to be the spiritual and charismatic heir of Baal Shem Tov, who founded hasidism; but Zalman distinguished himself by working out a particular interpretation of the master's teaching. The Lubavitch version of hasidism, HaBaD (from the Hebrew *hokhmah, binah, daat,* meaning wisdom, intelligence, knowledge) is – so its disciples say – unique, in that it requires a personal intellectual effort and is not confined to the sphere of emotion and pietist activism. Ordinary hasidics believe that 'A deep understanding of the Torah can be the province simply of this one just man (the *rebbe*), who, when he studies, accumulates spiritual powers not only for himself but also for all his disciples. Against this, the HaBaD considers that deep understanding should be acquired by everyone. It was Rabbi Shneor Zalman who showed that intellectual analysis and emotion were not mutually exclusive.'[57]

Although the Lubavitch practise what they preach and make use of their intellectual capacities, they, like other hasidics, have a boundless veneration for their *admor* (*A*donenu, *Mo*renu, *R*abbinu; 'our Lord, Master and Teacher'). His pronouncements, under direct divine inspiration, are final, and evince a super-lucidity inaccessible to ordinary disciples. The *admors* of all the hasidic sects are like dynasts, surrounded by a 'court' organized on the lines of the courts of the Baltic and Polish petty nobility of the eighteenth century.

Rabbi Yossef Itzhak (1880–1950), direct lineal descendant of Shneor Zalman, became head of the Lubavitch in 1921. Although his father, Rabbi Rachab (1860–1920), did perforce take part in politics, and opposed Zionism from 1899 onwards, it fell to Yossef Itzhak to lead the sect in its confrontation with bolshevism and then with the Nazi holocaust, and to move its centre to the American continent. His battles with the Soviet authorities were aggravated by the Jewish section of the Communist Party of the USSR, the Yevsektsya, archetypal 'bad Jews' contaminated by the spirit of the Enlightenment even to its logical conclusion in communism. Imprisoned and sentenced on numerous occasions, he was allowed to leave the USSR for Lithuania in 1927, and then in 1934 went to Warsaw. In 1940, fleeing from the Nazis, he arrived in New York and went to live in Brooklyn, and it was from there that this hasidic sect – one of many – was to become, by 1990, the most important of all the movements for re-Judaization on a worldwide scale.

The main credit for this goes to Menachem Schneerson, known as Rabbi Shlita, who has presided over the destiny of the Lubavitch

---

57   Haïm Mellul, 'Introduction', in *'HaBaD Loubavitch: repères et définitions* (Paris: Beth Loubavitch, 1989), p. 7.

since 1950. The son-in-law of his predecessor, born in 1902, he had both training in hasidism and a secular education, graduating from the prestigious Ecole Supérieure d'Electricité in Paris in 1940. In 1941 he joined his father-in-law in Brooklyn and laboured to institutionalize the movement first in the United States, then in Israel, and later on anywhere in the world where Jews were to be found.

Rabbi Shlita was implacably opposed to both 'reform' and 'conservative'[58] Judaism, which was espoused by the majority of American Jews but which he accused of making unacceptable compromises with the values of the surrounding non-Jewish society. His attempt at re-Judaization from below hinged on strict observance of the *mitsvot* (commandments) in their entirety. He made a point of restoring ancient customs that had fallen out of use, and he developed a whole network of schools and attempted to create a complete social environment for children which would separate them from the non-practising Jews, or non-Jews, outside. No Lubavitch fails to light his candles for the feast of Hanukkah or wear *tefillin* (phylacteries rolled around the arm). They are constantly singing (in English) about their expectations of the imminent return of the Messiah, repeating the slogan 'We want Mashiah now', followed by the Hebrew word *mamasch. Mamasch* means 'now', but is also very conveniently the acronym of *Mena*chem *Mendel Sch*neerson, and the disciples are not really discouraged from identifying him with the Messiah. This has called down the wrath of Rav Eliezer Shakh on the Lubavitch, for he sees in them the seeds of a dangerous heterodox idolatry.

Every year the rabbi launches a 'campaign' and sets a particular target for re-Judaization. For example, in 1972 'he created the Committee for the Seventy-one Institutions, with the object of founding seventy-one Torah institutions in the shortest possible time.' In 1980 'he launched a campaign asking children to bring their parents back into the ways of Judaism, in fulfilment of the verse "He shall turn the hearts of the fathers by their sons" [. . .] He asked for processions of children to be organized throughout the world on Lag Baomer day [. . .] He encouraged large families

---

58 See above, p. 148.

and condemned family planning, basing himself on the verse "Go forth and multiply" . . .'[59]

Campaigns of this kind call to mind the preaching methods of the Protestant Evangelicals in the United States; one thinks of Oral Roberts's 'Crusades for Christ' with the objective of 'saving a million souls every year'.[60] Rabbi Shlita also makes much use of audiovisual media, telephone and fax. These allow projects to be tightly controlled from the Brooklyn headquarters at 770 Eastern Parkway, which disciples call simply '770' – a figure with magical virtues. The rabbi, himself an electrical engineer (a qualification similar to that of several other contemporary religious leaders) has succeeded in attracting many engineers, computer scientists, dentists and other young Jews highly qualified in science and technology (with a bias towards the applied sciences) who have done their *teshuvah* (repentance and return to Judaism) in the bosom of the Lubavitch.

Herman Branover, the magnetohydrodynamist whose road to repentance was described at the beginning of this chapter, is an edifying example of this process. There too, as in the case of Evangelical and Islamist science graduates, the point is to show that science and faith are eminently compatible, and that the writing of software or the management of databanks do not invalidate belief in the super-lucidity of Menachem Mendel Schneerson. On the contrary they strengthen it, by giving it the means of wide propagation.

The purpose of this propagation is to strengthen proselytism among Jews, to draw them into the community of the Lubavitch, and then to separate them from the mass of those who are tempted by the values and seductions of the society around them. This separation between practising Jews and those who simply belong is a 'redundancy' (in the etymological sense of 'overflow') of the separation between Israel and the other nations, the specific prohibitions which are the distinguishing mark of the Jew among the nations.[61] This differentiation from the rest of humanity is a very

59   *HaBaD Loubavitch: repères. . .*, op. cit., pp. 58 and 60.
60   See above, chap. 3, pp. 112–13.
61   See Laurence Podselver, 'La séparation, la redondance et l'identité: les hasidim de Lubavitch à Paris', *Pardès*, 3, p. 168.

marked feature of the disciples of Rabbi Shlita. The journal of Lubavitch youth in France explains to its readers: though 'God created the whole universe according to the fundamental division of the four kingdoms – mineral, vegetable, animal and human [. . .] it is written that there exists in reality a fifth kind: *Am Israel*, the Jewish people. [And] the distance separating it from the fourth kind – the whole of the "speaking" human species – is no less than the distance between the human and the animal.'[62] There could be no more explicit way of justifying a rejection of any universal value whatsoever.

Just as the *kosheruth* serves to distinguish between Jews and 'the whole of the speaking species', the *glat-kosher*, a more severe and restrictive *kosheruth* observed by the Lubavitch, maintains an impassable barrier between them and the rest of the Jews. The effect of this food law on new converts – the *baalei teshuvah* – is to distance them very rapidly from the circles in which they were born. As Laurence Podselver observes: 'By refusing family meals, the new disciple as it were causes the ties of kinship to shift into the sphere of the other.'[63] This process is perpetuated by the custom of intermarriage solely within the Lubavitch movement, which strengthens its hold as an emotional community defined by rites of separation from the rest of the world.

This definition of identity by exaggerated ritual and the systematic search for points of differentiation is reminiscent of a pietist Muslim group, the Tabligh.[64] In order to protect its members against assimilation by the surrounding society, the Tabligh, which was founded in 1927 in India, where Muslims formed an island in the ocean of Hinduism, instituted a great number of signs that would identify their bearers as Muslims in daily life. In a literal imitation of the custom of the prophet Mohammed during his earthly existence, members of the Tabligh allow their beards to grow, wear the white djellaba, and scrupulously observe the most minute and demanding rules of ritual, plus the sexual and food prohibitions. Even their rigorist attitude to *halal* (ritually

62   Rav Yoël Kahn, 'La cinquième dimension', *Rencontres 'HaBaD*, 25 (summer 1989), p. 15.
63   Laurence Podselver, 'La séparation. . .', op. cit., p. 172.
64   See above, chap. 1, p. 34ff.

slaughtered) food constitutes a striking parallel to the practice of *glat-kosher*, for they will not 'trust' *halal* that they have not supervised themselves.

To exponents of this re-Islamization from below, Muslims outside the group are 'those who have strayed', who have to be won back to the true way by the intensive practice of congregational prayer; all others are 'ungodly' vessels of corruption and moral perdition.

What distinguishes the Tabligh from the Lubavitch is their respective attitudes to politics. Each practises a strategy of re-Islamization (or re-Judaization) from below, with the intention of winning over the whole of the Muslim (or Jewish) societies or populations in the long term. And where they control communities containing a significant number of their disciples, they have to define their attitude in relation to the political system that shapes the society in which they are operating. In any event, that society takes an interest in them. The Lubavitch, who are citizens of democratic countries, have votes, and the various candidates for office in the United States, France and Israel seek those votes. Generally speaking, members of the Tabligh are citizens of authoritarian Muslim states or foreign immigrants into Western countries. They are not electors, or only marginally so, but because of their apolitical pietism governments regard them as an alternative to the revolutionary movements working for re-Islamization from above and aiming to achieve power.

Both the Tablighis and the Lubavitch at first adopted a 'minimalist' attitude of non-confrontation with the authorities, giving priority to their social work with young people in their community – who, once within the fold, would no longer pose problems (particularly of delinquency) because they would be, as it were, withdrawn from the body of society. Often this has brought them more status, backing for their associations, permission to bring in staff from abroad and so forth. But although the Tablighis as such have seldom got beyond this stage, the Lubavitch have realized that, among the Jews of the diaspora, they have electoral power – at least at local level – and that in Israel itself they have means of influencing policy choices at national level.

At Sarcelles, a Paris suburb with a large Sephardi population among whom the Lubavitch wield some influence, they have contrived to deploy the votes available to them skilfully in close-run elections. In 1989 they dashed the hopes of the socialist candidate, who made a point of his Jewish origins in order to gain the community vote, by voting for the outgoing mayor who had generously subsidized a kindergarten organized on the principles of HaBaD hasidism.[65] In Paris itself it is well known that some leading members of the Lubavitch community were supporters of Mayor Jacques Chirac, and he amply repaid them by furthering the establishment of community schools and giving the go-ahead for marches and demonstrations.[66]

But it is in Israel that the Lubavitch movement has made a particularly high-profile, successful entry into politics. According to his hagiographer, it was in 1967 that Rabbi Shlita 'began his campaign to prevent Israel giving back the territories won during the Six Day War'. In 1970 he made a fresh intervention in the political life of Israel by 'beginning his fight against the dreadful decree of "Who is a Jew?", under which a non-Jew who had made a show of conversion could be regarded in Israel as a full-blooded Jew.' 'Then (1978) he severely criticized the tragic Camp David accord.'[67] Although he did not recognize the legitimacy of the Zionist state of Israel, the rabbi of the Lubavitch considered that Jewish domination over the whole of the territory of *Eretz Yisrael* was an indispensable preliminary to the coming of the Messiah, and that everything that might cleanse Israel of its Zionist accretions and steer it towards 'Torahcracy' should be encouraged. With this in mind, he made a decisive contribution to the successful election campaign of Agudat Israel in 1988.

In the Jewish world, movements for the reaffirmation of religion 'from below' had gained wide access to the political domain by the end of the 1980s. That is largely due to the exceptional conditions obtaining in the state of Israel, whose electoral system, based on full proportional representation, has enabled the *haredi* parties, though supported by only 15 per cent of the population,

---

65   See V. Linhart, G. Mace and N. Offenstadt, *La Communauté loubavitch de Sarcelles: Mémoire* (Paris: Institut d'études politiques, 1989).
66   See the story that appeared in the monthly *Passages* (January 1989), by Batrice Szwec.
67   *HaBaD Loubavitch: repères*, op. cit. pp. 56, 57, 59.

to control several ministries and to obtain large subsidies in order to go on strengthening their network of practising Jewish communities. But, even outside the Jewish state, this model for entry into politics by movements of re-Judaization 'from below' had been widely followed in the diaspora, in the United States and, more recently, in France. It is giving fresh life to an idea of 'community' that is undermining one of the main foundations of democratic societies, the equality of all citizens before the state and the law. This egalitarian, universalist principle is rejected as being a product of the hated spirit of the Enlightenment, which extolled the emancipation of reason from faith, the end of obedience to the special religious Law of the Chosen People.

In the Jewish world, present-day communalism owes many of its successes to its links with a tradition whose logical outcome was the autonomy of the ghetto – which is now being glorified by the most orthodox disciples of re-Judaization. In the Christian and Muslim worlds, which have no such history behind them, the community pattern is the most effective way to counteract a secularized society and state which have proved resistant to conquest by the movements of re-Christianization or re-Islamization 'from above' that appeared between 1975 and 1985. But Judaism is not a universalist, 'missionary' culture pledged to limitless expansion. Communities which are so pledged find it infinitely more difficult to translate their ideals into specific political action than does the Jewish community, whose frontiers are closed around a people whose distinguishing feature is its uniqueness.

5

CONCLUSION
Reconquering the World

Movements for the reaffirmation of religious identity have under-gone a considerable change between 1975 and 1990.

In fifteen years they have succeeded in transforming the con-fused reaction of their adherents to the 'crisis of modernity' into plans for rebuilding the world, and in those plans their holy scriptures provide the basis for tomorrow's society.

These movements have arisen in a world which has lost the assurance born of scientific and technological progress since the 1950s. Just as the barriers of poverty, disease and inhuman work-ing conditions seemed to be yielding, the population explosion, the spread of AIDS, pollution and the energy crises burst upon the scene – and all of these scourges lent themselves to presentation in apocalyptic terms.

During this same period the great atheist messianic ideology of the twentieth century, communism, which had left its mark on most of our social utopias, went into its death throes, and finally succumbed in the autumn of 1989 when its most potent symbol, the Berlin wall, was destroyed.

The Christian, Jewish and Muslim movements we have been observing are to be viewed in this dual perspective. Their first task was to fix labels on to the confusion and disorder in the world as perceived by their adherents, breathing fresh life into the vocabulary and the categories of religious thought as applied to the contemporary world. Next they conceived plans for changing the social order so as to bring it into line with the commands and values of the Old Testament, the Koran or the Gospels; for, as they saw it, nothing else could ensure the advent of a world of justice and truth.

These movements have a great deal in common beyond mere historical simultaneity. They are at one in rejecting a secularism that they trace back to the philosophy of the Enlightenment. They regard the vainglorious emancipation of reason from faith as the prime cause of all the ills of the twentieth century, the beginning of a process leading straight to Nazi and Stalinist totalitarianism.

This radical challenge to the foundations of secular modernism is uttered by its own children, who have had access to today's education. They see no contradiction between their mastery of science and technology and their acceptance of a faith not bounded by the tenets of reason. In fact, people like Herman Branover consciously symbolize the fact that a 'godfearing Jew' can also be a 'great scientist'. And the self-image favoured by Islamist militants is that of a girl student, muffled in a veil with only a slit for the eyes, bent over a microscope and doing research in biology.

All these movements agree that the modern secular city is now completely lacking in legitimacy. But while Christians, Muslims and Jews all consider that only a fundamental transformation in the organization of society can restore the holy scriptures as the prime source of inspiration for the city of the future, they have differing ideas of what that city will be like. Each of these religious cultures had developed specific truths which, insofar as they provide the basis for a strong reassertion of identity, are mutually exclusive. All they have in common is a rejection of secularism; beyond that point their plans for society diverge and then become deeply antagonistic, with a potential for bitter conflict in which none of these doctrines of truth can afford to compromise, on pain of losing followers.

Their short-term prospects will depend upon the relationship between their base in society and their respective political objectives. For re-Islamization, re-Judaization and re-Christianization do not have the same impact, the same significance, in their respective societies – despite the parallel courses they have followed since the mid-1970s. Their respective intensities can be gauged and their probable futures deduced by comparing the successes and setbacks experienced by movements 'from above' and 'from below', the methods of action they most favour, and whether or not they accept that democracy as such has an independent right to existence.

The extension of the jihad

In the 1990s the re-Islamization movements appear to have the greatest potential. The Muslim world of the Mediterranean shows signs of social breakdown that are causing deep discouragement, especially among its teeming youth, on a much larger scale than is so far discernible in Catholic Europe, the United States or the Jewish world. In Muslim countries Islamic fervour usually gathers strength just when the generation born after independence comes of age and the first government of indigenous elites is in power. In Egypt twenty-five years elapsed between the rise of Nasser and the triumph of the *Jamaat islamiyya* in the universities of Cairo. In Algeria, which became independent in 1962, it was only after the 1980s that the Islamic Salvation Front achieved its first successes, with a crushing victory in the municipal elections of June 1990. In Palestine, occupied by Israel since 1967, the PLO leadership got along without much competition for two decades; only with the Intifada did the Islamic Resistance Movement mount a challenge to it.

The successes of the Islamists are the clearest indication of the political, economic and social bankruptcy of the post-independence ruling elites. To criticize them in the name of the sacred writings of Islam was specifically to challenge the alien, Western-import nature of the modernity they had tried to build. It was a radical criticism that refused to borrow anything from a political system which it held to be intrinsically wrong. 'Democracy' itself is rejected out of hand, as is incessantly repeated by Imam Ali Belhaj, the spokesman of the contemporary Islamist movement in Algeria; there is no basis in the Koran for the idea of the *demos*, the people as sovereign. On the contrary, it affronts the only legitimate sovereignty: that exercised by Allah over the *umma*, the community of believers, through a government which must implement the divine commands as found in the sacred writings of Islam.

Islamist condemnation of the democratic system is absolute on two counts. Firstly, the 'democracy' to which the rulers of Algeria or other countries paid lip-service was only a meaningless catchword, because the military regimes and the one-party states were dictatorships, and the people knew it. Thus it is easy nowadays to cast 'democracy' as the ugly sister, because it has remained largely unknown in the Muslim world as an operative political system. But, in addition, the rejection of even a chimerical notion of democracy is actually inherent in Islamic religious doctrine, which, in its present-day militant reaffirmation, is fervently monist: there is only one organizing principle in the world – God – and human freedom is reduced virtually to zero. In Islamist thinking there could be no room for autonomous political activity outside the control of the *shar'ia*, the Law codified by Islamic scholars from the revealed scriptures. To introduce democracy is to destroy the case put forward by the re-Islamization movements.

Thus there is very little chance of a democratic alternative that could mount a real challenge to the growing success of the Islamization movements in the deeply inegalitarian societies of the contemporary Muslim world. When unemployment is the most likely prospect for most young adults, the *jihad* seems more attractive than public freedoms.

The nature of these societies, combined with the specific characteristics of Islamic religious culture, also explains why movements 'from above' play such a large part. Ever since the later 1970s groups wishing to act directly on the state in order to re-Islamize it have employed various forms of political violence, sometimes including armed conflict. The Iranian revolution has had its would-be imitators, and in those closed political systems such aspirations tend to become channelled into insurrection. Such insurrections have been severely repressed – most of all in 1982 when the Syrian town of Hama was bombed during an uprising instigated by the Muslim Brothers. Violence, not only against 'ungodly' states but also against 'Westernised' Muslims or non-Muslims (from the Copts in Egypt to the hostages in Lebanon) has now become inseparable from our image of the Islamist militant.

The Kingdom of Israel

Just as many of the Islamist movements arose in Muslim countries twenty-five years after independence, so Gush Emunim, the most important of the movements battling for re-Judaization 'from above', was formed in 1974, twenty-six years after the foundation of Israel, by young militants who had never known any government other than the Zionist Labour party. Their bitterness after the psychological defeat of the October 1973 war calls to mind the feelings aroused in the Islamists by the failure of Arab regimes. But there was a distinct difference in the social conditions of the two groups. Granted that the Israeli economy was not exactly flourishing at the time, the present welfare and future prospects of the young Emunists were incomparably better than those of the Islamist students who at that very time were forming their underground associations in the suburbs of Cairo.

Both their respective intellectual leaders, Rav Kook and Sayyid Qutb, had the same wish – to build, on the ruins of the secular state, a social system based on their holy scriptures. For the former it was to be the Kingdom of Israel, built on the *halakah*, the Jewish Law, and for the latter the Islamic state, built on the *shar'ia*, the Law of Islam. But they envisaged that transition differently. Rav Kook believed that the secular state of Israel was unconsciously serving the will of the Messiah; it had to be changed more quickly, not destroyed by force of arms. Sayyid Qutb and his followers, on the other hand, held that Nasser's state and its surrogates were completely alienated from Islam and must be destroyed.

Gush took part in the politics of Israel, but never formed a party, though it did have some of its members elected on the ticket of parties whose aims were compatible with its own. It was most active in the Occupied Territories and Sinai, pressing for a thorough colonization so as to align the frontiers of biblical Israël with those of the longed-for kingdom of the Messiah.

From this viewpoint, non-Jews had no right to the land that had been promised to the Chosen People. Carried to its logical extreme, this way of thinking led to the plot to blow up the mosques on the Temple Mount in Jerusalem, which, its authors believed, would provoke a war between Arabs and Israelis that would end in victory for the Jews and the expulsion of the Palestinians from the Occupied Territories.

This is an extreme incidence of something which was bound to emerge from the reaffirmation of religious identities: a clash between holders of opposed, but equally radical, beliefs. In the case of Gush Emunim, the phenomenon was carried to extremes by its ultra-nationalist nature. Unlike the movements of re-Islamization from above, working for the violent destruction of Arab regimes, the violence of the movements of re-Judaization from above was not aimed directly against the state of Israel, but against foreigners, non-Jews, with Palestinians in the forefront.

There was a sharp decrease in the more extreme manifestations of Gush activism after the 'Jewish underground' network was broken up in 1984, but its ideology gained currency in government circles. The religious–conservative coalition that came to power in Israel in June 1990 shared several of the ideals that Gush had proclaimed between 1974 and 1984; and the serious clashes between Jews and Arabs that occurred in October 1990, when some twenty Palestinians were killed in a single day, were the result of a demonstration organized by a group that wanted to lay the first stone of the Third Temple – unless that was merely a pretext. In the context of the Middle Eastern conflict, whipped to fury by the Iraqi invasion of Kuwait in August 1990, any provocative act centring on Temple precincts and the Dome of the Rock would be likely to trigger escalating violence, which would hit the Palestinians first, but could widen into the international conflict to which the conspirators of 1984 in fact aspired.

Countering secularism

There is one fundamental difference between the movements of re-Christianization 'from above' and the Islamist or Gush Emunim: the former have never had recourse to political violence – either in Western Europe and the United States, or under the communist regimes which persecuted them.

This fundamental distinction betokens a different attitude to democracy. Islamists reject the very idea of it, aspiring to found a society based on the *shar'ia*; the Emunists regard it as a temporary situation that can be exploited to hasten the coming of the messianic kingdom in which the *halakah* will have the force of law. Both follow a monist pattern in which the sole principle of social organization is God's revealed Law. Any human intervention which might constrain the total application of that Law is perverse and blasphemous, and must be fought until the wrongdoers recant.

By contrast, the movements of re-Christianization from above – even the most uncompromising, like Jerry Falwell's Moral Majority – have never questioned the dualism symbolized in Christ's saying 'Render unto Caesar the things that are Caesar's, and to God the things that are God's.' Christianity has no equivalent to the *shar'ia* or the *halakah*, and Christendom nurtured the process which was to lead to modern democracy via the Reformation and the Enlightenment; though modern democracy had to struggle to throw off the Church's hegemony over civil society. In other words, the various movements of re-Christianization from above cannot reject democracy as an alien graft on to their own system. They *have* to speak the language of democracy if they want to be heard by the citizens of present-day Europe or America. This 'democratic constraint'[1] does more than forbid the use of violence. It also influences what these movements actually say. Communion and Liberation combats the 'dominant culture' of the secular state in Italy, accusing it of hampering freedom to express Christian values in the state schools, for example. And the freedom of man, as a creature of God, was the last stockade against the totalitarian oppression of the communist system, as seen by re-Christianization movements in the Soviet bloc.

As for political objectives, these groups show no desire to force the state into applying a Law drawn from the holy scriptures, as do their opposite numbers in Islam and Judaism. They wish rather to defeat the legal enshrinement of secularism, which relegates the expression of religious identity to the private sphere, and to replace it with a system in which, in the words of Cardinal Ratzinger, this identity may acquire 'public legal status'. That should enable Christians to introduce Gospel values into certain aspects of public activity. The idea is not to make the state apply divine Law, but to spread the faith without interference from Caesar – to drive back the frontiers of secularism. It is inconceivable that such a process could be consummated without re-Christianization from below as a necessary complement.

There could never be a Christian equivalent to the Islamic Republic in Iran. When the televangelist Pat Robertson put forward his name as a candidate in the 1988 American presidential election, he failed. But Jerry Falwell's Moral Majority successfully built up a gigantic educational project, Liberty University, to train

---

1 It also has an effect on the re-Judaization and re-Islamization movements 'from below' among the Jews of the diaspora and among Muslim immigrants in Europe (see below).

re-Christianized elites whose medium-term mission is to penetrate the machinery of US politics, economics and culture.

Thus, despite their similarities, the re-Islamization, re-Judaization and re-Christianization movements 'from above' differ significantly in their attitudes to the state, the law and the constraint of democracy, and these differences have their origin in their respective religious doctrines. They are exacerbated by the political and social context of the societies in which these movements are developing. The Muslim world, with its closed political system and bleak economic outlook for young people, naturally induces a resort to various forms of violence, and a marked intolerance fed by a monist conception of the universe. Israel combines an open political system with a monist religious doctrine taken to extremes by (for example) Gush Emunim, which has directed its violence only against non-Jews. In Christian Europe and America, the democratic constraint resulting from a dualism inherent in the religious doctrine itself has steered the movements for re-Christianization towards the reacquisition of public legal status and an attempt to loosen the grip of secularism. This has not led to violence, even under communist regimes in which there was no scope for free expression.

In each of these three cases, the movements 'from above' reached an impassable threshold in the mid-1980s, after which movements 'from below' came to the fore. Sometimes these were different groups, different militants; in other situations the group was the same, but the strategy had changed. Movements 'from below', whether Islamic, Jewish or Christian, set to work on the individual in similar ways: he was induced to break with the values and customs of the surrounding society and acclimatized to a new society within communities of believers. These communities live by commands or values drawn from their sacred writings, interpreted literally, and they aim to influence the whole of society in the long term.

Nevertheless the intensity of this process varies greatly in each of our three religious cultures. The break with the world may be more or less radical, and not all movements are equally capable of enlarging their grasp or influencing the political system. These differences are due to the extent to which the different religious cultures lend support to the aims and objectives of the respective movements. They are also due to the social context, and to the ability of the various groups to respond to the demands of individuals affected in varying degrees by the lawlessness and disarray in society as a whole.

The return of the ghetto

It is in the Jewish world that the consequences of 'return' and 'repentance' (*teshuvah*) are most visible. Both in Israel and in the diaspora, the *haredim* (ultra-orthodox) groups have built up an extremely large network of closed communities based on the most uncompromising observance of the *mitsvot* (the sacred duties and prohibitions). The *haredim*, with their network of religious schools and colleges (*yeshivot and kolellim*), their efficient distribution of strictly *kosher* food and their highly fertile endogamic system, have pushed the break with the customs and values of the surrounding society to the limit. Their attitude is grounded in a culture of separation and refusal to assimilate that has enabled the 'Chosen People' to remain distinct throughout the centuries of the diaspora. But here it is reactivated and reinforced: the orthodox preserve themselves first and foremost against the seductions of secularized Judaism, marked by the 'false universalism' born of the Enlightenment. But, as the journal of the French Lubavitch remarked, in the eyes of the Creator there is as much difference between Jews and non-Jews as between non-Jews and animals. Any failure to observe the *mitsvot* entails the dissolution of the Jewish identity in the said 'universalism' and threatens to compromise this hierarchy.

In cultural and social terms, the considerable growth in the orthodox community movement since the mid-1970s is attributable to the confusion and anxiety induced by the crisis of secular modernity evidenced by the writings of those who have experienced 'repentance and return'. Because of the comparatively large size of this community in Israel it has been able to play a considerable role in politics, because the proportional representation voting system enables minority religious parties to control the government. In this particular case, orthodox movements participate in government; but, while demanding changes in Israeli law to bring it into line with the *halakah*, they exploit this situation mainly to obtain large public subsidies that enable them to cover the operating costs of religious institutions which are not in themselves productive of material wealth.

In Jerusalem and Bnei Brak, barriers are set up on the eve of the *shabbat*. This concrete delineation of a circumscribed space – a ghetto – is not yet systematized among the Jews of the diaspora, where the ghetto is more a matter of choosing one's social acquaintances, organizing one's time to ensure strict observance of the *shabbat*, praying and going back to the rite in its entirety. It is also built around the control exercised over the young, who are educated in private ultra-orthodox schools which withdraw the children from the influences of the outside world and from the temptations of assimilation. Life in a community system of this kind plays down as far as possible ideas such as a citizenship shared with American or French non-Jews, or a shared nationhood. For example, in Lubavitch primary schools in Paris, French and mathematics are the only 'profane' subjects taught. History, geography, civic education and other 'mind-broadening' disciplines that shape the world view of other French boys and girls are replaced by the learning of Hebrew and the reading of the Bible and the Talmud. Cultural interaction with the non-Jewish world is reduced to its most basic terms: you learn to read and add up. Here we see the communal phenomenon at work in its most absolute expression.

Imitating the Prophet

In the Muslim world, movements 'from below' do not draw their sustenance from a religious culture of perpetual separation from the environment, as does re-Judaization. There is no wish to rescue a Chosen People from the dangers of assimilation; here the aim is to participate in a dynamic process of spreading Islam to the whole of humanity, while defending an identity that is under threat during temporary 'phases of weakness'. The pattern provided by tradition is that of the prophet Mohammed, whom one must imitate to the letter in all aspects of behaviour so as not to lose one's way and risk seeing one's religious identity adulterated by the surrounding 'ungodliness'. The *Jama'at al Tabligh* ('Society for the Propagation of the Faith') which has taken the logic of re-

Islamization 'from below' to its uttermost extreme, began operations in India in the 1920s because, as the Tabligh saw it, there was a risk that the Hindu majority would swamp the Muslim minority. Fifty years later this tactic has surfaced again among Muslim immigrants into Western Europe. To imitate the Prophet in his way of dressing, eating and looking at the world, of treating his wife (or wives) and educating his children, is to break with the social environment in France, Germany or Britain, as manifested in education, housing and so on. It is to build a self-sufficient world, subject to a corpus of prohibitions and constraints rather like those of the re-Judaization movements, but directed towards a different end. The re-Islamized equivalent of the ghetto is not an end in itself: it must expand as soon as it can, first to embrace 'strayed' Muslims and then to win over the rest of humanity.

In present-day Europe this strategy of gaining spatial or symbolic re-Islamized areas is part of a larger thrust towards communalization with a religious or ethnic slant. Its primary function is to provide stable reference points for the national and religious groups concerned, who are usually searching for a redefinition of a socio-cultural identity that has been eroded by migration and lack of job security and who do not feel at home with traditional models of state citizenship. But this 'communalization' can turn the constraint of democracy to its own advantage in a way reminiscent of the 'orthodox vote' in Israel. Citizenship, when acquired, leads to group votes which are traded for ever-increasing concessions made by the state, allowing communal leaders to assume more and more control over the education of children and all kinds of social activity.

In the Muslim countries themselves, the process of re-Islamization from below has resulted in the creation of networks of mutual help and control of the population in urban areas, especially in outer suburbs. The example of Algeria has shown how a political party could capitalize on this phenomenon, as was done by the Islamic Salvation Front in June 1990, in the first free elections held in the country since 1962.

Communion and community

The movements of re-Christianization from below cover a much wider spectrum, ranging from Catholic charismatic or Protestant evangelical groups reliving the daily presence of miracles, to other networks which, like Communion and Liberation in Italy or the Moral Majority in the United States, pursue Christian social action by the methods of big business. These latter groups have shown great flexibility, and have learnt to switch their activism from the political to the social sphere when it suited their interests. In particular they reacted swiftly when they realized that identifying too closely with narrowly Christian moral prohibitions was bad for their image. When they made the fight against abortion or divorce their main campaigning issues, threw themselves into referenda in Italy or lobbied in the United States, they received an enthusiastic response from the already converted, but did not win any new recruits. So, in order to gain a wider hearing, Communion and Liberation, and Jerry Falwell and his friends, decided from the mid-1980s onwards to switch most of their activities into the social and cultural sphere; they created structures to deal with needs which state institutions could no longer meet. Thus the Company of Deeds, which was founded in 1986 under the auspices of Communion and Liberation, has become a very important intermediary in the labour market in present-day Italy. This does not mean that its founders have given up their aversion to divorce or abortion, but they are now getting the message across in the context of charitable works and mutual assistance, which is better suited to winning over those who would be repelled by too much harping on such moral themes. They too are adapting to the 'democratic constraint' while pointing out the main evils that disfigure the organization of society.

In America in the autumn of 1990, Jerry Falwell considerably reduced his televised preaching, in the wake of the general discredit brought on televangelism in 1989 by the spate of scandals involving the Bakker, Swaggart and Oral Roberts brigades generally. The flow of gifts from the faithful dried up, until they did not even cover the cost of broadcasting the programmes. But Liberty University is training thousands of preachers and influential people, and when the next economic recession hits America, with the accompanying social and moral crisis, they will be all ready to explain it in terms of an apocalypse caused by man's disobedience to God and his separation from Jesus Christ.

At the same time, Falwell is offering scholarships to a growing number of foreigners – South Americans, Africans, West and East Europeans, who intend to create institutions similar to Liberty University in their own countries.

In both Catholic Europe and Protestant America, movements of re-Christianization 'from above' have successfully moved back into the social field and joined up with Charismatics, Evangelicals and Pentecostals. The latter groups specialize in an uncompromising 'Christian break' with the habits and customs of 'secular humanism'; the former, while carrying out various offensives against the frontiers of secularism, are finding areas in which evangelization can be made truly effective. Education is one of those priority areas: one great advantage of controlling institutions of higher education is the chance to train re-Christianized elites who will be able to combat the values propagated by the 'dominant culture' of the secular intelligentsia.

But this process can extend its hold over significant sectors of the population only if it is able to respond adequately – as it says it can – to crises in society and culture. As the twentieth century draws to a close, re-Christianization movements are finally gathering strength and marshalling their militants to confront the society whose culture gave birth to secularism. It is far more difficult to expel secularism from Western society than from today's Jewish or Muslim world. Compared with the expansion of the *jihad* or the rebuilding of the ghetto, Catholics and Protestants are only at the 'beginnings of the Christian era': their concern is still the prevalence of 'paganism', equivalent to the 1960s *jahiliyya* of the Islamists. The time for the conversion of Constantine or for starting a crusade is not yet. But, in the medium term, it is the logic of conflict which underlies the parallel development of different religious movements setting out to reconquer the world. Such conflict is ultimately a war between 'believers' who make the reaffirmation of their religious identity into the criterion of truths that are both exclusive of others and peculiar to themselves.

Index

141–2, 144, 147–8, 153,
171–80, 189–90
hasidism movement in Judaism
174–5
Haskalah (Jewish
Enlightenment) 144, 147,
174
Havel, Vaclav 80, 94–5
Hearst, William Randolph 112
Heidegger, Martin 55
Helms, Senator Jesse 103
Heritage USA 100, 114
Hervieu-Léger, Danièle 76
Hinduism 2, 35, 187, 201
Hitler, Adolf 56–7, 151
Hruza, Karel 91
human rights, and Catholicism
59–60
Hungary, Catholicism in 84
Hunter, J. D. 123–4, 132
Hurwitz, Shimon 143, 145
Hus, John 87, 89
Hussein, King of Jordan 21
Hussein, Mahmoud 15–16

Ibn Taimiya 30
Ilyas, Muhammad 34
imams, in Algeria 45
India, and Islam 35, 187, 201
Intifada, Palestinian 36, 41–2,
193
Iran 5
American hostage-taking in
32, 119
and Egypt 29–30
and France 40
and Islam 7, 15, 17, 27–9,
30, 194
and re-Islamization 'from
above' 32
and the Rushdie affair in
Britain 33, 39

universities 27, 28
Iran–Iraq war 13, 32, 33, 39
Iraq 15, 32, 33, 39
Islam 13–46, 193–4, 200–1
in Algeria 13, 14, 15, 16, 18,
193
and American Blacks 149
and American Evangelicalism
137–8, 139
and Catholicism 40–1,
49–50, 59–60
and democracy 46, 193–4,
196
in Egypt 10, 15–16, 17,
18–19, 25–7, 29–30, 193
intégrisme and
'fundamentalism' 3
in Iran 7, 15, 17, 27–9, 30,
194
Islamic 'break' 22, 33, 34–6
and *jahiliyya* 20–1, 33, 38,
46, 156, 169
and Judaism 156
and Marxism 13, 14, 15,
15–17, 22–3
in the modern world 2, 7–8
Shi'ite 28–9, 31, 139
Sunni 28, 29–33
and terrorism 13, 33–4
ulemas 30–2, 45
see also re-Islamization
movements
Israel 140–2, 152–90
and the Arab–Israeli war
(1973) 5, 22, 140, 156,
157, 195
Bnei Brak settlement 176–7,
178, 179, 200
Council of Torah Sages 175,
179, 182–3
and Egypt 21, 161, 164–5,
166, 195

ADIRONDACK COMMUNITY COLLEGE

8 3341 0009 040 3

BL 238 .K4613 1994

Kepel, Gilles.

The revenge of God

DISCARDED